AN AMERICAN FAMILY:
FOUR CENTURIES. TWO CONTINENTS

S. Frederick Starr

The contents of this work, including, but not limited to, the accuracy of events, people, and places depicted; opinions expressed; permission to use previously published materials included; and any advice given or actions advocated are solely the responsibility of the author, who assumes all liability for said work and indemnifies the publisher against any claims stemming from publication of the work.

All Rights Reserved
Copyright © 2023 by S. Frederick Starr

No part of this book may be reproduced or transmitted, downloaded, distributed, reverse engineered, or stored in or introduced into any information storage and retrieval system, in any form or by any means, including photocopying and recording, whether electronic or mechanical, now known or hereinafter invented without permission in writing from the publisher.

Dorrance Publishing Co
585 Alpha Drive
Suite 103
Pittsburgh, PA 15238
Visit our website at *www.dorrancebookstore.com*

ISBN: 979-8-88729-418-6
eISBN: 979-8-88729-918-1

Table of Contents

A Note to Readers iii

I. The Sterns/Csillags/Starrs 1

II. Two Centuries of Quaker Edmondsons 44

III. George Edmondson, 1797-1863 69

IV. American Edmondsons 107

V. Two Lives: Work and Days 190

Ending 239

Afterword 241

A Note to Readers:

The text you have in your hands, or have loaded onto your screen, is so fat as to demand an explanation. Why was it written, and why, in heaven's name, should you even start to peruse it, let alone read it through?

Here, spread out over several hundred pages, is the history of my family. Besides myself, the audience for such a story is therefore limited to my three siblings, for it is they alone among everyone on our planet who fully share the same family whose history is recounted here. The death of my sister Ivy, known as "Buffy," before this text was completed brings the core audience down to two. I cannot exclude the possibility that either of my daughters might someday leaf through these pages out of curiosity about half of their background or to find out what their father was doing when he should have been paying attention to them, their families, and their children.

It is not out of the question that one or two of the four children of my brother George or sister Diana might also delve into the book, perhaps in an effort to trace the eccentricity of one of their parents to its origin. But beyond this, it is hard to imagine a grandchild being inclined to pore through such a long tome, for by then it would cover at best a quarter of his or her ancestry. But there may be hope, for on both my father's and mother's side there are cousins, for whom at least half of the following story may have some relevance, and they have many children, although statistically they fall into the category of those who are only "quarter interested."

If the immediately possible readership does not exceed fifty, and if many of them might have better ways to spend their time, why would I have written this? One thing is certain: it was not because I thought that the fruits of my research would somehow "explain" my parents. For my parents lived forthright lives that don't need to be explained. Anyway, why should the reminiscences and research of just one of their four children dominate the record when the memories of the others might be very different yet equally valid?

Nor have I been driven by some kind of genetic determinism that assumes that the past shapes and limits the present. True, my mother once pointed out to me that when I sit I often hold my left foot on its side, just as her father had done. But so what? We know far too much about genes and inheritance to fall for such simplistic explanations today. This is why I puzzle at my friends from Central Asia, Afghanistan, and Iran, all of whom can easily recount their genealogy over a canonic seven generations. Why seven, I asked them, and not six or eight? And do not such recitals pass on as many legends and fabrications as facts?

The main impetus to set down this story of my family was simple curiosity. Like every other human being, as a child I heard many stories about my parents, about their parents, and about their parents as well. Taken together, these fragments formed a picture of the past that was frustratingly incomplete and utterly confusing. At the simplest level, I wanted to bring some order to this mess of tidbits imprinted on my memory.

Since I was more concerned with human beings than mere genes, I did not bother to avail myself of the several genetic tracing services now available. Nor did I resort to the Mormons' profitable Ancestry.com. More than a few of the revelations that arose from my research caused me to emit an audible "Aha!" But these were lower case exclamations and not the kind that arise from real revelations that would explain some heretofore curtained-off aspect of life as I had experienced it. The "big picture" I grew up with survived all my enquiries largely intact. To be sure, it was vastly expanded and deepened, but it was not changed fundamentally.

What, then, does this leave us with? The answer is simple, and compelling. The stories of my father's and mother's families differ dramatically from each other. They involve different countries, languages, religions, cultures, educational experiences, professions, and careers. No less important, both families changed radically and fundamentally over the four centuries encompassed by this history. As a devoted fan of Russian literature it pains me to pick a bone with Lev Tolstoy, but I do so just the same. On the opening pages of War and Peace the novelist proclaimed that "All happy families are alike; each unhappy family is unhappy in its own way." The volume that follows provides solid testimony that Tolstoy was wrong. In fact, all families are both unhappy and happy in their own way, and all those ways are worthy of attention.

My counterparts in many countries and on several continents could recount family histories that are equally rich in complexities and dramatic changes through time. If there is anything distinctive about the following story it is that its main elements came together in America. More than that, it is distinctive because the impulse to explore them and to set them down is itself deeply American. This quest is distinctly (though not exclusively) American, for

America, more than any other country on earth, has been and remains the place where men and women from dramatically different backgrounds and cultures come together to form new families. Many Americans who are the products of such whirlwinds feel a natural compulsion to learn about and document the story.

This, then, is above all an American story, the history of a typically mongrel American family. It is a story of constant and intense change and conflict, but also of adaptation and resolution.

It is also, whether or not I choose to admit it, my personal story. While preparing these notes, I came across Ralph Waldo Emerson's stunning declaration that "In different hours a man represents each of several of his ancestors." Over and over I have found myself sympathizing with one or another of my forebears, squirming at them, grimacing with them, or cheering them on as if they were some earlier version of me. Emerson understood this, too, declaring that [ancestors] "constitute the variety of notes for the new piece of music which [one's own] life is."

Whether or not anyone finds something of interest in all this, investigating the lives of my immediate and more remote forebears has been great fun. It has challenged me at every turn and opened as many questions as it has resolved. Perhaps some of that excitement comes through on the following pages and will inspire readers to conduct their own explorations.

S. Frederick Starr
Washington and New Orleans, 2017.

I. The Sterns/Csillags/Starrs

How little we know of our parents' world, let alone the world of their parents! Of course, much may be communicated in the course of daily interaction between parents and children. But some parents are more given to reminiscing than others, and not all children are good at posing the questions that overcome inhibitions or taboos. Worse, the demands of daily life claim time that in an earlier day might have been filled in part by reminiscing. And because more and more of us live at a distance from grandparents, we lack the easy interaction with them that is most conducive to talking about the past.

My parents' days were filled with earning a salary and raising four children. Even when they had time, they did not talk much of themselves (and my father notoriously so), preferring instead to hear from us. By contrast, my maternal Grandma Wilhelmina "Minnie" Edmondson lived with us for quite a few years, thanks to which we children learned quite a lot about her and her husband's family, the Edmondsons. Beyond this, I was to spend eleven years in Oberlin, Ohio, the epicenter of a micro-region in which both sides of my mother's family had dwelled for a century. I literally wallowed in connections with the Edmondson family. But I grew up knowing next to nothing about the Starrs beyond the fact that they had come from Hungary.

My father was a dutiful son. My older brother's middle name, Alexander, honors Grandpa Alexander Starr. Father corresponded with his parents in both English and Hungarian and paid perfunctory visits twice a year, one of them alone. When he would pack the entire family in our Pontiac station wagon for our annual trip to his parents, we all knew that the best part of the day would not be the visit itself but the ice-cream cones promised on the return trip. This is quite understandable, as both of my Starr grandparents spoke with such thick, sing-song Hungarian accents as to make sustained conversation difficult, even had any of us grandchildren been interested in engaging in one. The far-off world from which they came was as inaccessible to us as their native language. I cannot recall a single fact about them or their world that I heard directly from them.

This accounts for the imbalance in these sketches. Whereas three chapters are devoted to the Edmondson family stretching back to specific forebears at the end of the sixteenth century, there is only this one chapter on my father's family. And although I have been able to trace Starr forebears back from Hungary to Moravia in the early eighteenth century, no specifically named and identified individuals enter the story until as late as 1877, when Grandpa Starr was born. They existed, of course, but I have not been able to pin specific identities on any of my father's ancestors prior to that date.

We children knew that our father, Stephen Zoltan Starr, had spent his first fourteen years in Hungary and Central Europe. But beyond what seemed to me his rather bizarre middle name (what real name begins with a "Z"?), that world left practically no traces in his daily life. I never heard him speak a word of his native language except to his parents during rare visits to Cleveland, and there were no more than two Hungarian books in our house. While he apparently had a relative, also named Zoltan, who had worked in Hollywood scoring the music for Walt Disney's Fantasia, I have no evidence that they were in contact. He and my mother had a couple of Hungarian friends in Cincinnati but he kept at arm's length the few "professional Hungarians" who sought him out. True, he loved the music of Vienna in general and fin de-siècle Vienna in particular, and relished rye bread, pickles, chicken paprikash, and goulash. But the same can probably be said of thousands of Americans who have merely travelled to Central Europe or taken a course on it, but otherwise have no family connection to it.

Stephen Starr's indifference towards the land of his birth bordered on contempt, but he despised even more the Communists whom Stalin installed in Hungary in 1949. He ridiculed the Communist government and grinned with delight—even punched the air-- when the Hungarians beat the USSR in water polo in the famous "blood in the water" match at the 1956 Olympics. Except for such moments, he considered Hungarians to be lazy or worse: hence his tired but revealing joke, "How do you make chicken paprikash?" Answer: "First, steal a chicken." His library was filled with books on the ancient world and on American and British history. Large portraits of Lincoln and Churchill hung in gold and black frames above the entry table in our house. I knew my father's library well, but can recall only a handful of books touching on Hungary in the entire collection and those pertained to the golden era of Habsburg rule before World War I.

These circumstances and others left me quite ignorant of my father's family and of his upbringing. What I did know can be quickly summarized, namely, that he was born in Budapest, where his father had been a lawyer; that the family emigrated to America at some time in the early 1920s, settling in Cleveland; and that at some point they had changed their name from the un-spellable and un-pronounceable "Csillag," which in Hungarian means "star," to "Starr."

My ignorance and indifference regarding the Csillag family would have remained solidly intact had my father himself not volunteered several tidbits of information that intrigued me. The first appeared as a result of a post-card I sent home from the German city of Passau. I was nineteen and hitch-hiking from Amsterdam to Ankara in order to join the excavation at the ancient city of Gordium. The card was simply to tell my parents that I had safely reached that point. When I returned home that autumn Mother told me that my father had been excited to receive the card because he had spent several years as a student in Passau. I was amazed. Why Passau? What did he study there? And in what years did that take place?

The second tidbit came when he and I were discussing my study of the Russian language. This was the high Cold War era and, as noted already, my father held Communism and the Soviet government in utter contempt. But he told me how a kind Russian POW during the First World War had carved for him a beautiful model of a Volga boat. When I asked how this had occurred, he explained that his father had commanded a POW camp on the Eastern Front and that the soldier had been one of the thousands of Russians interned there. Again, how did it happen that my grandfather, the bald-headed man with a pince-nez whom I had met at his modest apartment in Cleveland, had been running an Austro-Hungarian POW camp?

The third tidbit appeared when my father and I were discussing the system of serfdom in Russia and Central Europe. I mentioned Tolstoy's evocative description of long rows of scythe-wielding peasants slowing moving across a field harvesting grain. He enthusiastically recalled seeing precisely such a scene in Hungary, and how at a fixed number of steps the entire row of harvesters would all halt together, pull sharpening stones from their hip pockets with their right hand, slowly and mechanically stroke the blade three times, return the sharpening stones to their pockets, and then continue their cutting. This puzzled me. I thought his family was from Budapest. What was he doing in the countryside?

Peasants harvesting wheat, Nagykata, Hungary, ca. 1920.

I was not the only one of my four siblings to come across such provocative tidbits. During the 1960s my elder brother George, a young faculty member at Berkeley, expressed sympathy for the student protestors on his campus. My father, who had never been able to pursue his dream of becoming an academic historian, considered the protest to be the work of spoiled and ungrateful students and any sympathy for them from young faculty members to be treachery. About this time, George met and married a lively and engaging Hungarian emigre of the 1956 generation, Julia Bader, then a Berkeley graduate student. Being herself of a Jewish family, Julia explained to George that in Hungary the name Csillag is commonly considered to be Jewish and a literal translation of the common German-Jewish name Stern.

George, who did not appreciate paternal criticism, gleefully reported this to me. I considered it yet another intriguing and unexplained tidbit, but he treated it as a gambit to be used in his stand-off with our father. George and Julia later married. He learned Hungarian, they acquired a grand residence in Buda, and thereafter spent half of each year at their palazzo high above the curving Danube.

The fifth and final tidbit of disconnected information on Grandpa Starr came to me during my installation as President of Oberlin College in September, 1983. My father's younger brother, George came out for the day from his home in Cleveland. Uncle George was a seventy-two-year-old bachelor and had long since retired from the florist shop that he had run since returning from the war in the Pacific in 1945. During a reception at our house Uncle George casually dropped the fact that Grandpa Starr, Alexander Csillag, was born not in Budapest, as I had always assumed, but in a place called Nyregyhaza. This was totally new to me, and I had to write down the five-syllable unpronounceable town name in order to remember it.

This series of accidental revelations served as a vivid reminder that I really knew nothing about my father's early life or the entire Csillag family. But I was just beginning a new and demanding job, so I did nothing about it. I did not even begin to delve into these mysteries for another twelve years, and even then my investigation proceeded fitfully, producing nothing more than scraps of penciled notes that I lodged in folders and promptly forgot about. It took me another twenty years to find time to examine these fragments and to set down what I found in them. The results of that enquiry are presented here. Readers will quickly discover that I have managed to clarify many old enigmas but a still larger number of new ones emerged in the process. Significantly, the gaps pertain not to what my grandfather and his forbears did, but what they actually thought and felt about their world and their responses to it. In the absence of direct evidence from their own mouths or pens, I am left to do as any historian would do under the circumstances, namely, offer my own speculations. So here, for better or worse, is what I've learned.

Victor Karady, a professor at the Central European University in Budapest and the leading authority on the history of the Hungarian legal profession, maintains a digital file covering every member of the Budapest bar in the late nineteenth and early twentieth centuries.[1] When I asked him about my grandfather's purported life as a lawyer, he promptly responded with welcome news. His file included two Csillag Sandors. I knew that Sandor is the Hungarian form of Alexander, and that Hungarians state their last names first. Since the birthdate of only one of these fit that of Grandpa Starr, I knew I had found my man. The file entry recorded further that Sandor Csillag was born on April 12, 1877, in the town of Nyrluga in Szabolcs County. Since these are data provided by Csillag himself when he received his law degree, we can assume they are correct.

Both statements came as surprises. US Census records during the time of Csillag/Starr's life in Cleveland date his birth to 1878, not 1877. And his son George had clearly informed me that the birthplace of his father, and my grandfather, was Nyiregyhaza and not Nyrluga. Since both places were totally unknown to me I turned to old maps. These indicated that both are in the far northeast of Hungary, close to the borders of present-day Slovakia, Ukraine and Romania, and that they are a mere twenty-three miles apart. Nyiregyhaza has long been a thriving small city while Nyrluga is even today a small village, a mere spot on the map. Nyrluga is only seven miles from the Rumanian border and twenty-five miles from the borders with Ukraine and Slovakia. The obvious conclusion is that Csillag's birthplace was so insignificant a place that he found it more convenient to tell his younger son that he was from the nearest big city. But this hypothesis fell apart when I went on to discover that an even bigger city, Debrecen, today Hungary's second largest metropolis, is a few miles closer to Nyrluga than Nyiregyhjaza. Evidently, there were reasons other than proximity for Csillag to have told his son he was from Nyiregyhaza.

Professor Karady's file, based on the records of the Budapest University School of Law, goes on to describe Csillag as an "Israelite." Here, finally, was confirmation of the fact that Csillag was born Jewish and that at the time he enrolled as a law student in Budapest he still considered himself Jewish. My brother George's mischievous claim that the family must have been originally Jewish was right!

At the time of Csillag Sandor's birth in Nyrluga, he was one of only 115 Jews in that small village.[2] But Jews were by no means strangers in Hungary. A document from 1421 ordered Jewish residents of Budapest to wear red pointy caps and a yellow spot on their tunics.[3] A century after this law, many eastern (Sephardic) Jews had emigrated to Hungary from Turkish lands, and in the late seventeenth century yet another fresh wave of European or Ashkenazy Jews arrived from Austria and Germany, settling mainly along the Austrian border. To which of these groups did the Csillags trace their origins?

It turned out that none of these earlier waves of newcomers were at all relevant to the Csillags, whose forebears arrived in Hungary only in the 1700s. The Holy Roman Emperor of Austria, Charles VI, lived from 1685 to 1740. Early in his reign he grew concerned over the demographic explosion taking place in Jewish communities in Bohemia and Moravia. Clearly, they had prospered, and were producing large families. In order to cap the Jewish population, Charles VI issued the so-called Familiants Law of 1727, which limited the number of Jewish families in Moravia to 5,106. Just why he chose this number is only one of many mysteries surrounding these events. To keep the total constant he order that only one son per household would henceforth be allowed to marry and establish a family. Predictably, and as Charles VI doubtless hoped, this triggered an emigration of younger sons from Moravia. Some went to Silesia while at least some looked to the underpopulated eastern reaches of Hungary.

But for one fact, this suggests that the immigrant family in Nyrluga came early, after 1727. The family's name complicates this hypothesis, In to the eighteenth century Jews in the Austrian Empire did not have last names, preferring instead to be known simply as "Son of Avram" or Abramsohn" or "Son of Mendel," or "Mendelsohn." Only in 1783 did the reform-minded Holy Roman Emperor Joseph II (who ruled Hungary, as well as Austria and Moravia) ordered all Jews to adopt German last names. This demand arose from his government's eagerness to identify all inhabitants and fix their names on the tax rolls. To the credit of this Habsburg ruler, he also issued an edict allowing Jews to enter universities, establish schools, run businesses, and found synagogues--as long as they gained a knowledge of the German language and adopted German last names.

Following this imperial decree of 1783, Austro-Hungarian tax records listed quite a few families that had adopted the name Stern, which presumably denoted the Star of David. The family in Nyrluga was one of these. What we don't know is whether they arrived in Hungary only after 1783 or if they came earlier and, maintaining contact with family members in Moravia, decided to change their last names upon learning that the rest of their family had done so.

The record is also silent on the question of where in Moravia these ancestors came from. However, one thing is all but certain: they did not hail from one of the larger towns around Brno, places like Trebic, Holesov, or Mikulov. These were all well-developed and handsome towns in the eighteenth century. Not only did they boast elegant baronial residences but active and sophisticated Jewish communities. These were the folks whose descendants included such Moravian-born luminaries as composers Gustav Mahler and Erich Korngold, or psychiatrist Sigmund Freud.

The families that produced such geniuses were a world away from the progenitors of the Csillag family, who almost certainly hailed from the one of the dozens of small villages on lands owned by members of the nobility. On what basis can we say this? It is nearly impossible to imagine a young couple from one of the sophisticated Moravian towns emigrating to a tiny, remote, and foreign agricultural settlement, whereas it would be quite natural for a young couple from a rural commune to do so.

We can therefore safely conclude that this unnamed earliest known Hungarian male ancestor was in fact not Hungarian but a Jew from Moravia, that he hailed from an anonymous farming settlement in Habsburg Moravia, and that he arrived on Hungary's eastern border after 1727.

What profession did the earliest known progenitor of the Csillag family in Nyrluga follow, and what were the occupations of Nyrluga's handful of other immigrants from Moravia? In Central Europe during the eighteenth century the scarce commodity was not land but labor. Because of this labor shortage, the large landowners of Hungary campaigned for the admission of Jews and welcomed the wave of newcomers as agricultural workers. A village like Nyrluga would also have needed merchants and small craftsmen. We can therefore safely conclude that in the eighteenth and early nineteenth century the Sterns/Csillags either worked the land or were petty tradesmen.

In spite of the fact that the Germanization of their name opened many doors to ambitious Jews throughout the Austro-Hungarian Empire, the life of the Stern family at Nyrluga continued as it had for generations, as farmers or village tradesmen. In other words, they did not cash in on the opportunities that their name change opened to them and which were to expand thereafter.

The next wave of change came in the 1840s, when a fresh wave of reforms brought about profound changes in the lives of all Jews in Hungary. These trace to the end of the Napoleonic era, when members of the Hungarian nobility began lobbying the Austrian emperor in Vienna for greater self-government. As they intensified their campaign in the 1830s and 1840s, a handsome, eloquent, poor, intensely patriotic, but egotistical young Lutheran aristocrat, Lajos (Louis) Kossuth appeared on the scene.

Kossuth, a lawyer by training, spent a number of years as a staff member of the Hungarian Diet, a quasi-parliament made up of landed aristocrats. When the Diet was dissolved, he launched a career as a crusading journalist and campaigned relentless for freedom of the press and what he termed "Magyarization." He had a point, for ethnic Hungarians, or Magyars, were a minority in their own land, far outnumbered by the Slovaks, Romanian, Croats and other ethnic minorities living along Hungary's borders. Initially Kossuth had hoped to "Magyarize" these groups, but none wanted to abandon its own language and identity and rebrand itself as Hungarian. Worse, as nationalism arose among these peoples of Central Europe, each wanted to be united with its co-nationals on the other side of Hungary's borders. None were content to view themselves as a minority within Hungary. Kossuth came to realize that the only non-Magyar group that was prepared to make common cause with the Hungarian Magyars and form a majority bloc with them were the Hungarian Jews.

When the arch-reactionary Austrian Foreign Minister Count Metternich died in 1848, and with a Croatian army already on Hungarian territory, Kossuth made his move. In a series of powerful pamphlets, he called for independence from Austria, democratic elections, freedom of the press, the abolition of aristocratic rights, a national currency, and a single Hungarian nation, in which the Hungarian language would become the sole lingua franca for government (members of the Diet had heretofore debated in Latin!).

Kossuth's pamphlets and ringing oratory made him the leading figure in what had become a Europe-wide year of democratic uprisings. His name was heralded in Paris, Prague, and Berlin. In far-off America Senator Daniel Webster of Massachusetts read Kossuth's speeches into the Congressional record and began penning his biography, while the journalist Horace Greeley ("Go West, young man!") wrote of Kossuth that "Among the orators, patriots, statesmen, and exiles, he has, living or dead, no superior."

No group more warmly welcomed Kossuth's call to arms than Hungary's Jews, for they saw in his program the culmination of the process of emancipation that had begun back in 1783. Ten thousand young Jewish Hungarians joined Kossuth's army and were among those who cheered when, in April, 1849, he issued a Hungarian Declaration of Independence and declared himself, in a bow to both republicans and royalists, "regent-president."

Significantly for our story, Lajos Kossuth issued this ringing declaration in the Protestant Great Church in Debrecen, today Hungary's second biggest city, only fifteen miles distance from Nyrluga. It is inconceivable that the grandfather of Csillag Sandor was not among those local Jews who welcomed this call to emancipation and Magyar citizenship. Indeed, it is quite possible that he was present for Kossuth's great speech at the Cathedral in Debrecen and that he joined his army.

Unfortunately, Kossuth high-minded but endless rhetoric soon fell to earth. The military tide had already turned against him when he issued his Hungarian declaration of independence in April, 1849. Meanwhile, Kossuth's bold move and the possible demise of the Austrian monarchy had deeply alarmed Tsar Nicholas I in Russia. Wasting not a moment, he rushed his army to Hungary and forced Kossuth to abdicate on 11 August, barely four months after his ringing oratory in Debrecen.

The ideals advanced by Kossuth lived on among large numbers of the Magyar elite, and also among the many Hungarian Jews who had wholeheartedly embraced them. The interests of these two parties were complementary. The Magyars, by linking up with Hungary's Jews, could form a ruling majority. To draw Hungary's Jews to their cause, they annulled all discriminatory laws against the Jews and allowed them to function as full citizens of Hungary. From their side, Hungary's Jews realized that by entering into a political alliance with the Magyars and offering their full support to the Austro-Hungarian state, and adopting the Hungarian language (rather than German or Yiddish), they could achieve full emancipation and become free and normal citizens.

Because neither party could achieve its goals without the other, each was prepared to make a deal, the key result of which being that Hungary could thrive as a sovereign state and Jews would become, for all practical purposes, Magyars. This "deal" remained solidly in place down to 1919. It was reinforced by a Compromise (Ausgleich) that Hungary struck with Austria in 1867. This important agreement enabled the new Hungary to enjoy full autonomy but under the same crown as Austria, and confirmed the rights and civil liberties of the Kossuth era, including Jewish emancipation.

The new Magyar-Jewish coalition inspired many Jews, eager to take advantage of the new rights and opportunities accorded to them, to flood into Hungary's cities and into all the main urban professions. In 1850, there had been only 60 Jews in Nyiregyhaza, but by 1869 their number had increased to 1,129 and by 1880 to 2,097, or 8.7% of the population. In that year construction began on a grand new synagogue honoring the golden jubilee of the Habsburg Emperor Franz Joseph. By then Nyiregyhaza's Jewish community was one of the largest in Hungary. Most of the newcomers came from the surrounding villages, places like Nyrluga.

Driven in part by this migration, Nyiregyhaza gained full self-governance in 1865 and in 1876 (the year before Csillag Sandor's birth) it became a county seat. By the next census four years later the population had grown to 22,625. With new parks, schools, and civic buildings Nyiregyhaza was a city on the move. With the great Tokaj wine district only a few miles to the West, it was also a very pleasant place, as it remains today.

What is notable is that the Csillags of Nyrluga held back from joining this tide of migrants to the city. Only with the birth of their son Csillag Sandor in 1878 did Csillag Sr. (we don't yet know his first name!) and his family relocate to Nyriregyhaza. This was a full generation after Kossuth's reforms. Csillag Sr. and his father would surely have supported Kossuth and the Compromise of 1867 and welcomed their positive gestures towards Hungary's Jews. But for whatever reason, Csillag Sr. and his wife stayed on in tiny Nyrluga until after Sandor's birth. was born.

However, they had definitely relocated to the city by the time Sandor entered school, for it was only through successful studies at Nyriregyhaza's excellent new primary and secondary schools that one could even think of applying to the prestigious Faculty of Law at Budapest University, as Sandor was to do in 1895 or 1896. Both schools were new, having been organized a decade earlier by leaders of the rapidly expanding Jewish community there. A successful candidate for the Faculty of Law in Budapest would also have to have had some grasp of modern government and business, which could be gained in Nyiregyhaza but not in Nyrluga. Given his debt to his training there and to the insignificance of his home village, Nyrluga, it is no surprise that Sandor would later tell his younger son that he was from Nyiregyhaza. After all, it was there that Sandor first glimpsed the possibility of redefining himself as a self-made man.

As the pace of social and cultural change in the expanding city quickened, divisions appeared within the Jewish community of Nyiregyhaza. An Orthodox group split off from the Magyarizing "Status Quo" majority, which was busy raising money to construct the large new synagogue that opened three years after Sandor's birth. Meanwhile a growing number of more secular Jews disengaged from both groups, while a small but steadily increasing number of Hungarian Jews converted to Catholicism as a means of integrating themselves yet more fully integrated into the life of the newly constituted country.

This would not have shielded any of these groups from the wave of anti-Semitism that swept the city of Nyiregyhaza in 1883 and briefly spread throughout Hungary. This arose when the mother of a teenage girl in the small town of Tiszaezlar, fifteen miles northwest of Nyiregyhaza, reported the disappearance of her daughter. Then two brothers, one five years old and the other twelve, told neighbors that their father, the sexton of the Tiszaezlar synagogue, had ordered the girl killed and decapitated in order to get Christian blood that could be mixed with matzah for Passover. The older brother even claimed to have watched the gruesome scene through a keyhole at the synagogue.

The "Tiszaezlar blood libel case" became a sensation throughout Hungary and beyond. But when members of the Hungarian judiciary travelled to Tiszaezlar to examine the scene, they discovered that the keyhole in question did not open onto the synagogue and that the boy could not have observed any activity within. On August 3, 1882, the judge pronounced the defendants not guilty.

Even though justice prevailed, the damage was done. Venomous anti-Semitic pogroms occurred in many towns. In Budapest authorities had to call out the army to quell attacks on Jewish students at the University. Csillag Sandor was five years old and a resident of Nyrigyhaza when all this occurred.

How did the Jews of Nyiregyhaza react to the Tiszaezlar trial? On the one hand, a Hungarian court had completely exonerated the accused. On the other hand, the city's Jews had experienced at first hand a nasty strain of anti-Semitism that had remained largely out of sight during the years they were expanding their community and building their synagogue and schools. Some of them concluded that it was dangerous to engage too closely with the Gentile world and the new government in Budapest. These Orthodox Jews withdrew into their own community and sought to limit their contact with the new political order that had been introduced by Kossuth and the Compromise of 1867. Eventually they abandoned Nyiregyhazy.

On the other side, more worldly Jews, both active participants in the new "modern" synagogue and those who had become fully secular, embraced the new political order ever more closely. In other words, the Tiszaezlar affair broadened the split that already existed among the Jews of Nyiregyhaza and, for some at least, confirmed the case for full assimilation and even secularization.

Csillag Sandor stood emphatically with the assimilationists and the secularists. His entire career confirms his unwavering commitment to these ideals. Sandor's bold stance raises the question of whether his father held similar views or, alternatively, that it was Sandor who was the first member of his family to break with Judaism. Either way, Sandor's rejection of Judaism was final. The records of Budapest University continued to identify him as an "Israelite," but this was pro forma, since the only other recognized categories were Catholic and Protestant. "None of the above" was not an option. But there is no evidence of Csillag Sandor ever having been a practicing Jew. He was among those Jews who fully embraced Kossuth's proposal that the Jews of Hungary become fully "Magyar." This is how he viewed himself and how he expected others to view him.

We have presented indirect evidence that the Nyrluga Jewish family took the name Stern shortly after 1783, abandoning whatever earlier name it may have carried. But who then changed Stern to Csillag and when did this happen? In the complete absence of evidence on this important point, let us simply note the two possibilities. First, if Csillag Sandor's father or grandfather did it, then we can conclude that even if they stayed in backward Nyrluga, the family had embraced Kossuth's ideal of assimilation. Second, if Sandor himself changed the name, it indicates that it was he, not his father, who was the first in the family to grasp the promise of Magyarism and to recast his own identity to achieve it. Such a path paralleled that of many other Jews from Hungary's East. For example, Oszkar Jakubovits, who was born just east of Nyiregyhaza, changed his name to Jaszi in 1881 and, after emigrating to America in 1920, became a distinguished historian of Hungary at Oberlin College.

Whoever made the name change, by the time Csillag Sandor signed in at Budapest University around 1895-6 his last name had been changed for the second time in a century and the young law student was solidly on a course to full assimilation as a Magyar.

The Sterns of Nyiregyhaza were not the only people by that name who took this path to assimilation and Magyarization. Curiously, the two best known Stern-Csillags both achieved distinction in the arts. Thus, Terez (Therese) Stern (b. 1862) adopted the name Csillag and converted to Catholicism along the path to becoming a famous actress at the Hungarian National Theater in Budapest. Similarly, Hermann Stern changed his name to Csillag and gained distinction in Vienna as a violinist and teacher, one of whose students was the Finnish composer Sibelius. A third and older artist who adopted the name Csillag was Roza Goldstein who, as Rosa Csillag (b.1832), became a beloved mezzo-soprano at the Vienna Opera. None of these are known to have been related to Csillag Sandor. But all three indicate that when Sandor or his father changed its name to Csillag he was following what was already a well-trodden path.

Sandor's decision to seek admission to the Faculty of Law at Budapest University was also a natural one for any upwardly mobile Jewish graduate seeking to participate in what the Hungarian historian Victor Karady calls "the Jewish-Magyar symbiosis."[4] Kossuth himself had been a lawyer and it was Jewish lawyers who had heroically led the defense at the famous Tiszaezlar blood libel trial back in 1882. Law, more than any other field, served and embodied the liberal ideals that lay at the heart of the new Hungary created by Kossuth and the Compromise of 1867.

Law was also by far the most popular field of study the late nineteenth century, accounting for a majority of all degrees. There were twelve institutions at which one could study law when Csillag applied, and Budapest's Faculty of Law was by far the best and most prestigious of them. Thanks to careful research by Victor Karady, we know that twenty-four-year-old Sandor Csillag passed his first exam (ominously called the "Rigurosum") in the Law Faculty of Budapest University in 1901.[5]

Once again, Csillag was far from alone. Between the decade of his birth and 1910, the number of lawyers in Hungary soared from about 2,700 to 3,750. Wags said that Hungary was becoming "a nation of jurists." Moreover, nearly all this growth was due to the large number of Jews who flooded into the field. Whereas they had constituted only 21% of lawyers in 1890, by 1910 they made up fully 45% of the profession; in Budapest, which claimed a quarter of all Hungarian lawyers, their number reached 63% in the same period. If Jewish converts to Catholicism were added to that total the percentage would rise to more than three quarters. In short, Sandor had entered an extremely competitive field, and one which had grown so rapidly as to lead people to talk of an over-supply of lawyers.

Professors responded by making the curriculum ever more demanding. Whether because of this or for some other reason, Sandor twice failed the next and highest level of exams, obtaining his doctorate only in 1907. The topic of his dissertation is not known. He was twenty-nine years old.

Armed with his law degree, Csillag proceeded to set up a civil practice in Budapest and to live the life of which he had long dreamed. This meant, above all, finding a wife, a task which he went about with speed and determination. Within months he had proposed to lively and well-educated Irene Friedenberg. She and Sandor were of the same age.[6] Like Csillag, she came from Hungary's easternmost region. In later documents she identified her home town as Mikolec, which is only sixty-four miles west of Nyiregyhaza. In fact, she had been born in a nearby village, Mad, in the heart of the famed Tokaj-Hegyalja wine country. In spite of its small size—Mad had only 897 inhabitants in 1890—it was an important center of Orthodox Jewry, as well as viniculture. Most of the Jews of Mad had migrated from Moravia, which meant her background was nearly identical to Csillag's. Like him, she was fully secular in her interests and aspirations—her father, Marton Friedenberg was a merchant born in nearby Zalkod-- but it is notable that the Friedenbergs had not Magyarized their name. Eventually Irene was to look far beyond the borders of Hungary.

*Irene Friedenberg's birth certificate, from Mormon archives,
Boca Raton, courtesy of Dr. Joan Friedenberg, Florida.*

As the twentieth century dawned, some Hungarian women concluded that the chief beneficiaries of Hungary's liberal reforms had been men, and that women had been left with no vote, no role in government, and a menial role in the economy. A few genteel ladies might preside at well-appointed dinner tables but far larger numbers of their less fortunate sisters were condemned to drudge work of various sorts. To correct this, Rosika Schwimmer, an exact contemporary of Csillag and also a secular Jew, founded the Association of Feminists. In 1906, she and like-minded Hungarian women took note when Finland introduced women's suffrage, the first country to do so.

All this was was very much in the air when Csillag Sandor went courting. Intent on gaining a place in polite society and not on changing it, he had a decidedly old-fashioned and patriarchal view of women. This became alarmingly clear to Irene Friedenberg when she invited him to dine at her home. As they finished the last course, she proudly announced that she herself had prepared the entire meal. Sandor was horrified. After all, he was looking for a wife who would grace his table, not a cook. Their engagement ended that evening and within months she departed Hungary for a new life, and a career, in New York.

Sandor wasted no time in finding another marriageable lady. By 1908 he had proposed to Regina ("Reszi") Roth, who was only seventeen and presumably could not, or would not, cook. Unfortunately, as of this writing we know absolutely nothing of Reszi Roth's background other than the fact, recorded in a document discussed below, that she, too, was an "Israelite." A single surviving picture of Regina shows a petit young woman with round nose and full cheeks, elegantly coiffed hair, pearls, and a chic dress with long, ornamental sleeves. The dress is in fact a kimono, and her hair, gathered into a loose bun, is also in a style intended as "Japanese." This is no accident, for Puccini's opera Madame Butterfly had premiered in Milan and Brescia in 1904 and was brought to Budapest in the same year that Csillag Sandor was courting Reszi Roth. Clearly, she was a young lady of fashion, and someone who could assume that the society in which she moved would appreciate the up-to-the-moment operatic allusion.

Regina Roth in Japanese dress, c. 1906. S.F. Starr

Sandor and Reszi settled into a large apartment in Szondi ut, a street in the respectable Sixth District of Pest.[7]

They presumably began their married life with a small staff. However, their son Istvan (e.g. Stephen Starr) reported later to his wife that they soon maintained a staff of seven, including a coachman, cook, butler, a German governess, doorman, Hungarian maid, and laundress.[8] Clearly, Sandor had successfully launched his legal practice and his career.

As Csillag Sandor's career developed, he sought to acquire all the trappings of a successful member of the emerging upper class created by Hungary's unique "Jewish-Magyar symbiosis." These included a country residence. Besides being a social statement, a country place provided a welcome alternative to spending the humid Budapest summers in a downtown apartment building. At some point before 1912 the Csillag family took possession of a country house in the town of Nagykata, 37 miles southeast of Budapest and an hour's ride by train from Keleti Station.

The residence at Nagykata stood in the very center of the rural town. Its appearance and age are unknown, aside from the fact that it had an expansive beamed dining room with a chandelier. The house was large enough to accommodate the immediate family, several in-laws, as well as the staff of seven.

Each spring Sandor would hire a wagon to transport his library to Nagykata. There the family, which often included Sandor's widowed half sister, Irene Farkas, participated fully in the unchanging life of a Hungarian village. They lived close by the Catholic church, with its graveyard full of statues of saints. The church itself had two doors into the nave, one for peasants and the other reserved for well-born citizens. Just outside the doors was a low hillock where the town crier would appear each Sunday after mass and, gathering the parishioners with a hand bell, relate the local news of the day. The family would stay in Nagykata through the autumn harvest and then return to Buda.

Csillag Sandor ca. 1908. S.F. Starr

During these idyllic years following their marriage, the Csillag family grew to five with the births of Istvan

(Stephen) Zoltan in 1909, Gyorgi (George) in 1911, and Clara in 1912. A photograph from a couple of years later shows Istvan, with his mother's round nose and round cheeks, perched on a three-wheeler and Sandor with a pince-nez, sitting by proudly and somewhat stiffly in a black suit with high collar. Then tragedy struck, when Resci Roth Csillag died while giving birth to her fourth child. This happened in 1913, when she was only twenty-three years old. Her eldest son's sole memory of her was riding with her through the countryside in a carriage. Neither Clara nor Gyogi retained any memory of their mother.

And so Csillag Sandor became a single father. In an effort to help the bereaved father and orphaned children, their grandmother, Aunt Irene Farkas, and another aunt moved in with the family. These adoring ladies spoiled all three children, lavishing on them rich foods cooked with ample amounts of goose fat. In their eyes Istvan in particular could do no wrong. Thoroughly spoiled by their attention, he fell into the habit of simply stepping out of his clothes at night and leaving them on the floor, confident that an aunt or one of the bevy of servants would pick up after him. His wife, Ivy Jane Edmondson Starr, reported that his habit continued into the early years of his married life.

The rhythm of normal life returned. The children grew, going to school in Budapest during the year and spending summers in Nagykata. Stephen Starr remembered a sense of foreboding each autumn as the return to city life approached. He knew it was only days away when he would spot long lines of peasants advancing slowly through the fields of ripened wheat with theirs scythes swinging, pausing every few strokes to sharpen their blades.

Living right next to the Catholic Church meant that the Csillag family could observe at close hand the life of the parish and participate informally in some of its events. When Istvan was about six, the entire town celebrated the installation of two new bells in the church's steeple. The mayor spoke, and then the priest offered a blessing. Before doing so he asked for all the "virgins" present to step forward. The boy was puzzled when the crowd tittering mischievously and not one of the local maidens responded to his call. Only much later did he understand the cause of their mirth.

As the Csillag children grew, their relation to the Catholic Church at Nagykata grew ever closer. This process calls for close examination, but all those involved are now dead and the written sources are meager. The best we can do is to conduct a forensic examination of the little evidence that survives and draw whatever conclusions it warrants.

The key document is a certificate of baptism issued by the Catholic Church of Nagykata. It certifies that Csillag Istvan Zoltan was baptized at the church on the 18 July, 1919, and that this action was officially entered into the registry on 15 September, 1921. It also identifies Istvan's parents as "Csillag Sandor, lawyer, Catholic" and "Roth

Regina Israelite."

The message is clear: the Csillag's oldest son was baptized and presumably his sister Clara and brother Gyorgi were baptized at the same time. But when did these baptisms occur? Note that the document also provides the surprising information that Csillag Sandor was already a Catholic when the baptism took place, but that Regina Roth was not. Of course, it is quite possible that one partner in a Jewish couple might convert to Catholicism while the other remained Jewish. But it would be unusual for a young woman whose husband was thirteen years older to defy his views on a matter as fundamental as the choice of their family's religion. Yet the certificate clearly identifies him as being Catholic. The only logical conclusion is that the Csillag Sandor's conversion and baptism took place only after Regina's death, in other words, at some date between late 1914 and November 19, 1919.

Csillag Zoltan's certificate of baptism, 18 July, 1919. S.F. Starr

Does this imply that the father converted first and then waited a decade to baptize his eldest son and, presumably, his other children? Contradicting this hypothesis is Istvan (Stephen Starr's) clear recollection, related several times to both his wife and younger son, that he served several years as an altar boy at the church in Nagykata. In the 1980s Istvan, by then Stephen Starr, returned with his wife to Nagykata as tourists. The Csillags' house had long since been demolished and most of what he remembered of the town had been replaced with ugly Communist era buildings. But as he and his wife trudged up the steps to the church he looked down and with a shock of recognition spotted the old familiar flagstones. The sight of them immediately called to mind his racing "hell bent" up that flagstone walk as the priest stood at the top urgently waving to him to hurry and nervously complaining that he was already late. The other acolytes all stood by grinning.

Church of St George (Szent Gyorgi), Nagykata

The incident with the priest could not have taken place after the baptism in November, 1919, because within days of the ceremony all three Csillag children were sent out of the country for their safety. Given that altar boys rarely are allowed to attend at Mass before they are seven, and that even then they are required to take classes for several months, then we can conclude that the incident on the steps took place shortly after 1916.

But this implies that Istvan was serving as an altar boy before his very late baptism. Could the failure to have him baptized earlier have been due to an oversight? Given the chaos of World War I this is entirely possible. Hence, the most logical conclusion is that Csillag Sandor converted to Christianity after the death of his wife in 1915. Two events followed: first, he was elevated to a higher military rank and, second, he immediately enrolled his children in the life of the church, which included Istvan's service as an altar boy. But with Sandor himself rushing back and forth to the Eastern Front and with the home front in a state of confusion, he simply forgot to attend to his children's baptism, an oversight that he corrected in November, 1919.

These details turn out to be important to our understanding of Csillag Sandor at this critical moment of his life. He had clearly accomplished much. Back in Nyiregyhaza he had received a solid education that gained him entry into the prestigious Faculty of Law at Budapest University. And after a struggle he had earned his doctoral degree and set himself up in what was manifestly a lucrative legal practice. He had married a woman whose background was similar to his own, and they had three growing children. Except for the tragic death of his wife, Reszi, his life had followed a steady upward trajectory.

The rapid rise of Csillag Sandor epitomizes the ideals and hopes of liberal Hungary as propounded by Lazlo Kossuth back in 1848-1849, enshrined in the Compromise of 1867 establishing the dual Austro-Hungarian monarchy, and elaborated in legislation since then. We don't know if it was Sandor or his father who changed the name from Stern to Csillag, but this action initiated the family's Magyarization, which proceeded steadily and successfully thereafter. By 1910 or so Csillag Sandor was a living embodiment of the practical "philosemitism" underlying the deal that had been struck between Catholic Magyars and the more secular Jews. This unwritten "assimilationist social contract"[9] was based on mutual understanding and the recognition of the two parties' interdependence. It enabled them together to do what neither could do alone, namely, to form a majority bloc and rule the country. And it opened attractive careers to the brightest and most ambitious members of both groups.

It is no wonder that Csillag Sandor became an ardent patriot of the Hungary that had enabled him to advance and prosper, and a keen supporter of the Dual Monarchy of Franz Joseph II. Indeed, he retained these loyalties down to the end of his life. Hungary went further in its "philosemitism" than practically any other country in continental Europe at the time, but informal but real barriers remained. Jewish lawyers could rise to the top of the Hungarian bar, but the next two steps were largely closed to them.[10] They could practice before imperial courts of law but positions as notaries, judges, and members of the higher civil service were reserved mainly for ethnic Magyars and Catholics. Jews could wear swords and volunteer for the army but the officer corps was largely closed to them. As he faced these realities, Csillag Sandor came up against what today we would call a glass ceiling.

There is no doubt that Sandor Csillag thought of himself as a person of exceptional talent, which his early professional, intellectual, and financial success only confirmed. His family had long since rejected the traditionalism of Orthodox Jewry and by the time he finished law school he was thoroughly secularized. Why, then, should he not overcome this last barrier to his social an economic ascent by converting to Catholicism? This is the kind of reasoning that underlay his decision, taken shortly after the death of his wife in 1915, to become a Christian.

On 28 June, 1914, a mustachioed Bosnian Serb nationalist named Gavrilo Princip stepped out of a crowd that had assembled in the city of Sarajevo to greet members of the Austro-Hungarian royal family. Moving quickly, he fired two deadly shots. The assassination of Archduke Francis Ferdinand and his wife was a gravely serious act. Austria-Hungary immediately sent its army into Serbia for what was intended as a punitive and localized strike. But Tsar Nicholas II of Russia rushed to the defense of his ally, Serbia. As the Russian army advanced into Ukraine towards the Balkans, Germany seized the moment to attack Belgium and Luxembourg with the clear intent of invading France. All Europe descended into chaos.

When World War I broke out at the end of July, Csillag Sandor and his family were in the countryside. To meet the crisis the Hungarian government issued a general draft call. The Csillag's coachman was among those mobilized in the first call. Five year-old Istvan loved this man. He would sneak into the kitchen each morning to share the coachman's peasant breakfast of hot pork fat seasoned with paprika dripped onto a slice of black rye bread and chewed up with a clove of garlic.

Csillag Sandor with Klara, Gyorgi, and Istvan, Nagykata, 1914-15.

Csillag Sandor's children salute the Austro-Hungarian Emperor. 1914. S.F. Starr

When the day came for the coachman and other local draftees to depart, the entire town of Nagykata drove or walked the six miles to the rail head at Tapioszele to wish them off. Members of the Csillag household crowded into two coaches and sang as they bumped along. The cook had prepared trays of food for the untested soldiers, who were already strutting about the platform like heroes when the family arrived. It was a good-natured and festive occasion, with a band playing and flags flying. The Csillags gaily passed their baskets of fried chicken up to the soldiers, who leaned far out of the train windows, grinning and waving. Then followed bunches of flowers picked by the children. Five-year-old Istvan waved a cheerful goodbye to his friend, the coachman.

Sixty years later Istvan, now Stephen Starr, recalled that the departing soldiers had the air of people heading for a picnic. Everyone was sure these local heroes would return victorious in only a month, or two at the most. But scarcely any of those who departed for the front that day ever returned alive.

Coachman in Nagykata ca. 1910.

At the very time the villagers were celebrating at Tapioszele, the army of Tsar Nicholas II was advancing into Galicia, that part of the western Ukraine that had been under Austrian rule since the eighteenth century. The Russians' force was enormous, four armies numbering 1,200,000 men, and well-armed. As it crossed the Russia-Austrian frontier, an Austro-Hungarian army of 950,000 rushed eastward to head off an attack on the Galician capital of Lemberg (now Lviv). In a series of bloody encounters the Russians seized Lemberg and pushed the frontier one-hundred fifty miles westward into Austrian territory. The Russians killed 324,000 Austrians and Hungarians while losing 225,000 of their own men.

The Battle of Galicia was a humiliating defeat for Emperor Franz Joseph and for the Austro-Hungarian dual monarchy. Within a month after the Nagyhaza recruits waved their last goodbyes, it was clear that the Austro-Hungarian state itself, and the entire way of life it sustained, were in mortal danger.

Stephen Starr later told his wife, Ivy Jane, that his father, thirty-seven-year-old Csillag Sandor, had volunteered for service in the cavalry and had been lightly wounded in his unit's first encounter with the Russians. While documents regarding his military service have yet to be exhumed from the archives, this is not surprising, for thousands of other patriotic lawyers and professional men, including many of Csillag's age, also rushed to the colors. His conversion enabled him to rise in rank. Sandor was so enthusiastic that he dressed both of his young boys in Hungarian army uniforms and photographed them as they saluted the camera.

During the first days of war the Tsar's army took captive 130,000 Austrian troops, whom they quickly packed onto trains and sent to hard labor building a railroad to Murmansk on the White Sea and roads in distant Kazakhstan, along the frontier with China. Thousands perished in the work. At the same time, those who claim that World War I was a kind of dress rehearsal for the inhumanity of World War II surely overstate the case, if the treatment of captives is any measure. The Russian, German, and Austrian Red Cross organizations were in regular touch with each other, and officials from the captives' home countries regularly visited the internment camps.[11]

Neither Vienna nor Budapest had anticipated that the first battle of the war would leave them with 40,000 captive Russian soldiers on their hands. This was a fraction of the numbers of Austrians and Hungarians the Russians had captured but it was significant nonetheless. The governments in Vienna and Budapest had no plan for what to do with them. So they set up several POW camps near Hungary's eastern border and simply parked the captive Russians there.[12] By comparison with Germany's three-hundred POW camps housing 2,400,000 POWs or what eventually became the million captives in Russia, these Austro-Hungarian camps were modest affairs.[13] Their commandants were reminded of their duty to "treat the prisoners humanely" and in accordance with the 1907 Hague Convention that Emperor Franz Joseph had signed in 1909. Since all able-bodied officers were needed for the war effort, the management of these camps was entrusted to wounded officers and civilians. Csillag Sandor had been wounded and therefore met this criterion. With his solid grounding in the law and his background in the very regions of Eastern Hungary where the camps were situated, he was an ideal candidate to direct one of them. The appointment also provided this patriotic lawyer, who aspired to a career in the upper reaches of the civil administration, a welcome opportunity to exhibit his managerial skills.

And so Csillag took over the command of a large POW camp on Hungary's northeastern border. City Directories for Budapest after 1914 do not list the Csillags at their apartment in Pest, which suggests that during the war the family stayed in the country year-round rather than just in the summers. As a single father, Sandor was fortunate that his mother and sister could take care of the three children. But stationed far to the East, the widower Sandor missed what was left of his young family. He therefore arranged for Istvan, Clara, and Gyorgi to join him. They spent more than a year at the POW camp. After buying chickens from local farmers and planting a garden, the family was able to live there in relative comfort.

Csillag's tenure was apparently successful, for no incidents are recorded in the detailed documents preserved in the Hungarian archives. Stories passed on by both his son Istvan (Stephen Z. Starr) and his second wife, Irene, provide hints of his managerial style and how it was received. Both reported that Csillag believed that idleness posed the greatest threat to good order at the camp. Other camp commanders may have organized athletic events, but

Csillag followed a plan that was distinctly his own. Obtaining paints, brushes, and canvases, he soon had scores of prisoners painting landscapes and portraits.

He also set up a woodworking shop. Three quarters of a century later his son Istvan fondly recalled being befriended by a Russian who had worked as a barge hauler on the Volga before being drafted into the Tsar's army. One day this homesick POW proudly presented the six-year-old with an elaborately carved model of a Volga boat. Considering the deep antipathy towards Russia that had permeated Hungarian society since 1849, when the Tsar's army had crushed the liberal regime of Louis Kossuth, and considering that during World War II both Germans and Russians badly mistreated their prisoners of war, these incidents from the life of one Hungarian internment camp are a credit to its commandant.

A surviving report card confirms that Istvan spent the second grade at a city school in Budapest, but we have no idea whether other members of the family were in Budapest or back in Nagykata. That his sister and brother were too young to attend school suggests that they probably remained in Nagykata while he lived with his father in the city. These improvised arrangements continued throughout the war, with Istvan spending more and more time with his grandmother, aunt, and siblings at Nagykata and Sandor staying in Budapest and visiting Nagykata when he could.

During Istvan's winters in Budapest his father would sometimes spirit him away from his studies to spend an afternoon skating on Margaret Island, followed by dinner at a fine restaurant and then the theater. Aside from affording an opportunity to spoil his eldest son, who had only recently lost his mother, such indulgences in a time of war reminded Csillag of the kind of life to which his years of study and work entitled him, but which were receding into the past as Hungary's crisis deepened.

By 1918, tens of thousands of Hungarian troops had died in battles that left Hungary less secure than at the start of the war. At the war's end the Entente countries (Russia, France and Great Britain) demanded that Hungary hand over territory to them. Neighboring Slovaks, Croatians, and Romanians all saw their chance to set up their own states and looked covetously at Hungarian regions inhabited by their co-nationals. Irregular forces from these neighboring lands, furloughed Hungarian soldiers, and local Communists all roamed the countryside in marauding bands. The Hungarian government and the Austro-Hungarian monarchy to which it pledged its allegiance were powerless to reverse this downward spiral. Finally, on 31 October socialist forces led by Mihaly Karolyi seized power in Budapest. The "Chrysanthemum Revolution," so named for the flowers its jaunty backers wore in their lapels, brought many intellectuals into government. They were full of projects for rebuilding society but lacked any plan for rescuing the country from the deepening anarchy, let alone for dealing with the millions of non-Hungarians who wanted to secede and join their co-nationals in creating a Czechoslovakia or a Rumania. Trade ceased, food supplies vanished, and over the winter of 1918-1919 people grew desperate.

Like Csillag, Karolyi considered himself a true son of Kossuth and his revolution. His circle included many well-educated people like Csillag Sandor, one of them being the Minister of Nationalities, Oscar Jasci, the fellow easterner of partly Jewish background who, as we have noted, ended his days a professor at Oberlin College. But Csillag had no use for Karolyi's socialism, despised Karolyi's refusal to reinstate Habsburg rule, and saw at once that the Karolyi government was too weak to preserve the integrity of the Hungarian state. Csillag wanted nothing less than a full return to the former days of Habsburg rule under the Dual Monarchy.

Amidst this chaos, Csillag Istvan celebrated his ninth birthday on November 2, 1918. The Chrysanthemum Revolution had taken place only two days before and his father was in Budapest. Istvan and the rest of the family remained in Nagykata, where the local populace lived in fear of the armed bands of mounted fighters that had been spotted in the countryside nearby. Istvan and his young friends nonetheless gathered at the dining room table and broke out in applause when the cook brought in the birthday cake. Just at that moment a detachment of marauders swept into the village center on horseback. It is unknown to which faction they belonged or even if they were Hungarians, as opposed to the Romanian forces that were already roaming the land. Encountering no opposition and with no clear goal mind, they raced about the town's center wildly, shooting at random. Some of their bullets shattered the dining room window, glanced off the chandelier, or crashed into the beamed and plastered ceiling. As the children took refuge beneath the table, chunks of plaster rained down onto the table, ruining the cake.

Fortunately, no one was injured. But it was clear that Nagykata was no longer the safe refuge it had been since the outbreak of war. At dawn on the next day the entire family boarded the train back to Budapest. All the glass had been shot out of the car windows and the shooting still continued, especially at stations along the route. Young Istvan later recalled that each time the train approached a station the passengers huddled on the floor of the cars.

The family arrived safely, but precisely at the moment when the new Karolyi government was proving itself totally incapable of stabilizing the situation. Anarchy reigned in the capital as the political pendulum continued its leftward swing. Finally, on March 19, 1919, Communists forces led by a bellicose orator named Bela Kun seized power. Kun was a thoroughly secular Jew from Transylvania who had become a Communist while a POW in Russia. He and his Reds promptly nationalized all property, seized landholdings, cancelled all taxes on the peasantry, and took total control of cultural organizations, schools, and hospitals. Worse, after an attempted coup against them they instituted a Red Terror, murdering some six- hundred suspected enemies in Budapest alone. Those not murdered outright were brought before hastily convened revolutionary tribunals led by trusted Communists with no legal training whatsoever. The most common sentence for those judged guilty of anti-revolutionary activity was to be shot.

A handful of Budapest's lawyers supported the Communist coup,[14] just as some others had welcomed Karolyi. There may have been Communists among the pro-Kun faction but most of this small group acted on the expectation that if and when Kun were to fall there was sure to be an anti-Jewish backlash in which they would be the first to suffer. However, the overwhelming majority of Budapest lawyers of all religions, including Csillag Sandor, watched with horror as Kun and his followers tore down what was left of the system to which they had been committed and to which they owed their own advancement and place in society.

Csillag vehemently opposed Bela Kun and his Communists but we know next to nothing about the specific activities he engaged in during the one hundred thirty-three days of Kun's reign. Stephen Starr's wife, Ivy Jane, said directly that "Steve's father [i.e., Csillag Sandor] was involved in a vigilante group to put down the 1919 Communist rebellion." She had heard this directly from Sandor's son, her husband. Though only eight years old in 1917, Istvan was in Budapest at the time of these events and was bound to see them through his father's eyes, even if he did not understand them. And since he was to remain in regular contact with his father down to the latter's death, Istvan had ample opportunity to learn of his father's activities during that fateful autumn of 1917 and had neither a motive nor any need to invent such a story.

Two further detail are worth noting. Ivy Jane Starr also reported that her father-in-law, Sandor, had refused to take off his hat when Bela Kun passed by in a parade, and that he was briefly imprisoned by the Kun regime. She seems to have conflated these two events in her mind, but her brother in law, George Starr (Csillag Georgi), reported to this author in 1983 that Kun had jailed Csillag Sandor for his anti-Communist activities, a more plausible cause for imprisonment than failing to doff one's hat.

Communist leader Bela Kun (rt.), 1919, a year after his troops shot up Csillag Istvan's birthday party.

Unrest continued as Kun proved even less able than Karolyi to stabilize the situation. The Romanian army watched this downward spiral and seized the moment to invade Hungary in order to seize territory. Hungary was now in free fall. Two years earlier Vladimir Lenin and his Bolsheviks had pulled off a coup in St. Petersburg and installed their Communist government in Russia. Kun desperately appealed to Lenin to send the newly-formed Red Army to his rescue, but the promised help never arrived. Kun fled the country and spent the rest of his days in Bolshevik Russia. Stalin eventually rewarded Kun for his loyalty to the cause of Communism by having him shot.

For forty days after Kun fled Hungary the Romanian army occupied Budapest. This provided an opening for Miklos Horthy, head of what remained of the Hungarian army, to seize power in what was the third coup in three years. In a bizarre but bold diplomatic and military stroke he first managed to get the Romanians to support his entry into Budapest on November 16 and then proceeded to drive them out of the capital. As the Romanians departed they pillaged a wide swath through Hungary, taking with them hundreds of freight cars filled with equipment and loot.

Although a navy man, Admiral Horthy had the ego required of a "leader on horseback." He was a Calvinist nobleman from Transylvania who claimed to be a monarchist. A few months after restoring the Diet or parliament, he got that body to name him "His Serene Highness, the Regent if the Kingdom of Hungary." This was to be a temporary post until a new King was named, but when a genuine Habsburg, Charles IV, appeared on the scene Horthy drove him out. Charles committed suicide soon thereafter. Horthy then set about building a personal dictatorship. To achieve this, he and his supporters used the army to restore order and security, for which most Hungarians were grateful. Then they began systematically dismantling the liberal institutions and liberal values of the pre-war decades in order to make way for a regime based on narrow Hungarian chauvinism.

During Bela Kun's rule and the first year of Horthy's rule, a powerful and ruthless ultra-nationalist movement had arisen among demobilized soldiers, some of their officers, and many others embittered by their country's humiliation in battle and then at the hands of Bela Kun's Communists. Its aim was to punish those responsible for losing the war and to stamp out Communism and all those Hungarians who represented or supported it. In practice, this "White Terror" was fiercely anti-Semitic, directing its hostility above all against those Jews, including Jewish converts to Christianity, who had risen in the professions and in government. Their aim, they said, was to reverse the social forces that had turned Budapest into "Judapest." Not waiting to gain power, armed bands roamed Budapest to hunt down Jews, or suspected Jews, of all descriptions. In the latter months of 1919 and through most of 1920 hundreds of Jews or suspected Jews were murdered in the capital, most in daylight and in full public view.

A century after these events Hungarian historians still debate the extent to which Admiral Horthy supported the White Terror. He was certainly well aware of it, for many of his own soldiers were centrally involved. He even criticized one of his subordinate officers for allowing his men to commit senseless murders, especially of Jews. But, it is argued, he otherwise stood by passively, turning his silence into tacit support. The White Terror raged on during the months Horthy was consolidating his control. Jews and other professionals knew full well that in Budapest it was directed mainly against them, and that it threatened not only their careers but their lives. Many chose to wait it out, hoping it would soon run its course, which in fact happened. Others were not prepared to wait, and began leaving Hungary in droves.

Unfortunately, we have no concrete information on Csillag's views and activities during the crucial early months of Horthy's rule. Was the vigilante group in which he participated during the Bela Kun interlude one of the groups that later evolved into, or merged with, the White Terror? Did Csillag, as Horthy rose to power, briefly serve as a judge in one of the courts that tried and passed death sentences on Communists who did not leave with Kun? This is what Ivy Jane Starr believed, on the basis of what she had learned from her husband, Stephen Starr (Csillag Istvan). In the same recollection cited above, she went on to say that "Then [i.e., following Kun's fall], being a lawyer, he [i.e. Csillag] became a judge in the trials that followed." Now, for all her talents, Ivy Jane Starr was not a historian, and took little interest in history. She had no reason to invent a historical role--positive or negative-- for her father-in-law, for whom she had little affection. Thus, even though this report was based on a single recollection by his son, conveyed by his daughter-in-law sixty years after the events in question, it appears more than likely that Csillag Sandor did indeed serve briefly as a judge in Admiral Horthy's campaign to mete out justice to those who had helped Bela Kun's brief Communist revolution.

One further detail merits our attention. We have noted that Csillag Sandor travelled to Nagykata to obtain certification that his son Istvan had indeed been baptized in the Roman Catholic church there. This occurred on November 18, 1919, only two days after Admiral Horthy and his troops entered Budapest. The White Terror was already underway, so it would have been wise under any circumstances to have at hand as many documents as possible to prove that he himself and his children were Christians, as the church paper from Nagykata attested. But did he also welcome Horthy's early claim that he would restore the monarchy to which he, Csillag, remained loyal, and put the legal profession once more on that lofty pedestal in Hungarian society to which it was entitled? And on this basis did he serve briefly on one of Horthy's tribunals? And then, seeing the gangsterism and wanton murder that persisted after Horthy's rise to power, did he belatedly realize that Horthy was no better than Kun and that the Hungary he had supported was doomed?

Three more blows fell in quick succession, the first in the same month that Horthy seized the reins of power. Once the war was over, the victorious allies, led by Woodrow Wilson, Britain's Lloyd George, and France's Georges Clemenceau, convened in Versailles to plan the post-war world. Above all, this meant fixing blame for the war and hence responsibility for paying reparations to those countries that had suffered its consequences. Never mind that Russia bore at least as much responsibility for the conflagration as Germany, let alone Austria-Hungary, or that the blame could be extended to every other power as well. The Versailles conferees agreed that Germany and Austria-Hungary alone were responsible and therefore must be required to pay reparations. Lloyd George demanded that the treaty acknowledge Germany's and Austria's "war guilt," but thought that onerous reparations would destroy the German and Austro-Hungarian economies and make recovery impossible. But Clemenceau demanded reparations at all costs, while Woodrow Wilson felt that reparations could be extracted without the humiliating "war guilt" language that was eventually enshrined in Article 231. At this crucial moment Wilson failed to provide decisive leadership. And so the conferees kept intact the vengeful language drafted by American diplomat Norman Davis and John Foster Dulles, a thirty-one-year lawyer with three years' experience, thus opening a path to Hitler's rise to power and to World War II. After World War II Dulles became the U.S. Secretary of State.

The second blow flowed directly from the first. If Germany and Austria-Hungary bore sole responsibility for the outbreak of war in 1914, they should be punished by handing much of their territory over to new states that were to be based on the principle of national identity. The resulting Treaty of Trianon stripped Hungary of three-quarters of its former territory and two thirds of its population. Aside from the loss of more than half of its arable land and two fifths of its industry, one out of every three Hungarians was now stranded in neighboring countries. With no choice in the matter, Horthy's government signed the Treaty dismembering Hungary on June 4, 1920.

The final blow fell in July, 1920. Over the previous year the legal profession and the universities that trained its members had been singled out for vilification, mainly because so many lawyers were Jews. Anti-Jewish atrocities were committed in several university towns and even on the academic premises. Amidst this mayhem, Horthy's prime minister issued a numerus clausus law that imposed strict university admission quotas on elements deemed "politically insecure." The quota for Jews was set at 6% of each entering class.

In spite of all this, millions of Hungarian Jews and Jewish converts continued to hope against hope that an acceptable "new normal" would eventually emerge from the wreckage of Hungary, and that they would find an honorable place in it. Indeed, many succeeded. Scores of Jewish-owned industries, including some of the largest and most strategic in the land, began once more to function. Businesses reopened their doors. Jews once more figured in the country's commercial, intellectual, and cultural life, and a few even found honorable positions in government.

But this was not for Csillag Sandor. Whatever hopes he may earlier have held for Admiral Horthy, by the summer of 1920 (if not before) it was utterly clear to him that the world in which he had made his way so successfully would never be restored. Horthy himself had signed the bill instituting quotas for Jews in the legal profession. The Dual Monarchy was no more, and Hungary itself had been so thoroughly dismembered by the victorious Allies that it offered little scope for a successful and ambitious forty-three-year-old lawyer.

One further factor figured large in Csillag Sandor's thinking. He had followed published accounts of the discussions at the Paris Peace Conference at Versailles and knew well the ominous provisions of the Treaty of Trianon. He was also well informed on the discussions leading to the establishment of the League of Nations in 1920. He concluded that, far from introducing an era of peace, these actions by the world's leading diplomats were bound, sooner or later, to lead to another war. Csillag Sandor's decision to emigrate to America, and not to England or Germany, flowed from this conviction that another war was inevitable, and his desire at all cost to assure that his two sons would not have to fight in it. Both of his sons later confirmed that these were his views.

But how would Csillag manage to depart Hungary? Amidst the anarchy that prevailed under Bela Kun, he had decided to send all three of his children to safety abroad. As soon as he was able to make the necessary arrangements, he sent the children to Passau, the ancient German city at the confluence of the Inn and the Danube from which monks had spread Christianity into Bohemia a millennium earlier. Irene Friedenberg's brother Hugo was already there, studying metalwork and the field of horology. It was he who arranged for Csillag Istvan's schooling.

Young Csillag Istvan was enrolled at the Salvator Kolleg, a highly regarded Catholic boy's school that still exists, although now secularized. There he was tutored each morning in Latin. His teacher, a priest, strolled with the boy around the ancient cloister, all the while conversing with him in the language of Cicero. There was nothing unusual in the fact that this twelve year-old should have been taught to speak Latin during those walks, and not merely to read and write it. After all, down to the era of Lajos Kossuth the Hungarian parliament had conducted its business in that tongue. To the end of his life Istvan read at least one book in Latin each year and could never reconcile himself to the fact that his younger son had majored in classics at Yale but could not speak the language that embodied Europe's classical heritage.

Csillag Sandor's children were now out of danger, but the path to America remained closed to him for the simple reason that he did not have a valid passport. The Austro-Hungarian Empire no longer existed and Horthy's Hungary had yet to begin issuing passports. The so-called "Nansen Passports," created by an Intergovernmental Conference for use by Russian and other refugees, did not become available until the end of 1922.

To solve this problem Csillag travelled to Prague, since October, 1918, the capital of the new state of Czechoslovakia. This was a logical decision, for the government there had already begun issuing internationally recognized passports. Prague also appealed to Csillag because Czechoslovakia, under its founding president, Tomas Masaryk, was precisely the kind of open, democratic, and pluralistic society that Hungary was ceasing to be.

Besides having no passport, Csillag was broke. He somehow found work and was able to visit his children in Passau. Returning to Prague, the young widower made contact with Irene Friedenberg, the woman to whom he had briefly been engaged back in 1907 and who had responded to his breaking off the engagement by emigrating to America. She landed squarely on her feet. Once in New York Irene had acquired enough English to get a job with the Cunard Steamship Company, which had just launched its two superliners, Mauretania and Lusitania. She was still employed by Cunard in 1915 when a German submarine sank the Lusitania, which led directly to America's entering the First World War. She also found work in New York as a fashion model. Her future step-daughter in law, Ivy Jane Starr, drawing on statements by her husband, Stephen Starr, reported that a stylish picture of Irene, with soulful black eyes and jet-black hair, was even featured in Vanity Fair.

During the last year of her life Irene told Sarah Cory, wife of her grandson Guy Cory, that she had "marched for women's' suffrage in New York." The event in question took place on October 23, 1915, when more than 25,000 women trooped up Fifth Avenue to promote women's right to vote. The New York Times warned in an editorial that if women get the vote, they will "play havoc for themselves and society." Others rejected it as a passing fad. But this was no mere whim for the indignant young immigrant from Hungary for, as we have seen, her advocacy of women's rights nearly a decade before the march had been the cause of Sandor Csillag's breaking of their engagement.

1915 Women's Suffrage Parade, New York, in which Irene Friedenberg participated.
New York Historical Society Library

After an exchange of letters (none of which survive), Irene travelled to Europe to meet her former suitor. The reunion was a success and the couple decided to marry. It is not clear if the actual wedding took place in Prague in 1921 or 1922 or shortly after the couple arrived in the New World. Nor is it known what kind of wedding they agreed upon, as she was Jewish and he now a Catholic.

Irene Friedenberg at the time of her marriage to Csillag Sandor, ca. 1921. Guy Cory.

No less complicated was the planning needed to get the three Csillag children to America. Irene paid for their ocean passages but had to return immediately to work and therefore could not accompany them to New York. Sandor also had to work to raise money for the family's early days in America. In the end they confidently (or foolishly) decided to send the children across the ocean alone, under the care of the elder boy, Istvan, now thirteen years old. The plan was for them to sail to New York, where they would be met by Irene's brother. This brother, Hugo Friedenberg, is the same relative of Irene's who had been responsible for Csillag Istvan's studying in Passau. When he had migrated to Detroit Hugo abandoned his expertise in clocks and founded the Ring Tool and Dye Company, which promptly made him wealthy.

The trio of young Hungarians, age thirteen, eleven, and nine, were to board the Berengaria at Le Havre. Launched by the Hamburg-American line as and named Imperator, this vessel had been the largest passenger ship in the world by gross tonnage when it was launched by the Hamburg American line in 1913. Seized by the U.S. and turned into a troop ship, it was now managed by the Cunard Line. Conveniently, since Irene Friedenberg now worked at the Cunard Line's New York office, it was a simple matter for her to secure tickets for the unaccompanied children. But on their way to the Berengaria the trio of young Cillags got confused and took the train instead to Le Havre, and had to be hastily rerouted to the French port. By the time they reached the French port all their money was gone. Had a kind British purser not loaned them money they would have been stuck in France, with no mother and out of touch with their father.

The Berengaria in its earlier life for the Hamburg-America line, ca. 1913

The ocean passage was uneventful. Istvan recalled later that the dining room steward felt sorry for the three young Hungarians. Alarmed at how thin they were, he pumped them with large bowls of unfamiliar oatmeal, which they loathed, being accustomed to coffee and Viennese pastry for breakfast. Arriving in New York on October 22, 1922, they were pleased not to have to pass through Ellis Island, Irene having somehow arranged this legerdemain. They were met by Irene's brother Hugo, who swept them off by train to see Niagara Falls and then, after a day of tourism, they proceeded to his home in Detroit. All three children were immediately enrolled in classes in English for foreigners. Istvan later took grim delight in recalled that the first English expression he learned was "upside down." After a few months in the care of Irene's brother, both of their parents arrived, and solemnly informed them that the newly formed family would settle in Cleveland, Ohio.

Step-Uncle Hugo Friedenberg and the Csillag childen, 1922. Dr. Joan Friedenberg

Why Cleveland? This was the logical choice for a family of Hungarian emigres because in those years Cleveland—or that part of Cleveland tucked along both sides of Buckeye Road-- was the world's second largest Hungarian city. The fact that Buckeye Road was not a main thoroughfare to anywhere except the Hungarian area protected Hungarian Cleveland from nearby Shaker Heights and the still extant palaces on Euclid Avenue. Obviously, residents of those two fashionable areas would have said that it was they who were protected by Cleveland's geography from the teeming Hungarian neighborhoods.

Within the Hungarian areas were many Catholic and Protestant churches that conducted services in Hungarian, as well as shops, restaurants, social clubs, and societies of every description. Sharp social hierarchies mirroring those that had existed in the old world quickly emerged and demanded the respectful attention of new immigrants. The community had thrived, however, and before World War I it had celebrated the success of Hungarians in the New World by erecting on Cleveland's University Circle a statue of the Hungarian hero of freedom, Lajos Kossuth, and, later, a monument to Gyorgi Washington in Budapest. Citizens of two worlds, thousands of Cleveland Hungarians traveled in both directions each year.

The 1920s were the golden age of Hungarian Cleveland, but even then it had begun to turn in on itself. In 1921, two years before the Csillag children arrived in Detroit, Congress passed an Emergency Quota Act limiting Hungarian immigrants to 5,747 a year, a number that was cut by a further third in 1924. This signaled to those already here that their numbers would not continue to grow and that Hungarian Cleveland had taken definitive form.

Once in Cleveland the Csillags found a second-floor apartment at 2893 East 120th Street in the all-Hungarian Buckeye section, which they rented for $40 a month. The house was new, having been built in 1920, The children were enrolled in public schools and Irene became a full-time mother. Their apartment was in a shingled double house amidst a row of almost identical shingled double houses. Another person might have accepted this as the necessary first step along a path that lead to a dignified and fulfilling life in America. For Sandor Csillag it seemed from the outset as the New World's standing rebuke to a person of achievement and dignity.

Sandor Csillag's progress in the English language was slow. Forty-five years old when he arrived in Cleveland, he was either too old or too proud to master a new language. Of course, near-fluent English could have come over time. But time would not change the fact that Sandor did not get himself qualified as an Ohio lawyer. Maybe the intricacies of the common law baffled him; perhaps he couldn't afford the cost of additional schooling; maybe he was too proud to sit in classes with people half his age; or perhaps he was simply lazy. But he never undertook the study necessary to become an American lawyer and he never took the Ohio bar exam. Eventually he settled into the modest role of a consultant on Hungarian law to the Cleveland Probate Court for cases involving immigrants. He was also active at the ward level as an organizer for the Democratic Party. In spite of the fact that it was the Democrat Woodrow Wilson who had dismembered their country, Cleveland Hungarians were solidly Democratic in their politics throughout the twenties.

Csillag was isolated from American life, but he was also isolated from the inner circles of Hungarian émigré life. Poverty, his background in Budapest (widely equated with Judaism), and even his new Catholicism, kept him out of the Magyar Club, which was dominated by Protestant aristocrats from Hungary's East. There is no evidence that he and his wife had any relationship to St. Elizabeth's of Hungary, the Hungarian community's main Catholic church, or with any of the three Hungarian synagogues that served the east side of Cleveland.

This isolation from both his former life and the new land in which he found himself could not have been easy for a man who had known nothing but success during four decades of life in his native land. Faced with this assault on his self-respect, he adopted a pose of haughty aloofness towards all. With fellow Hungarians, he played the dignified but stand-offish role of one who considered his past achievements to be obvious and sufficient proof of his worth. With Americans, he fell into the role of a kind of professional Hungarian, looking down on the New World. His daughter-in-law later observed that "Alexander Starr (e.g., Csillag Sandor) hated everything in this country." He became a professional European. When years later he and his wife were invited to dine at the home of his son Stephen's beloved, Ivy Jane Edmondson, her mother, Minnie Edmondson, innocently asked if he enjoyed visiting the Cleveland Museum of Art, even then one of the world's great collections. No, he sighed, for he was accustomed to the much finer museums of Europe. The same arrogance determined his opposition to the idea of his son marrying a mere artist.

Sandor Csillag's sense of despair over his fate in the New World and the arrogance he displayed in an effort to preserve his waning self-respect only deepened with time. It was relieved mainly through escapism. He loved horses and the excitement of betting, and had often attended the races in Budapest. His resumption of this practice at Cleveland's Northfield Park may have been one of the few continuities between his old life and the new. He invariably returned home broke, much to the disgust of his wife, who by then was working, and his son Stephen (Istvan), who by 1925 was bringing home earnings from his after-school job at Kundtz's Furniture Factory.

As the children reached high school age it was clear that the Csillags were stuck in the modest niche in the Buckeye Road Hungarian community into which they had fallen when they first arrived in 1923. Cleveland's large and complex outpost of Hungarian life had itself reached a plateau in the 1920s. Up until the imposition of quotas, there had been a constant flow of new arrivals. Now that flood shrank to a trickle, which was balanced by the outflow of immigrants who decided to return to the old country. During World War I and the 1920s more than half of the one million Hungarian immigrants living in the U.S. returned to Hungary. Having rejected this path, Csillag began slipping into American life. Nothing more clearly reflected this than his newfound ardor as a Cleveland Indians fan. This passion for baseball, along with the aspiration for a legal career, is one of the few things Alexander Csillag passed on to his elder son.

Given the frustrations Sandor Csillag encountered in America, one may well ask why he didn't join those who chose to go back to Hungary? By 1927 all three of his children were teenagers, fluent English speakers, and had become more American than Hungarian. Besides the fact that a return to Hungary would have been nearly impossible for the children, Sandor was as convinced as ever that Europe would again descend into in war, and didn't want his sons to be there when it happened.

With the door back to Hungary firmly closed, Sandor Csillag decided that, for better or worse, his family was now irrevocably American. On February 4, 1927, he therefore took the family to the United States District Courthouse in Cleveland, where all of them--except Irene--took out U.S. citizenship.[15] On 18 December, 1928 they took the streetcar to the Ohio Probate Court and changed their name from Csillag to Starr, a literal translation of the word "csillag" or "star," plus an extra "r."[16] This was the family's third name change in a century-and a half.

Irene adopted American citizenship only in 1932. Up to that time had she, disenchanted with her life in Cleveland, still dreamt of returning to Hungary? Was her action the result of her job at the newspaper? Or was it simply a practical step taken in the awareness that Hungary had by then become an economic and political morass? We don't know. Nor do we know who initiated the family's trip to the U.S. District Court to change their name. However, Csillag's eldest son, Istvan/Stephen, is the most likely candidate, as he was eighteen and by then firmly determined to break free of Hungary, Buckeye Road, and even his parents if necessary, in order to become an American.

They might have Americanized their name, but the newly minted Starrs still had to eat and pay the rent. Sandor, now Alexander, continued to work at the Probate Court, but the pay was modest. Irene therefore decided to get a job as well. She had solid qualifications and experience in the business world but even before the 1929 Stock Market crash she could not find a position in Cleveland. She therefore felt herself lucky to land a job as a reporter for the city's main Hungarian newspaper, Szabadsag ("Liberty").

Founded in 1891 as the first Hungarian newspaper in North America, Szabadsag was no ordinary emigre news sheet. For one thing, it was a daily when all of its five Hungarian language competitors in Cleveland were weeklies. It was also distributed nationally, and for a while even had a separate New York edition. It continued to hold high the banner of Hungary's liberal democracy long after it had ceased to exist back home. Back in 1902 it had been patriotic Hungarian-American staff members of Szabadsag who had initiated the project to erect Kossuth's statue in Cleveland and to place a statue of Washington in Budapest four years later. Politically, the paper adhered staunchly to the Democratic Party.

Irene Csillag/Starr remained on the staff of this voice of Cleveland Hungarians down to her retirement. Unfortunately, we have not yet exhumed her writings from the archives so it is not possible to speak of her reportorial interests and inclinations. But one thing is clear: when she joined Szabadsag she became the family's main breadwinner and remained so for as long as she worked there.

Alexander Starr (Csillag Sandor) about 1950) S. F. Starr

At this point, with both parents set in their new routines, our attention shifts to the Starrs' three children, Stephen (Istvan), Gyorgi (George), and Clara. Steve enrolled at Cleveland's East High School, George in East Tech, and Clara in John Adams. Although a normal district public school, East High demanded rigorous study of English, science, and the classics. Moreover, it was organized to mirror America's urban democracy, with an elected mayor and council and nine judges chosen from each class by the students themselves. It also took athletics seriously, with its Blue Bombers defeating all comers in football and baseball. It's motto, unusual for a public high school, was "Noblesse Oblige."

Many young Cleveland Hungarians became active in the numerous Hungarian societies, social clubs, and church groups for young people. But of the three Starr children, only the more retiring George followed this course. As a result, he was more steeped in Cleveland's Hungarian life than either of his two siblings. Clara and Stephen were both too busy with school to take part.

Clara graduated with honors from East High and then worked her way through Ohio State University. After graduation she followed in her father's footsteps and went to law school, graduating with distinction from Ohio State. She married an American, Wilbur Cory, had a son, Guy and, as a Columbus attorney, became the first lawyer in America to invoke hypnosis in a murder trial. She won the case.

We have already noted that the eldest of the three Starr children, Stephen, was intent from an early age on embracing his new land and on rejecting every trace of his Hungarian origins. He was so assiduous and thorough in this endeavor that his future wife, Ivy Jane Edmondson, did not realize he was Hungarian until four months after they met. His rejection of all things Hungarian extended also to his parents, from whom he increasingly distanced himself. Whereas his father had been profligate in his spending, Stephen would walk the eight miles downtown and back to his summer jobs rather than pay the eight-cent fare on the streetcar.

And yet he retained at least one important trace of Hungary. At Western Reserve College (now Case Western Reserve University) he fell under the influence of an impressive young Hungarian-born novelist, playwright, and sometime contributor to Szabadsag, Joseph ("Soszy") Remenyi (1892-1956). Like his snobbish father, Stephen still believed that America was too young to have a real history. And Remenyi's lectures on European history and on Hungary impressed him. He resolved to become a historian and began amassing information on the life of the Hungarian patriot, liberal reformer, and revolutionary, Lajos Kossuth. He was fascinated by this romantic figure and intrigued that Kossuth, after the fall of his visionary regime, had travelled in America and even visited Cleveland. Walking past the Kossuth statue daily on his way to the Western Reserve campus, Starr resolved to write his biography.

This was not to be. Indeed, it took another forty years before Stephen Starr was able to return to his first love, history. In the meanwhile he married, studied law at night but failed to take the law boards because of a bout of mumps, raised four children, and had a career in business. Eventually he was to publish six volumes on American history and to establish himself as an expert not on Kossuth or Hungary but on the American Civil War.

Starr worked hard at becoming an American. During his college days he met an attractive Cleveland girl named Kate Messick. Her father, Homer Dwight Messick, president of the lordly Union Trust Bank, had his Ceveland office in one of the most imposing neo-Roman buildings ever built in America. Messick was impressed by the bright young immigrant and spent hours conversing with him on every subject. It was through these conversations that Starr was first introduced to American history. Messick treated his young friend as a member of the family, and would loan him his yellow double-cowled Packard touring car whenever he needed to go somewhere. Kate meanwhile had resolved that she would marry the young man. Stephen wasn't interested but he nonetheless continued to view Messick as a model for himself and assiduously studied his turn of mind and every mannerism. To the end of his days Starr carried the aura of a solid and old-fashioned Clevelander of the nineteen twenties.

For all his efforts to adapt to his new environment, Stephen Starr could not entirely shake off his spoiled early upbringing or the influence of his father's arrogance and rudeness. I knew him as a person of mild disposition, reserved, but with considerable charm. Especially earlier, though, he had a reputation for being blunt to the point of rudeness. Whatever the cause, it was to cost him more than one promotion. When his friends at the Literary Club in Cincinnati later memorialized him, they noted sardonically that, "He was only rarely rude."

Steve Starr had been raised as a Catholic since age six or seven, had served as an altar boy, and had attended a classical Catholic school in Passau. But once in America he never returned to the Catholic Church, though he retained a quiet affection for its ceremony and music. As to his Jewish origins, this was a subject best forgotten. When he was fifty-five years old, friends in Cincinnati invited the Starrs to a Bar Mitzvah celebration. Stephen Zoltan Starr, whose forebears had once been immersed in the rich world of eastern European Judaism, penned the following description of the experience:[17]

> "The Bar Mitzvah was as good as a field trip in cultural anthropology. The service was in an Orthodox synagogue, and conducted in Hebrew (an unpleasant-sounding language) and lasted for three solid hours of uninterrupted guttural jabber and clanging. All of us (men) had to wear skullcaps and prayer shawls. The strangest thing was that while the cantor, or one or another member of the congregation, was chanting a prayer or passage from the Pentateuch at what in a Christian church

would be called the altar, the rest of the congregation were muttering the same thing (I suppose) in the body of the church, and there seemed to be a race going on as to who could finish first. And while all this was going on, the chanting up front, and the steady drone in the body of the church, people walked in, walked out, walked around, shook hands with friends, smiled and chatted happily, walked up to the altar to say hello to the rabbi—all in all the most disorganized, casual performance I have ever seen. They are badly in need of being taken in hand by a good Catholic or Episcopalian (high church) ritualist. When the services were finally over, and none too soon (Judaism is no religion for anyone with weak kidneys) we retired to a sort of hospitality room for what is called a "Kiddush."

Many decades later Steve took his wife to explore the country he had left at age ten. There were moments of recognition and pleasure, but for the most part the return visit confirmed in Starr's mind the wisdom of his decision to turn his back on his native land and its people. The couple had several Hungarian friends but in every case their relationship existed in spite of the Hungarian connection rather than because of it.

We will now take leave of Stephen Starr just as he has graduated from Western Reserve College. It remains only to summarize the last three decades of the lives of Alexander and Irene Starr. Alexander never gained his feet in America and spent the years down to his death in 1959 much as he had lived during the 1920s and 1930s, still in their apartment on East 120th Street and still mourning the loss of the world he had so arduously built for himself in Budapest. His wife, known to her children as Anyuka, eventually retired from her job at Szabadsag and also sank into a state of despair, unrelieved by the successes of her step-children or contact with grandchildren. Ivy Jane Starr recalled that what had once been her attractively soulful expression gave way to "a perpetual mood of mourning." Yet even though Stephen had considered her an "unsympathetic step-mother," both he and his wife came to respect her for the determination and "spunk" she had shown in maintaining a job that enabled her to feed the family and maintain their Cleveland household. After the death of her husband she spent her last days with her step-daughter Clara and her family.

Csillag Sandor and his wife Irene had toiled through their younger years to create a place for themselves in an open, increasingly democratic, and largely tolerant society. They lived lives of aspiration, and overcame formidable obstacles to achieve what they reasonably expected would be serene and productive lives. The forebears of Csillag Sandor, now Alexander Starr, had changed their country and language once before he was born, and had twice changed their family name. Continuing this pattern, so typical of Hungarians of his background, he was to change his religion, name, and country, first to pave the way for his personal advancement and then in the face of brute necessity. His life and that of his wife, Irene, were dominated by constant and profound change. In the end, their children thrived and welcomed their new world as natural and good, having reached the state of which Alexander and Irene had once dreamed but which they themselves never attained.

This story would be incomplete without a coda. Csillag Sandor and Irene were both born Jewish in the complex multi-religious and multi-ethnic stew of eastern Hungary. Both abandoned their birthplaces for the rapidly advancing and enlightened world of Budapest. Those who stayed behind did not fare so well. On 22 May, 1944, the 916 Jews who were then living in Alexander's birthplace, Nyrluga, were herded into boxcars and sent to Auschwitz, where all of them perished in the Nazi gas chambers.[18] Also in 1944, more than 6,000 Jews from Nyiregyhaza met the same fate, while another 2,000 Jewish citizens from the same city were deported to Russian labor camps in Siberia. Few survived. As to others named Csillag from the same immediate region, twenty-three people from the nearby city of Debrecen who bore that family named died in the death camps, as did another twelve Csillags from the village of Derescske, twelve miles from Debrecen.

It is not known which, if any, of the many Cillags who perished at Auschwitz and other extermination camps were related to Csillag Sandor. What is certain is that all but two members of the family of his second wife, Irene Friedenberg, were killed at Auschwitz. A direct descendent of this extended family, Joan Friedenberg, a professor in Florida, commissioned a family plaque to be placed at Auschwitz, and kindly listed "the children of Stephen Z. Starr" among the living heirs and signatories of the memorial.

What, then, would have been the fate of Csillag Sandor and his three children had they stayed in Hungary? Thanks to a remarkable young women who was sent with her mother to Auschwitz, we have a picture that is all too vivid. The girl in question was born in Satu Mare, sixty-two miles southeast of Nyirgesyhaza and only thirty-two miles from Nyrluga, where Csillag Sandor's family had lived for a century and where he was born. Satu Mare is now across the border in Romania. We do not know whether or how she was related to Sandor's family, but her name, too, was Csillag.

The young woman's mother perished at Auschwitz but she herself miraculously survived, and wrote about her ordeal. Her account describes with certainty what would have been the inevitable fate of Csillag Sandor and his three children, Istvan, Gyorgi, and Klara, had he not made the firm decision to emigrate. Here is her testimony:

> I was born in 1925 in Satu Mare, which was Romanian at that time but in 1940 became part of Hungary.... The Jewish community was very large in Satu Mare in 1939. Most Jews were Orthodox

but there were some who were Neolog (something like Reform Judaism today, SFS.) The language spoken in our home was Hungarian even though my mother's background was Romanian. My father was Hungarian and he couldn't speak Romanian. We also learned to speak German from our father, who spoke it beautifully because, way back, his background was German.

Our life was good and I cannot remember that we had any problem with anti-Semitism while Satu Mare was Romanian. We had a very good relationship with our neighbors and were good friends with everyone in our small community.

When the Hungarians took over it was no longer the same. The situation definitely worsened and stayed that way until 1944, when the Germans occupied Hungary. Shortly after the occupation we had to wear the yellow star. Conditions in the ghetto, while crowded, were not too bad. We had enough food and our Gentile neighbors were very kind to us. We were not fenced in but the German SS was in charge of the ghetto and they stood on guard at all times. We were confined to the ghetto for approximately four weeks. Then, during the month of May, 1944, we were deported.

We all had to leave our houses in the ghetto and march through the town to the railway station. It was a very long march, especially for my grandparents, who were in their late seventies. The march took us through the Jewish cemetery and I visited my father's grave and told him what was happening to us.

The authorities told us that they were taking us to Debrecen, which is a large Hungarian city not too far away, and that we would be put to work there. So my mother baked a lot of dry cookies and put them all in a large flour sack. She also prepared rantas, a kind of white sauce, and put it in a large jar for emergencies. At the train station the SS packed us all into cattle cars. I have no idea how many of us were in one car. All I know is that we were standing in there like packed sardines. Then the train started to move and we travelled and travelled. There was no toilet or any sanitary facilities for our needs. Conditions were so bad that one of my sister's school friends died on the way. I was in a daze. I think we travelled three or four days. Some bread and some other things were thrown to us once, but basically we were traveling without food and water, unable to sit down or sleep. Then finally we arrived somewhere, but we didn't know where we were. Suddenly we saw this sign: "Arbeit Macht Frei." We were at Auschwitz-Birkenau in Poland. My mother was holding her brother's two-year-old child to help her pregnant sister-in-law. The Polish prisoner whose job was to get us out of the cattle car asked her whose baby it was. When my mother answered that the child was her sister-in-law's, he ordered her to give back the child to the pregnant mother. Then they took away my grandfather's cane, and he complained to my grandmother.

At this time all the others -- old people like my grandparents, pregnant women like my aunt, or my cousins who were very young—were ordered to the left. The Nazis didn't need them. We never saw them again. None of them returned. Nobody.

In the barrack there were three-tiered bunk beds. My mother had to climb to the top bunk. Naturally that wasn't easy for her, but she made it because at this point she was still in good shape. We were in that Camp-C for about six weeks. Every day there were "Zehl Appels" (roll calls ed.) No matter how hard it rained or how cold it was we had to stand there, twice a day, to be counted. I don't know why. Then one day something terrible happened. As we were standing for roll call, one of the women gave birth to a premature baby. None of us knew that she was pregnant. We just couldn't tell, but I don't think she was in her ninth month. Anyway, the tiny baby just slipped out as we were standing there and right then and there she made a hole with her feet in the sandy soil and buried the tiny infant. Only those of us who stood nearby saw this happening. It was so horribly sad.

On another day following the roll-call we had to line up to be have numbers tattooed on our arms. After a long a wait they suddenly announced that there would be no more tattooing but that we now had to stand in a row for "selection". This usually meant that some people were selected to stay and some to be taken away. I greatly feared that we would be separated from our mother. So I gathered up all my courage and went up to the man doing the selection, who turned out to be Dr. Mengele, although I didn't know then who he was. I told him in Romanian that my mother was forty-six years old, still young and in very good condition, and that we would like for him to let us stay together. He must have felt good at that moment because he said, "All right." Then all three of us were transported to another camp called Stutthof, again by cattle car.

The Stutthof concentration camp, while smaller than Auschwitz, had pretty much the same set-up and routine. Later on, I was allowed to work in the kitchen. That meant that after work I was allowed to collect the potato and beet peels, as well as the used coffee grounds, and take them to my mother and sister as extra food. But by then my mother couldn't eat. She was deteriorating rapidly, although she still liked to talk about cooking. She was dreaming of the time we would get back home and all the baking and cooking she would do. But even the food I brought her did not improve her condition.

I kept on hoping and working energetically. Maybe that helped me. I said to myself that even if everyone dies, I will live. I was determined to stay alive. On one very cold and snowy day I was freezing. Before I went to work I told my sister that I would like to wear the brown scarf we owned. She said, "I put it on Mother's neck last night because she was also cold." So I took the scarf off my mother's neck but noticed that she didn't move. I asked Olga what was wrong with Mother and she answered that "Mother died last night, but I didn't want to tell you because you had to get up so early in the morning to get to work." So, my mother was dead. [20]

II. Two Centuries of Quaker Edmondsons

My mother, Ivy Jane Starr, was born Ivy Jane Edmondson. By 1909, when she appeared in the world, the Edmondsons were solidly established in Cleveland. Her father, George M. Edmondson, was the court photographer for such local plutocrats as the Mathers and Rockefellers and politicians like kingmaker Mark Hanna. Ivy Janes' mother, Wilhelmina Niesen Edmondson, was a self-made woman who had been orphaned in Amherst Ohio, twenty-eight miles west of Cleveland, then survived as a house-girl in nearby Oberlin, Ohio, before coming to Cleveland with the intention of becoming a Catholic nun and nursing sister.

In sharp contrast to the Csillags of Budapest, Nyiregyhjaza, and Nyrluga, Hungary, the history of the Edmondson family in both America and England is reasonably well documented. The volume of records and papers from the Edmondson family accounts for the fact that I have devoted three chapters of this family history to them, and only one to the Csillags. Had the bureaucrats of the Austro-Hungarian Empire been more diligent record – keepers we would have been able to devote three chapters to them as well.

During the nineteenth and early twentieth centuries several members of the Edmondson family lived interesting, complicated, at times colorful, and always highly productive lives in many places on both sides of the Atlantic. Principal among them were the three George Edmondsons whose lives spanned the years 1797 to 1949. They are the main subject of these sketches. The first was an important educational reformer in England, the second a colorful pioneer photographer, and the third a master portraitist who was the equivalent in photography of the painter John Singer Sargent. However, it is worth asking about the antecedents of the three George Edmondsons of the nineteenth and twentieth centuries. Who were those people? What did they do in life? And was there anything about those antecedents of the three Georges that might help account for the strong but very different creative energies that the three later George Edmondsons manifested?

Throughout the eighteenth-century members of that branch of the Edmondson family that later produced the three Georges lived quiet and inconspicuous lives. There are no biographies or memorial writings on any of them, and they left no lasting mark on their communities. Indeed, the only way one can pick up their earthly footprints is through marriage and death records kept by English civil authorities and by the various Quaker Meetings to which they belonged, for they were all members of the Society of Friends. But even these carefully maintained records contain so much contradictory information on birthdates and birthplaces that one suspects the scribes of intentionally seeking to confuse later researchers.

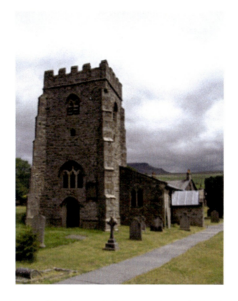

St. Oswald's Church, Horton in Ribblesdale

The earliest confirmed forebear of the "three Georges" was one John Edmondson, who was born in 1670 in "Horton in Ribblesdale," an ancient village dating to Norman times but inhabited today by fewer than four hundred residents, all of whom seem intent on distinguishing their home town from the larger town of Horton in nearby Lancashire. Although we don't know where precisely this John Edmondson lived, the village still preserves quite a number of yeoman's houses, any one of which could have been his. Alternatively, we know that one Alexander Edmondson, a kinsman, lived at Howgill, which came under the parish of Horton in the Pennines, and that these Edmondsons baptized a son, Richard, in 1671.[21] It is likely that our John Edmondson was also born at Howgill. John Edmondson was apparently quite content to stay in his remote area and at the age of thirty-one married Alice Burton, also from Horton in Ribblesdale.[22] They proceeded to have a brood of children, John Edmondson, Junior, a daughter and another son.

Gibbs Hall as it stands today, in ruin, but a Grade II Historic Landmark. Here two generations of Edmondsons lived, the last being George, who died in 1796 and after whom George Edmondson the educator was named.

This John Edmondson Junior, who was born in 1702,[23] moved some twenty-one miles northwest to the ancient village of Dent, founded by Norsemen but by the eighteenth century inhabited by yeoman farmers like the Edmondsons. Built of roughly coursed sandstone rubble and today standing in ruins, it is nonetheless considered an important example of a yeoman's farmhouse of the era, though it is in ruin. John Junior resided at "Gibbs Hall," a sold two-story sandstone farmer's dwelling with outbuildings that still stands, though in ruin. Even in its present ruinous state Gibbs Hall is designated by English Heritage as a Grade II historic landmark. Edmondson inherited this substantial house from his wife, Agnes Mason, who is described in the marriage record as being a "spinster" and native of Dent. The couple proceeded to have five children before John's early death. Like many rural folk in Dent, the Edmondsons were probably engaged in wool knitting.

By the early eighteenth century, the proliferation of Edmondsons in the area of Dent, Sedbergh, Deepdale, and Ribblesdale makes the tracing of their genealogy particularly difficult. Suffice it to say that the professional local genealogical researcher Jane Hanby encountered no fewer than three John Edmondsons in the immediate neighborhood! Prowling through this tangle, one finds that Thomas Edmondson, the middle son of John Edmondson, Junior, was baptized at Dent on 21 November, 1732. His siblings were John (baptized in 1728), Alice (1731), Sarah (1734), and George (1736).[24] Quaker records in London indicate that a Thomas Edmondson from Dent managed to get himself disowned "for misconduct." We don't know what nefarious deeds he perpetrated, but the timing suggests that this was not the John Edmondson we have been following but a relative by the same name residing in the same village. Indeed, the marriage of a second Thomas Edmondson, described as "a farmer from Deepdale," Dent, was recorded on July 7, 1754.[25]

Dent, Cumbria

Whatever the case, our Thomas Edmondson married Agnes Skelton and had several children, the eldest of whom was John, born on May 11, 1761.[26] This John Edmondson was raised at the family's home, Gibbs Hall, but eventually moved to Lancaster and set up shop as a ships chandler and general nautical outfitter and then shifted into the grocery business.[27] John Edmondson's youngest son, George, born in 1797 and the first of our three Georges, was to distinguish himself in Russia as a surveyor, expert on land reclamation, and agrarian reformer and then, back in England, as an important pioneer in scientific education.

We will turn to the life of this nineteenth-century George Edmondson in the next chapter. Meanwhile, let us return to his distant forebear, John Edmondson, who was born in 1670 in Horton in Ribbledale. Due to lapses in the archival record we cannot confirm the identity of John Edmondson's father, although there exists strong indirect evidence that his name was also John. This seems likely, because a year after the birth of the younger John, the parish records report on the birth of another son, Richard, and identify him as being the "son of John Edmondson."[28]

And so we have solid, if indirect evidence that the John Edmondson born in 1670 at Horton in Ribblesdale was also the son of one John Edmondson. Since most men married at around age twenty-five and immediately began producing children, we can confidently assume that this elder John Edmondson, who was the father of John and Richard Edmondson, was born between the years 1638 and 1645.

This is the point at which the story becomes complicated. During the years 1999-2008 archivist Jane Hanby of Lancaster, working at the behest of the author of this sketch, carried out a careful search of all extant birth and marriage records from villages and towns in the narrow band of inhabited valleys extending eastward from Sedbergh to Horton in Ribbledale. Her research led to two striking finds. First, she discovered that by the eighteenth century there were individuals or families named Edmondson in nearly every town, village, or crossroads in this remote, rural, isolated, and impoverished corner of England. With people by this name living in Sedbergh, Dent, Gawthorp, Deepdale, Cowgill, Horton in Ribbledale, and Clunter Bank, one is tempted to call it Edmondsonia. But it is important to stress that this concentration of Edmondsons dates only to the late seventeenth and eighteenth centuries. Most were related to one another, although the lines of descent are as complex and confusing as the Book of Genesis. Second, Jane Hanby found no documentation on the birth, baptism, or marriage of our earliest known John Edmondson. Her conclusion? That he was born, raised, and married elsewhere and only subsequently moved to the Horton area. Hanby even suggested that his progeny directly or indirectly accounted for most, if not all, of the rabbit-like proliferation of Edmondsons locally.

Before looking further into the background of this earliest Edmondson relative, we must pause to take note of the momentous events that seized all England in the years under discussion, and which account for the difficulty we experience today in tracing specific individuals during that age of turmoil. Between 1642 and 1651 England was wracked by not one but three civil wars, the first two between the supporters of King Charles I (Cavaliers) and Parliament (Roundheads), and the third between King Charles II and supporters of the so-called Long Parliament under Oliver Cromwell.

The English Civil War extended to both Ireland and Scotland. In 1649 Cromwell's army landed in Dublin to suppress both Royalists and Catholics, over whom it achieved a decisive and bloody victory at Draghena, when 3,500 royalists, as well as many Irish Catholic priests, were massacred. Cromwell proceeded to confiscate all Irish Church lands and the property of all Irish Catholics, which he then distributed to creditors and to his own troops. When Scottish royalists under Charles II mounted a strong counter-offensive, Cromwell rushed his army to Scotland, where they defeated the Royalist forces and occupied all of the Scotland's southern regions. This Scottish campaign was England's third civil war. Charles II escaped south into England, with Cromwell's army in hot pursuit. This ended with the Parliament's defeat of King Charles II at the Battle of Worcester on 3 September 1651 and Charles' exile to France.

England was now without a monarch, so the stalwart Puritan Oliver Cromwell, who led the Parliamentary forces, took the reins of state, first under a Commonwealth down to 1653 and then under his personal rule, called the "Protectorate," which lasted down to 1659. Only in 1688 was the rule of Parliament permanently established in law and the crown given the limited role in governance which continues to this day.

The human cost of England's Civil Wars was enormous, with nearly 4% of the English population, 6% of Scotland's, and fully 41% of the Irish people killed---a figure three times greater than losses during the Potato famine of 1845-8. The British Isles became an armed camp, with tens of thousands of young men enlisted into the contending armies and millions of ordinary citizens affected by the ensuing destruction, not to mention the taxes levied on them to maintain the enormous armies.

The impoverished northwestern regions of Westmoreland and Cumbria were swept into the turmoil. Large numbers of young men there rallied to Cromwell's army and marched with him to Ireland and Scotland. Those not in the fighting force seized on the assault on the throne and resulting turmoil as an opportunity to settle scores with the established Church and with their wealthy absentee landlords who had taken over Church lands seized a century and a half earlier by Henry VIII. As a result, the Civil War impacted the remote Northwest with particular virulence.

Given this prolonged period of turmoil, it is no wonder that record-keeping was spotty and at times even ceased at the local level, especially in Cumbria and Westmoreland, where so many abandoned their homes to fight under Cromwell. But the impact of the Civil Wars in the region went deeper. Thousands of those who left never returned, with some of Cromwell's soldiers taking up properties granted to them in Ireland and thousands of others simply fleeing the British Isles in hopes of establishing new lives for themselves in the more peaceful West Indies or North America.

All these developments together fall far short of describing the profound impact of the Civil Wars on Cumbria and Westmoreland. For the endless fighting between churchmen and dissenting Puritans caused many to view both parties with skepticism or outright hostility. Yet the local populace remained pious, and viewed the fights over religious faith and practice as a cardinal focus of their lives. Into this volatile atmosphere appeared a former shoemaker's apprentice from Leicestershire, George Fox. Literate, but otherwise without formal education, Fox as a young man had pondered the problems of faith. Travelling to London and across rural England, he was quick to detect hypocrisy and faithlessness in all whom he met. In the process he came to some very simple truths which, as he put it, "the Lord taught me," namely, "to be faithful…and to keep to Yea and Nay in all things."

George Fox, 1624-1691

Fox's faith was simple: "God dwells in the hearts of his obedient people," and men and women need only practice a form of silent, prayerful waiting to hear His voice. Englishmen could gain inspiration through personal faith and had no need for priests, theologians, or pastors to help them. Primitive Christianity could and will be revived. By individualizing the relationship of God and Man, Fox freed his followers from all the main religious and political controversies of the day---even while he generated an entire set of new ones.

By 1647 Fox began preaching at rural gatherings and in churchyards following services. He was often to be found standing at rural markets amidst stage players and rope dancers, bringing down fire and brimstone on the shoppers. In his own words, "So I stood in the marketplace and proclaimed the day of the Lord among them, and warned them all to repent."[29] Having memorized large parts of the New Testament, he spoke passionately about God's imminence and power as manifest in the Scriptures. Demanding that all lead sinless lines, he insisted that his followers abstain from alcohol and refuse to take oaths or pay tithes to the Church. Through faith and self-control, men and women were perfectible. Against doubters Fox rained down a torrent of Biblical texts, replete with warnings and threats against those who disobeyed God's will. He called on everyone from the King to Oliver Cromwell and the simplest yeoman to hearken to God's voice and "tremble at the word of the Lord", a Biblical phrase he repeated so often as to cause him and those who followed his preaching to be dubbed "Quakers."

In 1652 Fox's travels soon took him to Westmoreland and Cumbria. In his autobiography he recorded that:

> As we travelled, we came near a very great hill, called Pendle Hill, and I was moved of the Lord to go up to the top of it; which I did with difficulty, it was so very steep and high. When I was come to the top, I saw the sea bordering upon Lancashire. From the top of this hill the Lord let me see in what places he had a great people to be gathered.

Pendle Hill was only thirty miles east of Horton in Ribblesdale, where John Edmondson lived. From Pendle Hill Fox covered the thirty miles past Horton in Ribblesdale and on through Cowgill and Dent for another five miles to Sedbergh, where he delivered several memorable sermons at the local church. It is worth noting that about this time there were Edmondsons settled in all these places. Fox then moved northward into the Furness area of Cumbria, where he met his future wife, Margaret Fell, who lived with her family at Swarthmoor (i.e., Swarthmore) Hall. Not only the Fells but many other families in the vicinity were drawn to Fox's teachings.

Sedbergh Quaker meeting, Cumbria, where William Edmondson preached after joining the Quakers.

It is no exaggeration to say that the Religious Society of Friends, or Quakers, came into being in the course of Fox's visit to Pendle Hill, Westmoreland, and Cumbria, in other words, the precise area in which all the Edmondsons were living. A tenth of the local population openly declared themselves Quakers,[30] with many more who identified themselves as sympathizers. We do not know how many of the Edmondsons joined Fox's movement, but the absence of non-Quakers among local Edmondsons suggests that most, if not all, of them signed on, mainly in 1652 and the years immediately following.

One who definitely did so was William Edmondson from Little Musgrave, a small Cumbrian village in the Pennines just west of the ancient hilltop town of Great Musgrave, on the river Eden. Little Musgrave is only nineteen miles from Sedbergh, twenty-four miles from Dent, and thirty-five miles from Horton in Ribblesdale. Edmondsons are known to have lived in Little Musgrave since at least the 1540s, when Thomas Edmondson (ca. 1540-1590) was born there.[31] His son Edward, baptized in 1568, was the first to have his birth recorded, since record-keeping began there only in 1560. Since Little Musgrave had no place of worship, the baptism took place in the Anglo-Saxon era chancel of the Church of St. Andrew in nearby Crosby-Garrett. Edward in turn was the father of John Edmondson (1594-1635), who married Grace and between 1615 and 1625 and had six children: Eleanor, b. 1615, Dorothy, b. 1617, Thomas, b. 1619, Edward, b. 1622, John, b. 1625, and William, b. 1627.

At this point our search must pause to take note of two seventeenth century Edmondsons who gained a degree of fame, if not notoriety, William and John. William brought the Quaker movement to Ireland, became known as the "Hammer of Ireland" on account of his muscular proselytizing, and went on to debate Roger Williams, founder of Rhode Island. John moved to America, became the richest landowner in Maryland, and gave land for what is now the oldest house of worship in continuous use in America, the Third Haven Meeting House in Easton, Maryland. We shall trace the lives of both of these men. Then, having done so, we shall pin down their relationship to the line of Edmondsons who form the core of our story.

William, born in 1627, had a wretched upbringing. His mother died when he was six and his father died when he was eight, so he was sent to live with a brutal and abusive uncle. After a brief apprenticeship to a carpenter in York, William at age eighteen fled and joined Cromwell's Puritan army, in which he served down to 1652. His older brother John had fought with Cromwell in Ireland and decided to stay there when Cromwell handed out land seized from Catholics to his soldiers. In 1650 William saw combat in Scotland and ended up at the Battle of Worcester, where Charles II made his last stand before fleeing to France.[32]

In the year 1653 Edmondson joined his older brother Thomas and a third unidentified kinsman to attend a religious meeting in Westmoreland with one of Fox's early disciples, James Naylor (1616-1660). Naylor, too, had been a soldier under Cromwell but had turned his back on the Puritans after meeting Fox in 1652. Fox considered Naylor to be over-enthusiastic and erratic and with good reason: in 1656 Naylor was to enter the city of Bristol astride a donkey, claiming that he was reenacting Christ's entry into Jerusalem. The Puritans charged him with blasphemy and branded him with the letter "B." But the zealous Naylor swept up all three Edmondsons, who became Quakers on the spot.

Shortly after this meeting, William decided to join his brother John in Ireland. Taking advantage of Cromwell's expropriation of Catholic merchants, he purchased a shipload of goods and landed in Dublin in 1654, intend on becoming a storekeeper in the northern Irish town of Lurgan in County Armagh; After a brief stint at Cavan in Ulster, by 1657 he founded the village of Rosenallis near Mountmellick in County Laois in Central Ireland. There he acquired a farm and developed a tannery. Notwithstanding his embrace of the Quaker ideal of a sinless life, Edmondson still had to wrestle with his conscience over whether he should pay customs duties or evade them.

William Edmondson soon gathered the first Quaker Meeting in Ireland, one of the many he founded. In defending himself and his co-believers before local authorities he employed every tool in the book, including cool reason and fraternal bonhomie but, more frequently, defiance, bluster, invective, and crude abuse. In so doing, he quickly established himself as the human embodiment of the last and most radical phase of the English Reformation. Neither Catholics nor their English oppressors missed a chance to clap William Edmondson into jail and even burn down his house, but his fellow Quakers, not without wariness, viewed him as a hero. When he later published a Journal of his trials and tribulations (which the printer issued under the misspelled name "Edmundson," which he himself never used), it became a best-seller. Solid as a bull and portly when not recovering from time in jail, William Edmondson soon became known as "The Hammer of Ireland."

During a 1655 visit to England to restock his shop, Edmondson finally met George Fox, who had already heard of the Cumbrian's zeal and effectiveness in both argument and organization. The two immediately joined forces. Just as the Quaker movement was coming into being, William Edmondson became one of its most effective evangelists and the trusted companion of its founder.

Edmondson's adventures in Ireland continued until he was forty-four. Then in 1671 he had what he called "movings upon my spirit to travel to the West-Indies."[33] Reinforcing these movings was Fox's proposal that Edmondson join him and a small delegation to visit Quakers in the West Indies and North America. Edmondson eagerly assented and by late August, 1671, the party of six reached Barbados. After paying pastoral visits to Antigua and Barbados they sailed on to Nevis, where the governor refused to allow them to land, and then to Jamaica. After "some time of labour in the Gospel of Christ" in Jamaica, the band of Quaker pioneers sailed for Maryland. On the way they encountered fierce storms and powerful headwinds, which extended the trip to two weeks. When they finally landed at the mouth of the Petuxant River Edmondson was barely alive. He later recalled that as he emerged from the boat, "I could neither go nor stand, but as two bore me up, one by each arm, I had violent pains and weakness in my back and loins with piercing cold."[34]

There was already an active Friends meeting in Maryland, so after a few more weeks spent visiting there Edmondson proceeded alone to call on the isolated Quakers in the Carolinas. There he found "things were much out of order, but the Lord's power and testimony went over all." Following this uplifting moment Edmondson and two Friends then walked through uncharted paths to Virginia. It was a cold and rainy autumn and their route was marked only by slashes in the bark of trees. Soon Edmondson and his companions "were sorely foiled in swamps and on the third morning…I had rode but a few miles before I was seized with grievous gripes, and a weakness in the bowels occasioned by the great surfeit I got with those hardships in coming thither."[35] The other two Friends also fell sick and fainted.

Thus weakened, the band staggered into Jamestown and Green Springs, where they learned of rapaciousness by the provincial government and theological confusion among the Believers. Edmondson tried to address the former by visiting the Governor of Virginia, Sir William Barclay, but the representative of the Crown proved "very peevish and brittle." As to the deviant doctrines espoused by some of the local Quakers, Edmondson addressed them directly. In his telling, at least, the local Quakers "were glad thereof and much comforted, as sheep that had been astray and returned again to the shepherd, Jesus Christ."

It took Edmondson ten days to sail from Maryland to New York. There he convened "some of the chief officers, magistrates, and leading men of the town" for what he called "a large, brave meeting."[36] This was the first Quaker meeting ever in that future megapolis.[37] He then travelled to Shelter Island off the tip of Long Island, where he was joined once more by George Fox. On this 8,000 acre private domain a syndicate of Barbados sugar merchants led by Nathaniel Sylvester (1610-1680) had established the northern element of a three-cornered trade involving the West Indies and Africa; their main products were casks of preserved meats and other provisions prepared by slaves and indentured servants.[38] In addition to his farming and participation in the slave trade, the Dutch born Sylvester provided refuge to a number of Quakers, which is why Edmondson headed there.

Fox, who had just been in New England, implored Edmondson to accommodate Quakers there who were eager for him to pay them a pastoral visit. Winter had already set in and Edmondson was eager to return to Ireland. But instead he heeded the call and travelled to Newport in Rhode Island.

The first Quaker missionaries had arrived in Roger Williams' colony of Rhode Island back in 1657. After being thrown out of Massachusetts on account of his political views, Williams took care in his new colony to separate citizenship from religion. Although this was definitely not what he intended, this policy opened the door wide to Quakers. By the time Edmondson arrived there, Rhode Island had become one of the major centers of the Quaker movement in the New World.

This did not please the colony's founder. In spite of Roger Williams' well-earned reputation for tolerance, he drew the line at Quakers. Cambridge-educated Williams was erudite and, though inclined towards the Baptists, accepted most of the Boston Congregationalists doctrines, including the Calvinists' teachings on the rottenness of human nature, on predestination, and on the elect. All this put him squarely at odds with the Quakers, who viewed Williams as a mouthpiece of grim Calvinism. Williams in turn considered Edmondson and his gang as dangerous fanatics and disturbers of the peace.

Roger Williams, 1603-1683

Knowing that sooner or later a serious Quaker spokesman would arrive in Rhode Island from England, Williams had long since drafted fourteen propositions on which he and the Quakers held irreconcilable positions, and announced that he was prepared to defend his doctrines against all comers. Most of Williams' fourteen propositions pertained to questions of theology. Thus, he defended the orthodox doctrine of Christ's Incarnation; declared that the Quakers' "Spirit" had nothing in common with the Holy Spirit of Christian orthodoxy; accused the Quakers of pride and of putting their own supposed revelations above Scripture; attacked the contradictions and hypocrisies of Quaker teachings; faulted Quakers for locating God, Christ, and the Kingdom of God within each person; and accused them of offering a cheap and easy form of grace and of embracing a kind of conversion that was little more than a momentary enthusiasm that would obstruct true contrition and repentance.

When Edmondson arrived at Newport he was joined by three local American Quakers: John Burnyeat, John Stubbs, and John Cartwright. Fox had informed him of Williams' challenge and now Edmondson eagerly accepted it. Scarcely had Edmondson and his party arrived than he announced that he expected Roger Williams to appear at the Quaker Meeting House over a three-day period to debate the first seven of Williams' propositions, and then to move on to Providence to debate the other seven. Williams, born in 1603, was advancing in years but burned for the fight. Edmondson, who had devoted a quarter century to debating Puritans, Catholics, and Baptists, took to the confrontation like a hunting dog to red meat.

"A great concourse of people" showed up for all four sessions and hung on every word uttered. "When I came into the place," wrote Williams,

> "I found three able and noted preachers among them, viz., John Stubbs, John Burnyeat, and William Edmondson sitting together on an high bench with some of the magistrates of their judgment with them. I had heard that John Stubbs was learned in the Hebrew and the Greek and I found him so. As for John Burnyeat, I found him to be of a moderate spirit and a very able speaker. The third, W. Edmundson (sic.), was newly come, as was said, from Virginia, and he proved the chief speaker: a man not so able nor so moderate as the other two. For the two first would speak argument, and discuss and produce Scripture or any other learning; he [Edmondson] had been a soldier in the late wars, a stout and portly man of a great voice, and fit to make a braggadocio, as he did, and a constant exercise merely of my patience...."[39]

This was Williams' view at the start of the debate. After further exposure to the man, he concluded that Edmondson offered "a flash of wit, a Face of Brass, and a tongue set on fire from the Hell of Lyes and Fury." Edmondson, he concluded, was "an oppression of the mind."[40]

The Quakers packed the audience with their members and sympathizers, who constantly interrupted Williams and peppered him with taunts and question. The debate soon descended to an exchange of invectives. Edmondson considered Williams "pompous and unlikeable." He made clear that he considered Williams "an old priest and an enemy of truth," and saw all Williams' theses as nothing more than "slanders and accusations against the Quakers." In rebutting them he resorted to tirades and crude ad hominem arguments.

This put Williams off his stride. Of the first sessions Edmondson later boasted with un-Quaker-like pride that "The old man could make nothing out, but on the contrary [his propositions] were turned back upon himself; he was baffled, and the people saw his weakness, folly, envy, against the truth and Friends."[41]

Edmondson launched the second round of debates by standing up and declaring that so far Roger Williams had only "manifested his clamor and rash and false accusations." Since he, Edmondson, had "other service for the Lord" to perform, he was prepared to spend only one further day in debate. By this point the high-minded Williams had also had enough, having concluded that his opponent was "nothing but a bundle of ignorance and boisterousness."[42] And so the great debate ended, with Edmondson running off to Warwick, Rhode Island, to celebrate his self-proclaimed victory with old and newly-declared Quakers and Roger Williams retreating to his study, where he drafted a fat volume elucidating in excruciating detail the theological arguments underlying his fourteen theses and attacking the Quakers for heresy and all-consuming pride. He titled his book <u>George Fox Digg'd out of His Burrowes</u>."

It is worth pausing at this point to ask whether Edmondson's invective and rudeness arose solely from his personality or if they embodied Quaker principles as well. By any measure, early Quakers were fanatics. They declined to say "good evening" or "good morrow" because Christ had said that one should salute no man on the highway. For Quakers, politeness was merely a euphemism for snobbism and failure to treat others as true equals. Yet even among such people, Edmondson stood out as for his saber-tongued invective.

After making his way to Boston Edmondson sailed for Ireland. He was to make two further trips to America, one in 1675 and the last in 1683. The first was filled with more drama, as he managed to arrive in New England just as the so-called King Philip's War broke out, pitting native Indians against settlers and settlers against each other. He then showed up in Virginia just as Nathaniel Bacon was mounting a rebellion against Governor William Berkeley. During the years before and after these adventures Edmondson found himself thrown again into jail or placed in stocks, publicly excommunicated, and his house and store plundered by Catholics after their final defeat at the Battle of the Boyne in 1690. At one point he was sentenced to be hanged, but his captors then decided to shoot him because, as Edmondson confessed, "I was a stout man."[43]

Somehow the Hammer of Ireland managed to free himself. Indeed, he always seemed to slip out of tight situations and to prevail over all adversity. Thanks to this, he managed to raise a large family and live long enough to pen a lengthy autobiography. He spent his last years at Tineal House, his home near the thatched-roof village of Rosenallis in County Laois. "Tineal" refers to a form of ringworm. When he died at age eighty-five in 1712 he was buried at the Quaker graveyard that still exists on one of his former fields just outside Rosenallis.

Monument at Edmondson's otherwise unmarked grave at Rosenallis, Ireland.

It is tempting to paint the life and personality of William Edmondson in glowing colors, to describe him as a tireless defender of his faith, a passionate evangelist, a charismatic polemicist, and a hero who repeatedly escaped martyrdom only thanks to sheer willpower and an iron constitution. That, at least, is how Edmondson viewed himself. He was all this, to be sure, but this is far from a full picture of the man. He was also one of thousands of English opportunists who rushed across the Irish Sea to claim lands and businesses expropriated from Irish Catholics. He was literate but otherwise uneducated, but not once in his voluminous Autobiography did he regret his lack of education or indicate his interest in taking steps to rectify it.

In his personal dealings Edmondson was blunt and confrontational. Rather than debate points of difference, he preferred to overwhelm his critics with a torrent of abuse. Roger Williams was only one of many who found themselves on the receiving end of an Edmondson tongue-lashing. That a Quaker leader was widely known as "The Hammer of Ireland" indicates that, admired or despised, his modus operandi was known to all. In fairness, this was the style of the era. Fox himself, the founder of a faith later known for its mildness and opposition to conflict, joined forces with one of his early followers to publish a long and blistering attack on both Roman Catholicism and the Church of England, with various other malefactors thrown in for good measure. Entitled The Great Mystery of the Great Whore, the book was the same kind of caustic rejoinder to critics that became Edmondson's specialty. Typically, it was not enough for Edmondson to conclude that Jamaicans had what we now call "issues" in the ethical realm. Instead, he had to brand the whole island as a "debauched and wicked Sodom."[44] That Fox might have done the same does not make Edmondson's style of abuse less distasteful.

Nothing about William Edmondson was more praiseworthy to his friends or more offensive to his critics than the tone of infallible certainty in which he expressed himself on any subject. This arose directly from the Quaker belief that God speaks directly to each human. George Fox explained this with disarming candor:

> "And after our long seeking, the Lord appeared to us, and revealed His glory in us, and gave us His Spirit from heaven, and poured it upon us, and gave us His wisdom to guide us, whereby we saw all the world, and the true state of all things, and the true condition of the Church in her present state."[45]

Thus armed with the sword of infallibility, a Quaker was by definition invincible in debate, and therefore saw no reason to hear the other side of any argument. Edmondson was merely the most visible of the many who sallied forth against the enemies of God's truth.

William Edmondson suffered mightily for his beliefs. His steadfastness and staunchness in the face of man-made and natural adversity is admirable, or would be had he not chosen to detail every one of his "Sufferings" in a six-hundred-page Autobiography. Of course, the writing of such "spiritual autobiographies" was typical of the era. Scholar and Edmondson descendent George A. Starr wrote about this in his 1965 study Defoe and Spiritual Autobiography, explaining how such books as Edmondson's provided models and templates for the early English novel. But Edmondson's wallowed in his sufferings, reflected in his Autobiography and in his decision to name a son Tryal. Of his other eight children he complained about "my unhappy son William, my unruly son Samuel, my foolish and disobedient daughter Hindrance, and my rebellious daughter Anne."[1] More tha one of them manifested precisely the sort of willfulness and pride against which both Fox and Edmondson himself endlessly railed.

And yet there is another side to the man. In spite of long absences from home, he had a long and event-filled marriage and he and his wife Margaret successfully raised five children, whose descendants still gather from time to time in Ireland. When Margaret died in 1691 he penned a touching memorial to her:

> "She took charge of our outward concerns and family in my absence, and stood in her testimony against tithes, and the Lord increased things under her hand beyond ordinary, and in these times of great trouble and calamity which lay upon us in that part where we lived she was always ready to bear her full share of ye burden and in desperate danger would venture herself to save me, and I do not

---

[1] Autobiography, p. 141

remember if ever she was terrified or affrighted though occasion enough to affright anybody, but often on the contrary she would tell me she was not afraid……"

Of one such confrontation with angry Catholics Edmondson wrote that:

"…when I opened the door and they took me and my two sons from her prisoners, barelegged and bareheaded and left her stripped into her shift, and she many days not knowing if we were alive or dead, and about a week after this she fell into their hands a ye second time, they stripped her stark naked, except shoes and she went near two miles in cold winter, and all this she bore with much [illeg.] , and though they destroyed our house and all that was in it, and took away our stock, when it pleased God miraculously to restore me and my sons to her she was well content and satisfied…" [46]

Such passages as this are as endearing as they are chilling and go far towards humanizing this warrior of the faith. After Margaret's death Edmondson remarried and had two more children. When Edmondson died his second wife added to his Autobiography a touching tribute, praising his kindness and generosity.[47]

Even in his deep old age the great Quaker missionary maintained contact with his native corner of England. When he was in his eighties and living in Ireland he penned a letter or "paper of exhortation" to the Quaker meeting at Sedbergh, where the recording secretary described him as "our Ancient friend."[48] That he addressed this missive to the Sedbergh Friends, a district where he had found his vocation as a Quaker and where many Edmondsons were concentrated, reflects a rare link of continuity in his highly discontinuous life.

Whatever William Edmondson's ignorance, intolerance, vanity, and pride, he has one claim to fame that cannot be denied, and an important one: he was the first Englishman to speak out against negro slavery as a moral evil. During his second trip to America in 1676 Edmondson had justified slave rebellion in Barbados, where the governor had fined two other Quakers for the crime of "bringing negroes into their meetings for worship." Then, when he got to Newport amidst King Philip's War between settlers and Indians, he learned that New England Friends had opposed selling Indians into slavery. Their action might have elicited praise from anyone but Edmondson. Instead, he addressed a letter to New England Friends, noting that "…many of you count it unlawful to make slaves of Indians, and if so, then why the blacks?"[49] Edmondson also dispatched a letter from Newport to Quakers in all places in the West Indies and elsewhere where he knew slavery existed. In it he put forth the view that slavery should be unacceptable to a Christian, and that it was "an oppression of the mind." [50]

George Fox also criticized the holding of both Blacks and Indians as slaves, defending his position by citing I Corinthians 7:22: "God hath made all Nations of one Blood." But this came later, and was never as categorical or as emphatic as Edmondson's denunciations. *Indeed, no early Quaker, or anyone else in the seventeenth century, was so outspoken on the subject of slavery.* The demands of good manners never stopped The Hammer. Even though he was a guest at the Shelter Island home of Nathaniel Silvester he excoriated his host on the twenty-six slaves who worked the place. Silvester was unmoved by the criticism. Edmondson's principled persistence caused historian Hugh Thomas to cite Edmondson as the first person in the entire European world to categorically oppose African slavery and to use lines from Edmondson's first letter on slavery as the epigraph of his magisterial 1958 study <u>The Slave Trade</u>. Considering that even Philadelphia Quakers did not ban slavery until 1776, and that New Jersey was still freeing slaves in 1827, this is a noteworthy achievement.

This, then, is a brief portrait of William Edmondson from Little Musgrave who early joined the Quakers, became a close ally of their founder, George Fox, brought Quakerism to Ireland, and strove to keep American Quakers focused on their divine duties. But there was also another Quaker named Edmondson who made his mark on the world in the mid-seventeenth century, John Edmondson of Talbot County, Maryland. Let us therefore review the remarkable life of this second Edmondson of the era. Having done so, we will then be able to pose the question with which we launched this enquiry, namely, the relationship between the branch of the Edmondson family that eventually moved to Lancaster, England, and the two well-known Quaker stalwarts, William of Ireland and John of Maryland.

John Edmondson provided land and material to construct the Third Haven Meeting House, Easton, Maryland, 1681, the oldest continually used house of worship in America.

On the wooded edge of the town of Easton on Maryland's Eastern Shore stands an ancient building of hand-hewn timber, the Third Haven Meeting House of the Society of Friends.[51] It is surrounded by a field of unmarked Quaker graves and dwarfed by tall first-growth oak and maple trees. Erected in 1681, this is the oldest existing Quaker meeting house in the Americas and the second oldest intact house of worship in the United States. Down to the time it was remodeled at the beginning of the eighteenth century, it had a large second floor and two-story entrances on both sides, giving it a cruciform plan resembling the stone Quaker meeting house at Sedbergh. It was built on land given (or according to some sources, sold) by John Edmondson, a prominent Quaker landlord who lived on nearby Edmondson Neck (now called Cedar Point) off the Choptank River.

John Edmondson's house from the 1670s, incorporated into both its modest 18th century successor and then its grand 19th century successor, Cedar or "Edmondson" Point, Choptank River, Md., where Edmondson hosted George Fox and William Edmondson and where Edmondsons lived down to the mid-nineteenth century.

Prior to the construction of the Third Haven Meeting, Quakers had assembled for worship and community meetings at Edmondson's one-story house on Cedar Point. This pioneer three-bay structure, or its eighteenth century successor on the same spot, still stands today, although reduced to the status of a wing to a much grander residence. The historian H. Chandlee Forman, in his Old Buildings, Gardens and Furniture in Tidewater Maryland, proved that this is the site of Edmondson's original dwelling and argued that that building is in fact preserved in the structure one sees today. Chrisopher Weeks, however, in his Where Land and Water Intertwine: An Architectural History of Talbot County, Maryland, argues that while it is the same site, the existing structure dates to the eighteenth century. Archaeology could easily resolve this issue. At some point in the last third of the eighteenth century a later Edmondson incorporated the old house into a very large and imposing brick Georgian residence, which was in turn greatly remodeled in the 1920s.[2] Few homes in Maryland are more dramatically positioned at the confluence of two rivers leading into Chesapeake Bay.

The same year John Edmondson ceded the land for the meeting house he appeared in court to petition for a modification of the law on taking oaths. By 1681 the fury of the Civil War had passed and all parties were beginning to settle back into normal life. Presenting himself as a member of the Society of Friends, people who "in scorn are commonly called Quakers," Edmondson wrapped himself in the British flag. "Far from desiring the least breach of

---

[2] Christopher Weeks, Where Land and Water Intertwined: An Architectural History of Talbot County, Maryland, Baltimore, 1983, p. 201.

the Magna Carta or of the least privileges belonging to a free-born Englishman,"[52] he and his fellow petitioner were asking simply that the court accept their well-known loyalty and honesty in all dealings as being as good as an oath. Edmondson, exhibiting the heart of a lawyer, carried the day.

Over the following decades the name of this same John Edmondson was to appear on dozens of legal documents, most of them pertaining to the transfer of land. By furious rounds of deal-making during the 1670s he had amassed 40,000 acres in Talbot, Dorchester and Kent Counties. By comparison, George Washington's Mount Vernon never exceeded 7,000 acres. But Edmondson did not stop there. Back in 1666 he had petitioned for the right to trade with Indians in western Pennsylvania and he promptly poured his profits from that enterprise into yet more land. By the 1680s he owned 27,000 acres of land in Pennsylvania, which he supplemented with 4,000 acres in Delaware and further holdings across western Maryland. Edmondson must have been constantly on the move, and constantly juggling his finances for, as his biographer notes, "No other person in seventeenth century Maryland did a larger number of land transfers than he."[53] Edmondson also bought buildings, including the "Greathouse with the Blockhouse and Kitchen" in Newcastle, Delaware, Peter Stuyvesant's original Nieu Amstel, which the English had just captured in 1684.

As Edmondson's wealth grew he increasingly sought a role in public life. He appeared before the Provincial and Superior courts to defend Quakers in hundreds of cases, served twice in the lower house of the Maryland legislature, and in 1691 was among those proprietors who signed a letter to the King and helped draft Articles of complaint against the absentee but exceptionally tolerant Cecil Calvert, the second Lord Baltimore and founder of the colony. And when in 1692 a group of legislators took over the State House and spent several days drinking and carousing, it was the abstemious Edmondson who took their case. For good measure he also established the first school library in Maryland (at the Third Haven Meeting), served as overseer of Maryland roads, and was one of the commissioners who laid out the town of Oxford, Maryland.[54]

Who was this extraordinary entrepreneur, operator, and civic figure? Researchers have pored through the voluminous Maryland archives for information on him but he remains elusive.[55] In spite of his immense wealth in land he lived modestly, as can be seen from the small scale of his house at Cedar Point. He was one of America's largest landholders yet there is no evidence that Edmondson engaged in farming. We know that around 1667 he married Sarah Shoupe and that he had five sons, John, James, William, Thomas, and Samuel. Ignoring sermons and letters from George Fox and William Edmondson, he was a slaveholder, and at the time of his death in 1698 his property included nineteen chattel servants. Since this number included men, women and children of all ages and included house servants and craftsmen, it was scarcely enough to maintain more than a garden and small tobacco plot. But they remained Edmondson's slaves, and his will included no instructions to free them. This is the more striking since a Quaker neighbor, William Southeby, who provided the timber for the Third Haven Meeting House, became the first native-born American to write against slavery.[56] If Southeby had fallen under the influence of William Edmondson, "The Hammer," the same cannot be said for his neighbor John Edmondson.

What were the origins of this John Edmondson? Without a shred of evidence a family hagiographer from Mountain City, Tennessee, claimed that the family name was really Edmiston and that they were descendants of the titled Scottish Edmondstone family. This is nonsense. No one has succeeded in identifying John Edmondson's place of origin or tracing his ancestry. The best we know is that he showed up in Maryland in 1658, that he arrived from Barbados as a servant indentured to a London merchant named John Home,[57] that he first settled in the Quaker colony on the peninsula jutting out between the Potomac River and Chesapeake Bay, and around 1667 shifted his base of operation to the Eastern Shore. The same sources indicate that he was originally from Ireland.

This means that he was almost certainly the son of William Edmondson's older brother, John Edmondson, who had opportunistically moved to Ireland shortly after English royalists conquered the island and promptly set himself up there as a merchant. When his son also became a merchant and entrepreneur he simply followed in the family business. The decision by John Edmondson and his son to follow a worldly profession rather than become a Quaker crusader doubtless explains the fact that William Edmondson "The Hammer of Ireland" was glad to stay with his nephew in Maryland but otherwise showed no interest in him.

George Fox and William Edmondson paid two extended visits to John Edmondson's Cedar Point home during their first trip to America in 1671-2. Their arrival was heralded throughout the region and became a major public event. William Edmondson reported that "There were so many boats on the river that it was almost like the Thames.[58] The fact that he refers to the flotilla of boats indicates that the participants in this mass gathering assembled at the broad field between Edmondson's one-story house at Cedar Point at the confluence of the Tred Avon and Peach Blossom rivers rather than at the Third Meeting House, which had not yet been built. Among the thousand people who came to hear the renowned evangelists there were "papists and persons of chief account in the country," he boasted. This was doubtless one of the largest religious gatherings in seventeenth century America.

William Edmondson also visited John and the Third Haven Meeting on both of his successive trips to the New World. Along with the large and active Quaker circle in Newport, it ranked as the most important Meeting on the itinerary of "the Hammer of Ireland." Yet in his memoirs William makes no mention of his host, John Edmondson. This may seem strange, given that they came from the same remote area of England and were kinsmen.

Yet it was not William's habit in his memoirs to speak of any of his fellow Quakers by name unless they were travelling together or undergoing some terrible vicissitude together. Moreover, as we have suggested, William doubtless consider his nephew too worldly to be taken seriously.

Did this John Edmondson have other relatives in the New World? We know there were two other Edmondsons in Maryland at the time: William, also of Talbot County, and Archibald and his son Thomas, who appear in Prince George's County by 1680.[59] While it has been claimed that William was John's brother, which is entirely possible, there is no evidence to confirm this, nor do we know anything more about Archibald. No genealogical research on these two later Edmondsons has yet been carried out.

What can be said with certainty is that members of the family of John Edmondson, like that of William Edmondson in Ireland, soon assimilated to their new surroundings. Within three generations they had abandoned Quakerism and joined various Protestant churches. In due course they spread westward through Virginia to Tennessee and beyond, as probably did the descendants of the Marylanders John and Archibald. Many acquired land and slaves and many of those slaves gained freedom long before the Civil War. As that happened, many adopted the Edmondson name of their former masters.

One to do so was Paul Edmonson (sic.) of Montgomery County, Maryland, who was freed by the later Cedar Point Edmondsons by 1830, although his wife did not gain freedom for several more years. Two of their twelve children were light-skinned Mary (1832-1853) and Emily Edmonson (1835-1895), both of whom worked in the Washington area until a new law consigned them to their mother's legal status. They then tried unsuccessfully to escape to New Jersey on the schooner Pearl. The project failed but the two young women came to the attention of the Brooklyn preacher and abolitionist Henry Ward Beecher. His daughter, Harriet Beecher Stowe, incorporated scenes from the Edmonson girls' life in her Uncle Tom's Cabin and wrote of them more directly in her Keys to Uncle Tom's Cabin. They were emancipated in 1848, studied at Oberlin College in Ohio, and thereafter acted in mock slave auctions throughout New York State organized by Beecher. A monument to the Edmonson sisters stands in Alexandria, Virginia.

The Edmondson sisters of Alexandria, Virginia.

Another former Edmondson slave was George Edmondson (1836-1922) of Lexington, Virginia, who joined the 45th US Colored Infantry and fought through the last year of the Civil War. Wounded during the siege of Petersburg, he was promoted to the rank of corporal. His obituary identified him as "a leading citizen of Parkersburg (West Virginia) of the older generation."

Yet another was William Edmondson (1874-1951) of Davidson County, Tennessee. Born to freed slaves who had moved from Maryland, Edmondson began sculpting lawn ornaments and tombstones after sustaining a railroad injury. His day job as a janitor at Women's Hospital in Nashville enabled him to buy a house and continue sculpting. Discovered by neighbors Sidney Hirsch and Alfred and Elizabeth Starr, Edmondson's sculpture came to national attention. He was the first African American artist to be given a one-man show at the Museum of Modern Art in New York.

Sculptor William Edmondson, Davidson County, Tennessee.

After this lengthy diversion to explore the lives of two Edmondsons of the seventeenth century who gained prominence in Ireland and America, and after touching briefly on a few of the hundreds of their descendants and others who bore their name, we must now pose the question of what relationship, if any, did these two Irish and American Edmondsons have to the Edmondson family that is the subject of this investigation?

First, it is important to pinpoint the timetable of their lives and to place them in the context of the Edmondsons from Cumbria. For William "the Hammer" the evidence is solid: he was born in 1627 in Little Musgrave, Cumbria, the youngest of John and Grace Edmondson's six children. The birth date of John Edmondson of Maryland remains unknown, but we know he was in Maryland by 1658. Assuming he was between twenty-two and thirty at the time, this means he was born between 1628 and 1636.

This line of reasoning leads us back into the origins of that John Edmondson who was the father of the first well-documented Edmondson of the family that is the subject of this study. Recall that a careful search of records from the Sedbergh, Dent, Howgill, and Horton in Ribblesdale areas did not produce any record of the birth, baptism, or marriage of this John Edmondson. This caused the expert genealogist Jane Hanby to conclude that he came from elsewhere. We then explored the earlier concentration of Edmondsons in the area of Little Musgrave, seventeen miles to the north. In doing so we noted the absence of Edmondsons in the Sedbergh-Dent-Horton in Ribblesdale area in the sixteenth and earlier seventeenth centuries.

This suggests the likelihood that the John Edmondson who was the father of the John Edmondson who was born in 1670 might have come to Horton from Little Musgrave. Earlier, we estimated that this John Edmondson was born between 1638 and 1645. Given this, we should search for *his* father in the generation born between 1608 and 1620. The one who best fits that chronology is Thomas, the eldest son and born in 1619. That he would have stayed close to home was predetermined by the fact that as the eldest son he would have inherited his father's property and would have stayed there to preserve it and live off it. This being the case, we can hypothesize that John Edmondson of Talbot County, Maryland, William "The Hammer of Ireland," and Thomas were brothers. Thomas in turn had a son whom he named John, and this John Edmondson moved from Little Musgrave to Horton in Ribbledale, where he first enters the documentary record. *This means that William, "The Hammer of Ireland," John, whose son John Jr. became a wealthy landowner in Maryland, and Thomas, who founded the line that eventually moved to Lancaster and is the subject of this study, were all brothers who hailed from Little Musgrave.*

St. Andrews Church, Crosby Garrett

No other conclusion fits all the available evidence. To be sure, there remain gaps in the evidence, especially on the paternity and birthplace pf John Edmondson of Horton in Ribblesdale. This should not be difficult to verify, since the area of search is defined by the triangle of Little Musgrave, Sedbergh, and Horton in Ribblesdale. But the conclusion remains solid.

Meanwhile, at least seven conclusions can be drawn from what we know with certainty:

First, the Edmondson family that emerged into pubic visibility with the career of surveyor, agricultural reformer and educator George Edmondson (1797-1861) originated not in the city of Lancaster, where he was born, but in the hardscrabble rural area twenty-five miles further north in Cumbria that is defined by the villages named above and which today adjoins the Yorkshire Dales National Park.

Second, the earliest known member of this family, Thomas Edmondson (ca. 1540-1600) was from Little Musgrave and was baptized at the Church of St. Andrew in nearby Crosby-Garrott. His son John Edmondson (1594-1635) had a large family, including Thomas (b. 1619), Edward (b. 1622), John (b. 1625), and William (b.1627).

Third, male embers of this generation of the Edmondson family from Cumbria joined the Puritan army under Oliver Cromwell and fought in England, Scotland, and Ireland.

Fourth, most, if not all, of these members of the Edmondson family, as well as many others from the same locale, joined the Society of Friends under the direct influence of the preaching of the founder of Quakerism, George Fox, who visited their area of Cumbria in 1652 and launched his proselytizing campaign in that year at nearby Pendle Hill.

Fifth, several male members of the Edmondson family left their native region during and after the chaos of the English Civil War. The two most prominent of them were John Edmondson, who moved to Ireland to set up a business there, and his younger brother, the Quaker evangelist William Edmondson ("the Hammer of Ireland"), who made several trips to America, during which he visited his brother's son (John Edmondson, Jr.) on Choptank River in Easton, Maryland, and debated Roger Williams in Rhode Island.

Sixth, the line of Edmondsons from whom the Lancaster Edmondsons descended from one of the two older sons of John Edmondson (1594-1635), whose father was Thomas Edmondson (ca. 1540—1600). These two were Thomas, b. 1619, and Edward, b. 1622. *Since the name Thomas reappears frequently in the Edmondson family that eventually settled in Lancaster, and since the name Edward never appeared in that line, one can safely conclude that the Lancaster Edmondsons were descended from Thomas Edmondson, 1540-1590) via his son, John Edmondson.*

Seventh, as the oldest son, Thomas Edmondson was expected to carry on his father's farm and therefore lived out his life in Cumbria. If he fought in the English Civil War or joined his brothers briefly in Ireland, he quickly returned to Cumbria and remained there throughout his life. Thomas Edmondson's family were the "stay-at-home" Edmondsons. Unlike the descendants of his brothers John and William, Thomas's descendants remained staunch members of the Society of Friends down to 1860.

III. George Edmondson, 1797-1863

By 1797, the year George Edmondson was born, Quakers in England had been free to worship as they wished for more than century. Most of the hundreds of Meetings founded during the pioneering era before 1680 continued to thrive. The passions of the Civil War era had burned out, but the Quakers as a group maintained the old fire. They based their daily actions on the prescripts of the Gospels, and viewed all life's events from the perspective of the Bible, large sections of which they had committed to memory. Thus, they based their refusal to take oaths on two texts from the New Testament. In silent meetings, they waited for God to inform their hearts, and the guidance thus gained was invariably couched in the words of Christ as recorded in the Gospels. Earthly life for them was a series of Tryals or Trials, which appears more than once as a male name among early Edmondsons. They were in no doubt that they would face God's judgment, which would be based on the constancy of their faith and the consistency of their actions in the face of life's challenges.

Banned from civil and political life because of their refusal to take oaths of loyalty to the Crown, they looked to each other for support. Thus isolated from England's national mainstream, they preserved the language of the seventeenth century in which their faith had been born. Like most north-country Quakers, the Edmondson family continued to use "Thee" and "Thou" down to the mid-nineteenth century.

City of Lancaster and the River Lune, looking towards Cumbria.

John Edmondson, George's father, was born in 1754 the town of Sedbergh in the Ribble Valley of Cumbria, a region northeast of Lancaster where various branches of the large Edmondson family had been living since at least the sixteenth century. Indeed, until he married Jane Skelton in 1787, all members of the Edmondson family had lived and worked on farms and very small towns within a radius of fifty miles centering on Sedbergh. Today the town is within the Yorkshire Dales National Park and is considered a quaint rural tourist attraction, especially by book collectors. But in the 1780s Sedbergh was a harsh backwater, and John and Jane therefore moved in search of work to the port town of Lancaster, twenty-seven miles to the southwest. In making this move, John stayed solidly within the geographical orbit of the early Quaker movement.

George Fox had preached in Lancaster (as he had also in Sedbergh) and many early Quakers, including Fox himself, had been imprisoned in Lancaster's Norman castle for interrupting sermons, refusing to pay tithes to the Church of England and, after the restoration of the monarchy, refusing to swear an oath of loyalty. Fox himself was imprisoned there, and demanded the judge personally inspect the foul conditions in the jail. Imprisoned with him was the Quaker Margaret Fell, who brazenly demanded that a High Sheriff stop whispering to the Judge and speak directly to her if he had anything to say. At one point in the late 1600s several hundred local Quakers were imprisoned there. Conditions were extremely harsh, with one Henry Wood beaten so hard that "blood came out of his eyes." Female Quaker preachers were sexually abused. Indeed, it was their collective experience as prisoners in Lancaster Castle that led later Quakers to pioneer prison reform in both England and America.

Lancaster Castle in 1778.

Notwithstanding these travails, by the time John and Jane Edmondson moved to Lancaster Quakers had managed to establish themselves as successful businessmen and to carve out for themselves a respected place in the city's life. Shortly after their arrival in Lancaster the Edmondson's purchased a gloomy sixteenth century stone house with mullioned windows called Stone Hall, at Friargate, adjacent to Castle Hill. The house has long since been demolished, but it stood just west of where China, Bridge, and Church Streets now come together. A short walk from this house local Quakers constructed an austere but handsome Meeting House, which can still be seen on

Meeting House Lane. It is the second oldest house of worship in the city. The Edmondsons prayed there down to John's death in 1815.

Local documents record that John Edmondson was a "trunk maker and linen draper." This misrepresents his actual business. Lancaster is situated on the River Lune just before the meandering river opens into a broad estuary. A flourishing trade with the Caribbean and America caused the port to thrive throughout the eighteenth century. A number of non-Quakers from Lancaster made fortunes in the slave trade. John Edmondson made a good living from a shop in his house selling provisions to the sailors, including trunks, which he himself manufactured. For many years he made a modest living as a ships chandler and nautical outfitter.

Beyond these fragments of information, we know next to nothing of John Edmondson. However, his granddaughter, basing her account on what she had heard from Edmondson's son, left us one intriguing observation, namely, that he was:

> "Timid and apt to be discouraged, but he had bursts of daring independence that were more disastrous in their results than his periods of greatest despondency and inertia. He was one of those warm-hearted, lovable men whom it would be least costly to their friends to maintain in idleness on condition that they kept entirely out of business." [60]

Unfortunately, we do not know what constituted those "bursts of daring independence." Curiously, much the same could have been said later of his grandson, George William Edmondson (1837-1915), who in just such a "burst of daring independence" ended up in America.

John and Jane Edmondson had twelve children. They were a hardworking business family, and remained steadfast Quakers. This was the era in which the British army was recruiting for the wars on the Continent and in the Caribbean. John's oldest brother refused to serve in the army or to send someone else in his place, which landed him in prison for a month. Jane, who thought her brother-in-law was glorifying his suffering, ordered him to read William Sewell's 1722 History of the Quakers to find out about real suffering.

In 1809, when their son George was twelve years old and had completed Quaker day school in Lancaster, he was sent off to the Quaker school at Ackworth. Situated in a quiet rural area southeast of Leeds, Ackworth School had originally been built as a foundling hospital. However, the local businessmen who ran it began to use it as a source of child labor and to treat the orphans with "little short of barbarity, and in more than one case murderous cruelty."⁶¹ When it was closed in 1777 a Quaker, Dr. John Fothergill, bought the property and buildings and transformed it into an institution to prepare young Quaker for careers as teachers and businessmen. Banned on account of their refusal to swear oaths from entering Cambridge or Oxford, upwardly mobile Quaker boys and girls—Ackworth was a pioneer in coeducation--now had their own Oxbridge. Inspired by the example set by Fothergill, a passionate naturalist, friend of Benjamin Franklin and founder of several schools in America, Ackworth was from the outset a high-minded institution.

It is not clear how John and Jane Edmondson scraped together the money for George's tuition. For even though the school prided itself on serving "those not in affluence," the annual tuition fee was eight pounds eight shillings, a large sum if one considers that a colonel in the British cavalry at the time earned a mere 32 shillings per annum. By the time young George made the sixty-five-mile trip from Lancaster to Ackworth, shipping was shifting from the Lune to the Mersey River, enriching Liverpool but leaving Lancaster merchants and shippers high and dry. John responded in 1810 by selling his nautical outfitting store and hanging a sign on the same premises advertising "Edmondson Grocer and Licensed Tea Dealer." John Edmondson's two enterprises were modest but they enabled the Edmondsons to cover the Ackworth tuition and to allow several of their other children to proceed beyond grammar school—an astonishing achievement.

Ackworth School, 1805, 2010.

Ackworth School still exists today. Its solid granite Georgian buildings lend it the air of an exclusive English public school, which indeed it has become. Wealthy British students from the surrounding region study there as day students, while the dormitories are filled with the children of oligarchs from Russia and eastern Europe, Singapore business tycoons, and Middle Eastern sheiks. But in Edmondson's day Ackworth elevated austerity in its students' lives to the level of a core moral principle, and took it to Himalayan heights. All students wore uniforms of rough, hand-loomed cloth provided by the school. They arose at six, or at 6:45 in winter months, and took their morning bath by plunging into a nearby pond, the ice on which had to be broken in winter; girls had their own screened bathing area but took the same frigid plunge. In a move later copies by institutions as far distant as Oberlin College in Ohio, Ackworth required all students to help with the work of maintaining the grounds, cooking, and so forth. As Dr. Fothergill put it, "learning and labor, properly intermixed, greatly assist the end of both."[62]

The prevailing austerity was particularly conspicuous at mealtime. Pliny Earle, an American Quaker and insane asylum doctor, visited Ackworth a generation after Edmondson's time and wrote that "The food of the scholars is much simpler than that in American schools, and the table set in a style that would hardly be tolerated by our republican pupils. Wooden trenchers and tin cups, which appeared as if taken from the ruins of Noah's ark, and from each of which cups four persons drink, form the chief table furniture."[63]

Earle did not mention the "sartans" or two-pronged tin forks, nor the food itself, which consisted of porridges and puddings, bread, butter, and fruit from the school's orchards. Recreation consisted of work in the school's gardens and, in the winter, ice-skating on frozen fields which the students tamped smooth with their rough boots. Skates consisted of home-made wooden clogs with broad iron bands imbedded in their soles. Discipline at Ackworth was strict, and enforced with generous applications of the rod. Repeat offenders were confined for a day in a special room for that purpose.

Since Edmondson left no account of his Ackworth days, we must assume that they were harsh and academically demanding, especially in mathematics, algebra, and reading. The school published various tables and bodies of data which students were expected to memorize. We can be sure that upon his arrival at Ackworth he spoke with a strong Cumbrian (Cumberland and Westmoreland) accent, and in the Lancashire dialect that transformed "cold" and "old" into "cowd" and "owd," "school" into "schoo," "fool" into "foo," and "man" into "mon." Twentieth century linguists gathered the following lingering examples of this dialect, which still included elements from three centuries earlier: "What art t' doin'?" "Tha must be jestin'!" "'Dost t' see yon mon o'er theer?" "Si thee!" "Ah'm talkin' to thee!" "Wheer's thi jackbit?'" "This is mine an' that's thine!" "Hast ta geet a fiver tha con lend me."[64] It fell to the reading master, William Singleton, to instruct Edmondson and his fellow students from the hinterlands in proper English.

John Edmondson had apprenticed his oldest son to a cabinet maker. But after observing George's ability at algebra, he decided that the Ackworth student should become a land surveyor,. He therefore apprenticed George to a Quaker surveyor in the village of Hallam, near Sheffield in Yorkshire. These skills were to prove important later on, but for now George had other ideas. Meanwhile, his reading master, William Singleton, had left Ackworth and set up a school of his own at Hallam. There, in an old house dating from the time of Henry VIII (which still stands today, and is known as Broom Hall), he established a school that focused more narrowly on the practical skills which Singleton believed every young Quaker should master. Singleton was pleased to find his former student in Hallam, and immediately arranged to train him in printing, bookbinding, and map-making—all skills that Edmondson would later to put to good use.

Singleton and his wife were "convinced Quakers,", in other words, converts. His desire to abide by the letter of Quaker teachings caused him to leave Ackworth under less than happy circumstances. Besides his desire to set up a school that would focus on practical skills, Singleton had strongly objected to the canings and other forms of physical discipline inflicted on students at Ackworth. An anonymous older friend of Singleton's had visited him at Ackworth and penned a poem about him. Entitled <u>Mentor and Amander, or a visit to Acworth's school by a Late Teacher</u>.[65] Here are the words he put in Singleton's mouth, calling him Amander:

> Inspir'd by these, the HAPPIER WAY,
> My spirit would secure,
> And learn that, to prevent a fault
> Is better than to cure.
>
> The rod, and all severity
> Whate'er its varied name,
> I wish entirely to expel
> And ever to disclaim.
>
> The harsh command, the stern rebuke
> Of loud authority,
> The 'mpatient haste; the nipping taunt:
> Odious are all to me.

Broome Hall today.

Life at Broom Hall presented a pleasant contrast to Ackworth's austerity. In the evenings Edmondson and his friends even recited canto after canto of Byron's Childe Harold. As he later told his daughter, they did so "with all the greater gusto because it was only half approved." [66] Byron was only nine years older than Edmondson and his recently-published narrative poem, describing how a world-weary young man sought distraction in foreign travel, found many readers among Edmondson's contemporaries. Edmondson was anything but world-weary, but the romantic life of Byron's hero clearly touched him. To this point, the closest contact he'd had with foreign lands was through "Sundance" and Mahmadee, two students from Sierra Leone who were preparing to become teachers back home. Even though "they were not always an agreeable addition,"[67] they may have further whetted Edmondson's appetite for travel.

Details of Edmondson's education and later life in Russia were recorded by his daughter, Jane Edmondson Benson, in an anonymous little volume entitled <u>From the Lune to the Neva Sixty Years Ago: With Ackworth and Quaker Life by the Way</u>. It is from Benson that we learn that one day Singleton asked Edmondson to deliver a note home for him. The Singleton's daughter Jane answered the door, promptly called her mother, and then disappeared. Jane was several years younger than George, and was kept under a strict Quaker regimen. When a Quaker friend of the family accused her of having curled her hair, Jane's mother dutifully cut off. But Jane achieved a kind of vindication when the hair grew back curly, as it had originally been. George, now sixteen years old, was immediately fascinated by Jane Singleton and, with Byronic resolve, vowed that one day he would marry her. He contrived various schemes to be with her, including digging her plot in the family garden. But except for their brief doorway meeting he had never spoken with her. Nor did the Singletons—especially Mrs. Singleton-- welcome his doing so.

Singleton had a problem. He wanted to advance the education and career of his young protégé but knew that the ardent young man's suit of his daughter could lead to unwelcome difficulties for all. Just at this moment a solution appeared in the person of Daniel Wheeler, a fellow member of the Hallam Friends' Meeting. Wheeler had just agreed to travel to St. Petersburg, Russia, at the request of the tsar, Alexander I. An agronomist, Wheeler had volunteered his services in response to a request the Tsar had made to London Quakers for a person who could organize the draining of a thousand acre of swamp land near the Russian capital and transform it into productive agricultural land. This, at least, was the formal pretext the tsar used to advance his deeper purpose.

To understand the broader program the forty-one-year-old Alexander had in mind it is necessary to sketch the peculiar relationship that had existed between Quakers and the Russian crown for more than a century. Back in 1697 the twenty-five-year-old Peter I ("the Great") had visited London and been fascinated by what he learned of a people that refused to doff their hats to royalty because "they bow to none but God." An Englishman explained to Peter that "…they acted as loyal citizens unless they felt that those in authority were on a wrong course, when they had no hesitation in expressing their opinions." This attitude appealed to Peter, an aggressive modernizer, and so he attended a Quaker meeting on the very next day.[68]

This Russian fascination with Quakers and Quakerism waxed throughout the eighteenth century. It was a Quaker doctor, Thomas Dimsdale, who persuaded Catherine II tthat he should inoculate her against smallpox, and then her son, the future Alexander I, as well. This led to the world's first mass inoculation. It was possible only because of the exceptionally high esteem in which the Russian court held Quakers.

Tsar Alexander I built on this tradition, but with a twist. He knew from first hand of the Quakers' technical and scientific competence, but unlike his mother, Alexander was attracted far more by their deeply pietistic brand of Christianity. Tutored as a boy by the rationalist Swiss philosophe La Harpe, Alexander started out as a typical son of the secular Enlightenment. But the decades-long struggle against Napoleon, the crowned philosophe, changed this, causing Alexander to embrace mysticism and various forms of direct spiritual communion with God, including Quakerism. Thus, on his way to celebrate the final victory over Napoleon with an Orthodox mass on the spot where the guillotine had stood, he detoured to a remote Alsatian village to pray with a humble Lutheran pastor, Johann Friedrich Oberlin. In his entourage was the Baroness Barbara de Krudener, a spiritualist aristocrat from Riga, who at the same time was finding inspiration among peasant mystics across Central Europe.

Tsar Alexander I of Russia.

At Alexander's request, on Sunday, June 20, 1814, he was escorted from the posh Pulteney Hotel to the Quaker meeting in Westminster. He arrived in time for the last fifteen minutes of silent worship. The clothing alone of those gathered in the simple room confirmed that this was a bizarre encounter of seeming opposite: the Quakers' plain homespun contrasted sharply to the opulent uniforms and dresses of the tsar, his sister, the Duchess of Oldenburg and her husband the King of Wurttemberg, and Count Christofor Lieven, the Russian ambassador to England. Alexander's outreach to the Quakers was sincere. The next day the clerk of the London Yearly Meeting, William Allan, a young French convert to Quakerism named Etienne (Stephen) Grellet, and representative of the Westminster Meeting, John Wilkinson, presented the tsar a statement prepared by the London Quakers. They met for an hour, during which Alexander invited a group of Quakers to come to his capital, St. Petersburg.

Alexander was well informed about the Quakers' technical expertise in many fields, and therefore couched his invitation in practical terms. He proposed that they find among their group people who could figure out how to drain the massive bogs surrounding the Russian capital and convert them into productive farm land. But it was their piety, far more than their mechanical skills, which caused Alexander to issue the invitation. As he commented to Grellet during their meeting, I consider you as safely landed whist I have to combat with trouble and difficulties and surrounded by many temptations."[69] "I am one with you respecting the spirituality of your worship. I wish to pray daily not in form but as I am animated by the divine principle in my own heart." For his part, Grellet concluded that "I feel [Alexander I] may justly be called the Christian Prince." [70]

In Daniel Wheeler Alexander found the ideal collaborator in his mission to introduce genuine Christian piety into Russia. Like Singleton, Wheeler was not a birthright Quaker but a recent convert. He recalled that as a child he "was cast upon the wide world an orphan boy; then cradled on a boisterous element and nursed I the free-school of iniquity, with sinners my companions–but myself was the chief!"[71] He joined first the Army and then the Navy, serving in the West Indies. His "remarkable preservation" during a terrible storm at sea convinced Wheeler that he had to change his life. After a stint at shop-keeping in Hallam, during which he made a fortune selling ale, he turned to what he considered more appropriate work for a new Quaker, as an innovating and successful farmer.

When Wheeler finally met Alexander the talk was not about draining swamps but about "the peculiar principles of our Society." When Wheeler agreed to the monarch's proposal he affirmed that he did so "on the grounds of religious sensibility."[72] Their meeting ended with the two of them holding hands, their heads bowed, and silently affirming "Christ crucified, the power of God, and the wisdom of God unto salvation." When Alexander followed up with a formal contract, he left the salary blank, for Wheeler to fill in.[73]

Wheeler, who invariably appeared in a worn, coffee-colored coat, approached Singleton because he needed a young man who could tutor his children during their stay in Russia. George Edmondson was the ideal candidate. Besides his solid schooling and obvious Quaker piety, he was a qualified land surveyor who could take a direct hand in the land reclamation project that was the pretext for Alexander's project to bring the Russian people back to lives of faith and spirituality. For Singleton it was particularly convenient, for it would get Edmondson out of his household and enable the young man and Jane Singleton to test their devotion to one another. Singleton set the condition that Edmondson and his daughter should not communicate with one another during George's stay in Russia. Only after Edmondson passed these hurdles would Singleton consider an engagement.

On June 22, 1818 Wheeler and a party of eighteen, including young Edmondson, set sail on the Aruthesa from Hull bound for St. Petersburg. At first the sea was rough and Edmondson spent so much of the first days throwing up that he was "glad to creep into my cell at night, which bears the greatest resemblance to the large cupboard in the parlor at Lancaster…"[74] All the others were seasick as well, but they still managed to hold regular Meetings aboard the Aruthesa. The rest of the voyage passed smoothly. The Quakers had stocked up on gooseberries, ham, bacon, flour, eggs, butter, ducks, and fowl and had brought two cows as well. Ample food and a calm sea left everyone in a good mood. They sailed past Elsinore and then Copenhagen, where Edmondson noted that the King's palace resembled the Sheffield Infirmary. The weather was now so fine that Edmondson could report to his parents that "even the sea did not disturb [the reading of the] scriptures," and that he had not heard an oath since coming on board.

On the sixteenth day they reached the Russian naval base at Kronstadt. The King of Prussia was departing from Kronstadt just as the Wheeler party arrived and Edmondson climbed the masthead to observe the festivities. They hired a smaller craft powered by twelve Russian oarsmen that took them to St. Petersburg and an inn kept by the widow of a drunken Englishman. The next day they reached the magnificent baroque palace of Prince Bezborodko on the Neva embankment opposite the Monastery of St. Alexander Nevsky, where they were to be housed until departing for the countryside. Stone lions along the Neva quay still greet the visitor arriving at the Neva embankment and the palace itself still stands, though internally in decay. The Tsar welcomed them on the day of their arrival. The fact that they kept their hats on during the audience presented no problem.

Prince Bezborodko's palace on the Neva in St. Petersburg, where Edmondson stayed.

Edmondson, twenty years old and travelling for the first time in the world beyond northwest England, was smitten by his new surroundings. He was impressed to learn that Alexander often walked alone through the city. He judged Russian cooking ovens "in many respects superior to the English" and concluded that St. Petersburg "far exceeds any place in appearance that I ever saw in England." As to the twenty-four rooms decorated in different styles that were reserved for their use in Bezborodko's mansion, they were arranged en suite without corridors, which renders them "much warmer in winter."[75] To Singleton he enthused that even the swamp-fed waters of the Neva were "very wholesome after the first effect, which is purgative in most cases…"[76] Overall, he concluded that "From the accounts we heard of Russia before we came here one might have supposed it was wild, inhabited by men little more than savages, but we find the contrary to be the case."[77]

There is no more vivid description of St. Petersburg's official and social world than that included in Tolstoy's novel War and Peace, which is set in precisely the years preceding and during Edmondson's time in Russia. Indeed, the novelist used Prince Bezborodko, which means "Beardless," as a thinly disguised model for his elder Prince Bezukhov, which means "Earless." In St. Petersburg the new arrivals met Stephen Grillet and William Allan. At Alexander's request these two Londoners now headed the British-based Russian Bible Society, which toiled to spread the Gospel among the people of Russia. Both Grellet and Allan, it should be noted, also made cameo appearances in Tolstoy's War and Peace. The Wheeler party, including Edmondson, also appeared before the Minister of Education, Minister of Spiritual Affairs, and patron of the Bible Society, Prince Alexander Golitsyn. Though his retainers were shocked when the visiting Quakers kept their hats on, he, too, admired their piety and, after praying with them, affirmed his strong support for their mission. Golitsyn, who emerges in most histories, as well as in Tolstoy's War and Peace, as an unalloyed reactionary, received his English visitors as brothers in the faith and remained in close touch with Wheeler and his team down to Alexander's death in 1825.

After a few weeks spent at Prince Bezborodko's palace, the Wheeler party travelled several miles further up the Neva to a spot called Okhta, where they launched their land reclamation work. Finnish natives of the territory had aptly named the river Neva, which means "swamp" in Finnish. One of the few buildings in the entire marshy region was a large wooden house on a rare high spot where Wheeler and his family, Edmondson, and their Russian cooks and helpers were all housed.

House at Okhta where young George Edmondson lived, worshipped, and worked along with Daniel Wheeler and his family, S.F. Starr

Work began at once on the thousand acres of swampy land. Edmondson had been hired as a tutor, but when the Russian surveyor assigned to the project proved totally incompetent, Wheeler immediately reassigned Edmondson to survey the entire plot. Weeks later he also called on the twenty-one year old to oversee the digging of drainage canals, removal of stumps, and preparation of the land for agriculture. To this point George Edmondson had dutifully tutored the Wheeler children, even earning praise from Prince Golitsyn and the Minister of Foreign Affairs, Count Nesselrode, for his use of the so-called "Lancastrian" system, whereby older students tutored those younger than them. The fact that the older children were already good students enabled Wheeler to shift full tutoring responsibilities to Wheeler's oldest son, freeing young George Edmondson to become the key organizer of the entire project launched by Tsar Alexander I and headed by Wheeler.

George waited impatiently for the government commission that came with his new responsibilities and reported to his parents that he expected to "receive pretty handsomely" from it.[78] Even before his salary began, he was shopping for an expensive Russian fur coat or shuba. In the spirit of Quaker mercantilism, he was also suggesting to his parents products that might profitably be imported into Russia, including worsted stockings, shoes, and furniture, and suggesting ways of minimizing or avoiding tariffs. He also maneuvered to get his brother a post teaching English in the hinterland at a salary of 200 pounds a year.[79]

Though he spoke no Russian at first, Edmondson somehow managed the hundred seventy Russian peasant soldiers whom Alexander had assigned to the project. Within months he was known by his name in Russian, Egor Ivanovich (George, son of John) and was functioning effectively in what must have been peasant Russian. This doubtless made a favorable impression on the many visitors from the imperial court who drove in carriages out to Okhta to satisfy their curiosity. As soon as he returned from the Congress of Aix–la-Chappelle, at which France was readmitted to the community of nations, Tsar Alexander himself came to inspect the work, as did his German-born wife, Elizabeth Alexeyevna, who thereafter often brought parties of her own. After inspecting the work in the fields, the tsar and grandees who followed him always stayed for tea with the Quakers. Edmondson noted that the tsar spoke bad English and was deaf in one ear, but refused the services of an interpreter. It was at this time that the Tsar Alexander ordered that English be taught in all government-funded schools.

Other visitors included the Commissioners of the Russian Admiralty and the powerful Minister of Internal Affairs. The latter's visit was greeted with some concern, for Wheeler had introduced the innovative practice of actually paying the soldiers for the work they performed and paying them extra for overtime. Surprisingly, the minister voiced no objections. Prince Golitsyn also made an appearance at Okhta and promised to share with the ruler the plan for a project that Edmondson had drafted.

In 1973 Arnold B. McMillan published an article on "Quakers in Early Nineteenth Century Russia." McMillan was eager to show the St. Petersburg Quakers in what he was considered a positive light so he underscored their practical work in land development and education and bent over backwards to insist that they were "in no sense missionaries."[80] This, after all was the 1970s, when everything connected with Western colonialism, including the entire missionary movement, was condemned as a denigration of local cultures and A form of soft imperialism. But substantial evidence on the motives of both the Russian leadership and the Quakers who answered their call contradicts this conclusion.

It has long been known that Alexander fell into a depression following the victory over Napoleon and the bewildering and, to him, threatening circumstances of the post-Napoleonic world. He placed his hope in what he called a "Holy Alliance" of the major powers, a system of collective security under the joint leadership of Orthodox Russia, Catholic France, and Anglican Britain. Praised by some for having fostered peace in Europe, it was equally attacked as a reactionary project created to quell popular unrest. On a personal level, Alexander found release and solace only through direct spiritual communion with God and in the company of people who shared his yearning to hear God's voice directly, without the mediation of priests or churches. This is what drew him to various Russian mystics and to German mystics like Heinrich Jung-Stilling and pietists like Johan Friedrich Oberlin, not to mention spiritualists like Baroness Krudener. The Quakers' conviction that God speaks to each of us through an inner voice exactly coincided with Alexander's frame of mind. Alexander became, in effect, a closet Quaker.

Alexander and his ministers opened their capital to the Quakers in hopes that their deep piety, sobriety, self-discipline, and penchant for hard work would set an attractive model for Russians, and especially for the Russian peasantry. As Alexander put it in a letter to Stephen Grellet, "It was not the cultivation of morasses, nor any outward object, that led me to wish to have some of your Friends come and settle here; but a desire that by their genuine piety and uprightness in life and conversation, an example may be set before my people for them to imitate...."*81* In other words, this was a rare instance where officials of the receiving country themselves devised and supported what was in fact a missionary project.

The Quakers saw their work in the same light. Wheeler, a farmer who acknowledged that he undertook the mission "on the grounds of religious sensibility," did not hesitate during his first meeting with the tsar to offer spiritual advice to the ruler of a country with a population twice that of France and four times that of Britain: "When time shall rob thee of thy earthly crown, an inheritance incorruptible and undefiled-- a crown immortal, may be thy happy portion."[82] Had Alexander's main concern been with draining swamps he would have brushed aside this astonishing homily as grossly inappropriate. That he instead welcomed it indicates clearly his intentions and hopes for the Quaker mission to Russia.

Once established at their large frame house at Okhta, the Quakers began convening twice-weekly Meetings for worship in a large room on the main floor, a practice that continued throughout Edmondson's time in Russia. Grellet, Allan, and other Quakers in St. Petersburg travelled the six miles to attend these Meetings, as did many grandees from the Russian court. These sessions became so well known among the aristocracy and intelligentsia of the capital, that the poet Alexander Pushkin, in his luminous novel in verse, Eugene Onegin, has his self-indulgent hero flirting with Quakerism. Thus, the poet asks of his hero, as he searches for a new identity,

> Tell us, what new impersonation,
> What pose is held for us in store?
> Well? Cosmopolitan, Melmotic,
> Childe Harold-esque or patriotic,
> Tartuffe or *Quaker*, may one ask,
> Or yet another faddish mask?[83]

George Edmondson participated in the Meetings throughout his stay in Okhta. In letters to Singleton he dutifully reports on them, noting, for example, the reading of the Yearly Meeting epistle sent from Sheffield. Also read to the group was a paper entitled "Address to Parents" which was included with the epistle. As if displaying his maturity to one whom he hoped might become his future father-in-law, the twenty-year-old Edmondson declared this a subject which "has long wanted the attention of the Society."[84]

The first seasons of work at Okhta were successful beyond all expectations. Pleased with the results, Alexander proposed greatly to expand it, by draining and developing a much larger tract of land—fully 50,000 acres—near the village of Volkovo, north of St. Petersburg along the road to Moscow. He and Wheeler agreed that they would turn over the entire project to Edmondson to manage. The Volkovo tract was six miles away, so this meant that Edmondson had to move to the site. However, the only structure in the area was a ramshackle old hut inhabited by an elderly and taciturn peasant.[85] Edmondson moved in with the man and began what turned out to be an arduous project extending over five years. During one bitterly cold winter savage winds blew the metal roof from their hut and they were unable to repair it. In the end the Tsar sent a team of soldiers to replace the roof, and also sent medicines for the ailing pair. For the project as a whole Tsar Alexander detailed two-hundred soldiers to carry out the work. Once again, full responsibility for their work and welfare fell on Edmondson's shoulders. For his entire time at Volkovo, he managed to write only four letters home each year, down from six in his first years. Fortunately, all are preserved in the archive of the Quaker Historical Society in London. These letters present a vivid picture of this heretofore neglected initiative.

Edmondson's first impressions of Russia had been warmly positive, the effusions of a young man travelling abroad for the first time. His enthusiasm was such that they distorted his understanding of much that he observed. Thus, in a letter to Singleton and his parents he told of the large rafts that serfs sailed down the Neva to St. Petersburg, where they were broken up for lumber. Even though they could have taken flight in the capital, the serfs dutifully returned to their masters. "This is proof of their attachment to their owners," he observed in the letter to Singleton, "as well as their fidelity."[86] The possibility that they returned to their masters out of fear of being punished for not doing so did not yet occur to him. In another moment of enthusiasm Edmondson even praised the cleanliness of the Russian peasant."[87]

When word reached Edmondson that Singleton suspected that his young correspondent presented only the bright side of things, he soberly responded that "Thou art too well acquainted with human nature to suppose that society in its present state can be free."[88]

On one important point--and a very important one--Edmondson's enthusiasm proved to be fully warranted. In the early nineteenth century fully nine-tenths of the Russian peasantry was irrevocably bound to the land. As serfs, they were obliged to work several days a week on the lord's land and to contribute to their village community's annual payment to the landlord as well. They were subject to corporal punishment by their landlord and could travel only with his permission. Russian serfdom had become, in fact, a form of slavery.

Edmondson knew at first hand the devastating impact of Russian chattel slavery on the mentality of individual serfs. One day a peasant soldier turned to him for help in dealing with a painful toothache. Puzzled that the peasant spoke about the tooth as if it was someone else's, Edmondson asked him to whom the tooth belonged? The peasant replied laconically that "It is my master's tooth, but it is in this head," pointing to himself."[89] Wheeler meanwhile reported that he had heard it said that among the serfs "life is not worth a kopeck, or the hundredth part of a shilling."[90]

Catherine I had greatly expanded serfdom by extending it into newly conquered territories and had strengthened the landlords' controls over the lives of their serfs. But under Alexander I there began a many-sided and strictly confidential discussion on how to abolish the institution of serfdom. Edmondson was well aware of this, and reported to his parents that "Now vassalage [e.g. serfdom] is much on the decline…Many noblemen have given liberty to all their slaves. The Emperor is continually giving a number their liberty. He is very desirous to have the feudal system banished entirely."[91]

Edmondson erred in saying that many noblemen had freed their serfs---scarcely a handful had actually done so. But his observation reflected the enthusiasm for emancipation that prevailed among many of the more cosmopolitan landlords, certain of the tsar's advisors, and Tsar Alexander himself. This led to a number of proposals and projects for emancipation that appeared throughout Alexander's reign. Far the most concrete were legislation for Lifland (Lithuania) and Estland (Estonia) which Alexander instituted in 1816-1819.[92] Three striking features of these laws were, first, that they gave peasants freedom but no land; second, that they refused to embrace the individual peasant as a full-fledged legal subject and instead continued to vest the collective peasant village commune with vast authority over its members; and, third, that they not only permitted but required the government to continue regulating the relationship between lord and peasant.

Daniel Wheeler was fully informed on these projects, probably by the tsar himself. In short order he came up with his own scheme for emancipation. Simply stated, he proposed a practical scheme that would transform Alexander's land reclamation project into a powerful engine for advancing the cause of emancipation:

> "My idea is to make a trial of placing peasants on farms at moderate fixed rent, on the land we have drained and cultivated, and if these are favored to prosper, I have a hope that the nobles will see it their interest to divide their large estates on a similar way, and place their peasants on the same footing; and I am persuaded their incomes would be greatly increased."[93]

Wheeler's proposal was as ingenious as it was simple. The state itself owned millions of acres of land worked by millions of enserfed "state peasants." Beginning with Okhta and Volkovo, he proposed to settle peasants on their own land, which they would buy by paying a moderate rent. They would be free to hire themselves out either to the government or large landlords, but they would do so as free peasants, not as serfs. Moreover, unlike Alexander's own

Baltic projects, Wheeler's scheme assured each peasant a plot of land, required little government involvement, and freed peasants from the control of their own village communities. In other words, Wheeler proposed to turn Russian serfs into free farmers.

With Alexander's approval, both Wheeler at Okhta and Edmondson at Volkovo set about applying this ingenious scheme in practice. Once they had drained the land and established conditions for farming, Wheeler and Edmondson designated plots of forty-five acres and, after designing a model farm house, began constructing them for the use of peasant farmers, who would work the land as individual smallholders.[94] Remarkably, the name they gave to this innovative arrangement was "The Free Village."[95]

At a time when nearly all Russian peasants were enserfed and worked the land collectively in traditional communes, this was indeed a bold step, and one which could not have been taken had the tsar himself not supported it. These were the very years when Alexander I's more public image was of a reactionary who opposed the very reforms he had himself earlier championed. Several score peasants jumped at the opportunity thus presented. But the tsarist government would not take the next step and grant them legal freedom. They remained enslaved. Moreover, among the peasantry as a whole, few were prepared to separate themselves from the traditional peasant communes and the security they brought--along with low productivity. Alexander's serfs, in short, were not prepared to assume the risk of individual entrepreneurship. And few landlords, if any, saw in the Quakers' plan a more favorable arrangement than what already existed, i.e., collective working of the land and collective payments to the landlord, all regulated by the state. Perhaps the Free Village concept could have advanced beyond Okhta and Volkovo had Alexander more actively supported it. But Alexander, as usual, vacillated, and in the end the Wheeler-Edmondson scheme for abolishing serfdom went nowhere.

But their effort nonetheless had lasting consequences. In effect, the two Quakers proposed a program whereby communal or village-based agriculture in Russia would gradually give way to private farming, as it had in England in the sixteenth century. As such, it was one of the few concrete and practical proposals truly to abolish serfdom in Russia and practically the only one to propose the abolition of the backward-looking institution of the peasant communes. It would have granted full rights to peasants and relied on voluntarism rather than a decree from the throne.

Serfdom in Russia was finally abolished in 1861, two years before the abolition of slavery in America and with a minimum of strife and bloodshed. But the Emancipation of 1861, like its American counterpart introduced by President Lincoln two years later, was a half measure. The Russian emancipation granted land to the peasants, but only through their village communes, which it perpetuated. The American emancipation granted freedom but no land, nor did it commit the federal government to regulating future relations between former landlords and the freed slaves, as the Russian legislation did. Only after 1905 did the private peasant farm gain a legal and economic foothold in Russia. But this was stopped by the Bolshevik revolution, leaving the way open for Stalin's brutal re-collectivization of agriculture after 1929. In America, the federal government abstained from intervening in the relationship between former masters and their freed slaves until the 1960s. The simple Wheeler-Edmondson proposal had addressed all these problems.

Had the proposal advanced by Wheeler and implemented on a trial basis by George Edmondson gained the tsar's wholehearted and decisive support, Russian history would have followed a very different course. In the end, private agriculture made real headway in Russia only after the collapse of the USSR in 1991.

On a stormy morning in late winter, 1822, Wheeler showed up at Volkovo and asked Edmondson what he was planning to do that afternoon. Edmondson replied that he didn't know, and that he wished he was with the others at Okhta. To which Wheeler responded, "Suppose thou wert to sit down and pen a long letter to Anne Singleton?"[96] Edmondson was stunned, for he had suffered under Singleton's four-year ban on communicating with his daughter. Edmondson was now twenty-five and had proven himself hard-working and responsible. The ban lifted, he poured out his heart to his beloved and shortly thereafter made plans to return to England to marry.[97] Anne even agreed to return with him to his grim and isolated outpost at Volkovo.

Watercolor by Edmondson of his new house at Volkovo (now on northern edge of St. Petersburg), where he and his wife Anne lived, and where their first daughter was born. Brad Edmondson.

When Tsar Alexander learned of this he sought out Edmondson and told him "Egor Ivanich, I hear you are intending to return to England for a wife." Edmondson acknowledged that "This is true, with the permission of the Emperor," to which Alexander responded, "And could you not, in my wide dominion, find a lady to suit you?" When Edmondson told the tsar that his mind was set, Alexander accepted it, but admonished him to "Bring the lady here. Do not be tempted to remain in England. I do not like to lose honest men from my empire."[98] Edmondson later told his daughter that he realized that he was far happier at that moment than was the increasingly melancholy Emperor.

The marriage of George Edmondson and Anne Singleton took place in Hallam on December 27, 1822, after which the couple sailed back to Russia and settled into a new house at Volkovo which the soldiers had constructed for them. Edmondson painted a small watercolor of this house, which remains in the Edmondson family. It shows a two and a half story wooden structure surrounded by a high wall designed to keep wolves at bay. As a bizarre concession to Edmondson's new bride, whom the Russians obviously considered a lady of fashion, it also featured a small ornamental garden in the style of a French parterre. The residence could not have been comfortable, or even healthy, for it was surrounded by swamps that were infested with mosquitoes.

Within a year Anne gave birth to a daughter. The new mother did not share her husband's enthusiasm for everything Russian, and declared in a letter to her sister that "An honest and clean Russian servant would be a wonder worth exhibiting. I have not heard of such a one to be found."[99] Removing his rose-colored glasses, George Edmondson acknowledged that while a typical peasant soldiers might cross himself and remove his hat in deference to him, "He would cross himself with one hand and rob you with the other." Russian Orthodox Christianity, he concluded, was purely external and exerted little or no influence on a believer's conduct. It engendered ignorance and superstition, or so Edmondson concluded as he watched a peasant crossing himself before an eight-day clock in the Okhta residence.[100] The same peasant was quite capable of showing dogged passive resistance to avoid tasks he didn't like.

Edmondson's dyspeptic view of Orthodoxy had formed during his first year, as he watched a priest conduct a mass christening in a hole cut through the frozen Neva. The priest immersed each infant three times and used a birch twig to sprinkle it with freezing water. In one case the priest lost his grip on the child and the river's current swept it away beneath the ice. "The Lord has taken it," the priest solemnly declared, and the mother stoically accepted her child's fate.[100]

Edmondson did not lack opportunities for aiding the Russians among whom he lived and showing compassion for them when they were beset by troubles. Of all the crises he encountered, none surpassed the momentous flood of November 6, 1824. A powerful wind from the west swept in from the Baltic Sea, generating a storm surge that churnedt up the Gulf of Finland and engulfed the Russian capital at ten AM. Parts of the central city were under twelve feet of water in what remains today the worst flood in the city's history. Daniel Wheeler got close enough to the city to see it standing, as it were, in an open sea.[102] Hundreds of people and thousands of horses and other dray animals drowned; their corpses floating in the streets created a sanitary crisis that worsened when the water breached tens of cesspools. Both Okhta and Volkovo were spared, but the soldiers working there were immediately detailed to keep order in the suffering city.

Many saw the natural disaster as an omen. One to do so was the poet Alexander Pushkin, who drew dark inspiration for his epic poem The Bronze Horseman from the image of the French sculptor Falconnet's immense bronze stature of Peter the Great and his rearing steed rising menacingly above the roiling flood waters. Not just Peter, but the city itself and the government that labored there posed a threat to normal men and women. It is not the flood that destroys Pushkin's anti-hero, a humble scribe named Evgenii, but the Bronze Horseman himself, who comes thundering down on simple folk.

Wheeler tried to defend Peter's heir, the hapless and vexed Alexander I, who increasingly was perceived as an obscurantist reactionary who oppressed simple folks. "I am grieved," he wrote a friend in England, "to find the character of our Emperor does not stand so high with many in England as it did; and fully believe he has been prompted by evil-disposed persons to do things he does not approve of, and would not have done, but at their instigation."[103] This defense, which echoes the oft-heard line that if only the tsar knew what his subordinates were doing he would set things right, had at least some basis in fact. The Bible Society, which had been flourishing when the Wheeler team arrived, was now increasingly under pressure from the Holy Synod and from influential members of the Orthodox clergy. Police surveillance had intensified to the point that even Alexander's revered Quakers were feeling the heat.

On November 5, 1824, the day before the great flood, Edmondson wrote a letter to Anne's sister, Agnes, in which he assessed the mood in the Russian capital:

"A report has got abroad, and we understand that you may shortly expect us home again. Although we cannot deny that there seems a great alteration in the state of things here, we see no immediate prospect of it ourselves. The minds of the clergy seem to be in a very irritated state against everything that exposes their superstitious practices; their power over the Emperor is on the increase we think, but what would lead directly to the [illegible] respecting our return in your minds, would be the banishment of two Catholic clergymen, who dissented a little from their own church, seeing beyond the superstition of it. One of them published a book, which caused his banishment and the book to be burnt, for a passage of no moment whatever, but which they deemed heresy. Neither schools, the distribution of Bibles, tracts, or anything of the kind is now encouraged. This is certainly an alteration of things which we cannot but lament, and from which our friends have drawn the conclusion we shall not remain here long. When the right time comes we can assure them we shall have no objections to leave this unprincipled land, but at present can see no certainty as to the event or the time when it may take place, if ever." [104]

The "right time" came less than a year after the flood of November, 1824. The tsar was not happy with Edmondson's decision to leave and offered his young friend a thousand acres of land on the northern edge of the rapidly expanding imperial capital. But the gift of a large gift of marshy land (situated in "Shushary," from the Finnish suosaari, or "marshy island") held no attraction for Edmondson. His wife Anne suffered from chronic fevers which threatened their young daughter as well. And so, with a total absence of ceremony the Edmondson family in late November, 1825, set sail once more for England. With the exception of his brief return to England to get married, he had been away for seven years.

Why did Edmondson leave Russia when he did? The family had lived for three years in what was a mosquito-ridden swamp that was subject to water-borne diseases and outbreaks of typhus. Conditions there remained so primitive as to make it all but impossible for the young couple to care for their two-year old daughter, Jane. It was not a fit place for family life. Most important, at the time of their departure both daughter Jane and Ann Edmondson herself were ill.

Also, the campaign against Protestants and Catholic campaign mounted by the Holy Synod and senior Orthodox clerics gained new momentum during the year following the flood. The Bible Society continued to limp on, but many of its British staff returned home, as did many other expats. Six months after the Edmondsons departed, the Russian government closed the Bible Society. Prominent Catholics were declared persona non grata. Quakers were not banned, but fell under constant police surveillance. We know from his letter to his sister-in-law a year earlier that Edmondson was acutely aware of these developments and viewed them with concern.[105]

Less clear is the extent to which Edmondson was conscious of deeper political intrigues taking place in the capital and which were to culminate in disaster only weeks after his departure. For several years before this fateful autumn the Quakers' patron, Tsar Alexander I, was mired in a fog of mystical piety and was rarely seen in public. During the autumn of 1825 his wife came down with typhus and the tsar himself was said to be in declining health. Day-to-day leadership fell to the tsar's reactionary ministers and courtiers. For several years Masonic groups and other secret societies had been gathering in the salons of St. Petersburg to discuss the increasingly ominous situation. Some of these groups hatched bold plans for liberal reforms and a constitutional government, while at least one called for a reinvigorated dictatorship. When Alexander took his wife to the Black Sea port of Taganrog to recuperate, hundreds of these conspirators concluded that the moment to make their move was approaching. On 1 December Alexander died under suspicious circumstances in Taganrog. Immediately a dispute arose as to whether he should be succeeded by his reformist brother Konstantin, or by his more despotic younger brother, Nicholas.

On December 26 some 12,000 troops from Guards regiments representing the opposing forces assembled on or near Senate Square in St. Petersburg. Edmondson had already departed but Daniel Wheeler was standing in the crowd that assembled around the statue of Peter the Great. He described the events that occurred late on that winter day when the Governor General announced that Konstantin had stepped aside in favor of Nicholas:

> "Before five o'clock…rebellion had thrown off the mask. As the army about us had most willingly declared for Konstantin only ten days before, some hesitation in several regiments became visible. This moment seemed favorable to the wishes of some who were aiming at a general overthrow; and they artfully spread a report among the troops that Konstantin was only 200 versts from hence, but was prevented from coming forward, and that the newly declared Emperor was only a usurper. This had the effect of drawing several large bodies of troops into the square; and I believe many of those poor fellows believed they were only acting faithfully to the oath they had so recently taken; it is very evident that they had no pre-concerted design against the government. However, an armed force collected in the neighborhood of the Senate House, and were joined by a number not in military garb, and a mob of intoxicated rabble who had been stirred up to act on the occasion. In vain did the new Emperor send to them and endeavor to persuade them to peace and quietude. At last the military governor, an old soldier and popular character, went to harangue them, and might probably have prevailed, but the real plotters among them, fearing the soldiers would become reasonable, had the audacity to fire upon him. This poor Count Miloradovich, who had been unhurt, it is said, in thirty-four engagements, was now mortally wounded.
>
> This circumstance led to a dreadful carnage. The Emperor [Nicholas] was very unwilling to resort to force, and at first a volley of blank cartridges were fired; but this only caused the rebels to advance. A fire of grape shot was opened upon them with terrible effect, followed by a charge of cavalry. As most of the rebels who were able fled towards the river, the cannons were pointed in that direction… It is believed that several hundred perished…. [106]

One can only speculate whether Edmondson, who had by now developed his own sources of information among the St. Petersburg elite, was aware of the mood of conspiracy that enveloped the city during the autumn of 1825, and whether this knowledge figured in his decision to leave Russia. Wheeler most certainly was well-informed, which is why he stood on Senate Square on December 26. At first Wheeler supported the overbearing new tsar and even launched a new phase of land reclamation and reform during the early phase of his reign. But eventually he, too, left Russia, leaving the new project to his son, Edmondson's replacement as tutor, to manage. Daniel Wheeler died in America in 1837. A persistent tradition maintains that at his wish his body was returned to Russia and buried in the Quaker cemetery at the royal estate of Tsarskoe Selo outside St. Petersburg.

Once back in England Edmondson headed directly to the town of Blackburn, a formerly quiet Lancashire wool-weaving center at the southern end of the Ribble Valley and twenty miles north-northwest of Manchester. On 5 May, 1826, he announced in the <u>Blackburn Mail</u> that he was available to teach Russian and that he was opening a school in town.[107] Only one student responded to the ad, but when Edmondson opened his door to this student he launched a career in education that was to extend down to his death in 1863.

"G. Edmondson's Academy, Lower Bank near Blackburn, Lancashire," first quarters. S.F. Starr

Blackburn was no ordinary place and in deciding to settle there Edmondson showed remarkable foresight. New long-fiber strains of cotton were increasingly available from the American South and inventors and entrepreneurs in Blackburn and neighboring towns plunged headlong into the work of inventing efficient means of converting this high-grade raw cotton into fibers that could be spun into thread, and financing and building water- and then steam-powered cotton mills on an enormous and unprecedented scale.

The Industrial Revolution arose first in the spinning of cotton and the production of cotton fabrics. All three of the great inventors and industrialists who pioneered this Industrial Revolution hailed from the immediate vicinity of Blackburn. The first of this group was James Hargreaves (1720-1778), inventor of the "spinning jenny" and a native of a village just outside Blackburn. Hargreaves, it should be noted, was one of those Lancashire industrialists who exploited the orphans from the Foundling Home that became Ackworth. The second was Richard Arkwright (1732-1792) from nearby Preston, whose "water frame" made it possible to industrialize the spinning process. And the third was Samuel Crompton from Bolton, twelve miles distant from Blackburn, whose "spinning mule" made possible the mass production of muslin cloth. More than anyone else on earth, these three inventors and industrialists may justly be called the fathers of the Industrial Revolution. Most of the inventors and entrepreneurs who followed in the steps of Hargreaves, Arkwright and Crompton were Non-Conformists in religion, i.e., not members of the Church of England, and the largest group among them were Quakers. While this revolution spread eventually over all of the North of England, its first center was Blackburn.

Edmondson arrived in Blackburn just as the first wave of new industrial wealth was transforming it into one of the world's first industrial cities. The sights and sounds of construction were everywhere, with locally financed new mills, alms houses, civic buildings, warehouses, a new cathedral, residential housing, and an impressive stone aqueduct carrying the Leeds and Liverpool Canal all being built at once. Edmondson's first pupil was followed by many more, and soon he was able to buy three adjacent row houses in Blackburn's Lower Bank neighborhood, one for his family, one for his now widowed mother-in-law, and one for the school. The curriculum by now included English, Latin, Greek, and French, as well as a solid program in mathematics that led to courses in plain and spherical trigonometry. In what at the time was a stunning innovation, Edmondson's school also offered instruction in architecture, basic mechanical engineering, map-making, and landscape drawing. He also set up a printing and bookbinding shop and a lathe and other tools for woodworking. Copies of four books produced on the school's press survive in Blackburn's Public Library.

The second building of Edmondson's Academy, Blackburn, 1841 and 1905. S.F. Starr

By 1841 Edmondson's "academy" was attracting students from all over the country. Tuition was high and Edmondson made no bones of the fact that the student body was comprised mainly of "sons of more affluent families." In a third and final expansion, he moved the school to a fourteenth century country house in Ashton-on-Ribble, a suburb of Preston, eleven miles west of Blackburn. In renting Tulketh Hall, a large, ancient, and much-remodeled estate (which was demolished in 1960, Edmondson followed in the footsteps of his mentor and father-in-law, William Singleton. But he went beyond Singleton in opening the curriculum to whatever skills he deemed necessary to function effectively in the era of Industrial Revolution. In practice this meant welcoming activities and fields that had heretofore not been considered "academic."

Edmondson drew inspiration from Singleton's school at Hallam, but his own family provided a more immediate model of inventiveness in the person of his elder brother, Thomas (1792-1851). Originally apprenticed to a cabinet maker, Thomas found his way to the post of stationmaster on the newly constructed Newcastle-Carlisle Railroad. Vexed by the handwritten tickets he issued in wearisome numbers, the devised a new system of pre-printed and numbered cardboard tickets to be validated by a date-stamping machine. Just at the time George Edmondson was setting up shop at Tulketh Hall, Thomas was cashing in on this invention, from which he eventually derived a small fortune. "Edmondson Tickets" became famous, and even today are collected by enthusiasts who buy them on Ebay!

Both Edmondson's school at Blackburn and his new institution at Tulketh Hall were unapologetically Quaker in character. What was new was the extent to which Edmondson stressed the practical aspects of learning. He regularly apprised the Quaker Education Society on his work, reporting in 1841, for example, that "land surveying, levelling, etc., are taught by us in the field as well as in the classroom; the art of using the requisite instruments is as important as the theory."[108] Unfortunately, there is practically no extant information on the life of what Edmondson called the Tulketh Academy. Edmondson was a stickler on defining all aspects of the curriculum and went so far as to print such information for the parents of prospective students. He also issued periodic reports, and the students issued a monthly news sheet called the Tulketh Hall Mercury. Unfortunately, no copies of any of these publications are known to have survived.

Tulketh Hall, Preston, by J. P. Neale, 1825 (left) and painting from ca. Edmondson's time (right).

What can be confidently reported is that, with Tulketh Hall, Edmondson positioned himself and his academy at the very forefront of educational reform in the English-speaking world. At a time when Oxford and Cambridge in England, and Harvard, Yale, and Princeton in the United States all clung to a strictly classical curriculum, Edmondson had blazed a path into the modern world. He embraced the technology of the day and offered it a home in his academy, alongside classical subjects. He clearly did not consider this either a trade school or a German-type vocational school. Rather, he seems to have viewed his Academy as a place where future inventors and entrepreneurs might gain those skills that would be useful to them in the emerging industrial order. He probably knew that neither Arkwright nor Compton had received any formal education and that Hargreaves remained illiterate throughout his life. Edmondson appears to have proceeded on the assumption that future Hargreaves, Arkwrights, and Cromptons would need much more in the way of education and "useful" training. He therefore designed his institution so it could provide them to all comers. Both in concept and realization Edmondson's Tulketh Hall marked an innovative and significant step towards the development of modern education.

In 1841, the year he moved his school to Tulketh Hall, Edmondson was forty-four. His family had expanded and now included, in addition to daughter Jane, a son, George William (b. 1837), who was now four years old. The school was so popular that Edmondson had to turn away students. Not only was he prospering to a degree his parents couldn't have imagined possible, but he was gaining national recognition as an educational reformer and even as a visionary in that field. It was his growing fame as an innovator that led a group of investors associated with the great industrialist-turned-reformer-turned-utopian-socialist, Robert Owen, to his door. The resulting project—Queenwood College—was --Edmondson's last and greatest initiative as an educational reformer.[109]

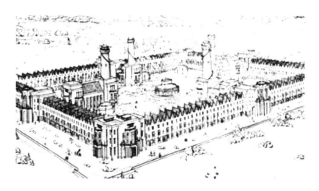

Robert Owen's proposal for "New Harmony" on the Wabash River in Indiana.

Owen was surely the most diversely talented, extravagant, and curious figures of the early industrial age. His march towards social reform began in 1813 when he and a group of investors that included philosopher Jeremy Bentham and the Quaker William Allan bought out his father-in-law's interest in the trend-setting cotton mill at New Lanarck, Scotland. Due to his effective management, Owen's work at New Lanarck brought him equal measures of wealth and dissatisfaction with the factory system that produced it. To improve the lot of his workers he introduced welfare programs that included clean housing, Britain's first pre-school program, recreational facilities, and a visionary Institute for the Formation of Character. Over time he became the first to champion an eight-hour work day and a leader in the movement that led in 1819 to Britain's first factory legislation.

Owen, like Rousseau before him, believed that human beings were innately good but were held back by perverse customs from the past and by ignorance. He was a perfectionist who believed human affairs could be so arranged as to bring about the Millennium, not in heaven (Owen was hostile to all religion) but on earth. Skeptical towards all government, he thought people should live in small, self-governing communities where property would be held in common. To advance that cause he sank much of his fortune into a utopian community on the Wabash River in Indiana. "New Harmony" failed even before residents could construct the enormous communal structure Owen had planned for them. Owen's son, who was in charge of the project, admitted that the men and women who assembled in Indiana to create utopia were "a heterogeneous collection of radicals, enthusiastic devotees to principle, honest], and lazy theorists, with a sprinkling of unprincipled sharpers thrown in."[110] This motley band of self-proclaimed] fired bricks to build the huge communal complex Owen had envisioned, but construction never took place.

Print of Robert Owen's Queenwood (left) and sketch from Edmondson era by student Fred Shields, ca 1858, (right), both from album given by GWE to GME, 1907. S.F. Starr

Owen's fortune was depleted but his boundless powers of persuasion enabled him to assemble the 30,000 pounds needed to lease eight-hundred acres of agricultural and park land near Stockbridge in Hampshire and to construct facilities for yet another utopian and socialist communitarian project. Queenwood Farm was, and remains today, a beautiful spot. Amidst the rich agricultural lands Owen constructed a magnificent headquarters building and related structures for a community of five hundred persons. The eighty-room main building was approached by a quarter-mile long alley of ancient yew trees. Surrounding it were promenades and landscaped gardens. "Harmony Hall," as it was named, was of solid brick construction, with gambrel roofs of Welsh slate, handsomely decorated assembly halls, and mahogany wainscoting. A stunned visitor noted that "There [are] few kitchens in London so expensively fitted up."[111] Engraved portentously over the main door were the letters "CM," for "Commencement of the Millennium." Overall, the structure was palatial in design and lavish in execution.

The yew alley at Queenwood, later the scene of a confrontation between two George Edmondson and his son. S.F. Starr

In fact, too lavish by far. By 1842 Owen had spent all his investors' money yet a mere ninety people had signed up to live in his utopia. "Harmony Hall," as the main building was called, had brought only disharmony. In 1842 the investors removed Owen from his leadership position. A splinter group of the Owen's communitarians set up a vegetarian commune nearby but this also went broke. By 1845 the Harmony Hall community was bankrupt, so the new leadership closed the project and decided to rent the entire complex and land to anyone who would take it.

Their first move was to contact George Edmondson. They did so because they perceived some relationship between what Edmondson was doing at Tulketh Hall and their own endeavors. As they explained in their letter to him, the Harmony Hall property was "admirably adapted to carry out the enlarged views of education they had heard he entertained."[112] Edmondson at first rejected the idea but, on further reflection, embraced it. Not only would the move give him facilities far superior to those at Tulketh Hall, but it would put him and his faculty within easy reach of London and its rich intellectual resources. The cost of the lease issued by Owens' partners must have been extremely low, as befitted businessmen who were committed to doing good, not well. Edmondson expected to cover the lease from tuition fees, as he had done at Tulketh Hall. The fact that the Society of Friends held the lease did not change the fact that the project depended entirely on Edmondson. Under any circumstances, Edmondson's hopes were justified by the ninety paying students who had enrolled by the end of the first year. He was riding high: a photograph of him taken about the time he founded Queenwood College shows a self-confident and deadly earnest personality, a true authority figure.

George Edmondson, about 1845. S.F. Starr

The main reason George Edmondson seized the opportunity presented by the Harmony Hall property is that it would enable him to extend his vision of education into new areas that had not been possible at Tulketh Hall, and to expand the range of his recruitment of both faculty and students. The main innovations at this new institution were in the fields of science and technology. In both areas Edmondson anticipated what was soon to become a major English concern. In the 1847, when Edmondson launched Queenwood College, England led the world in industrialization but it lagged in both science and technology. German scientists were already making their mark by that year, and France had long set the pace in technology and engineering, thanks to Napoleon's Ecole Polytechnique, which had been developed by another utopian socialist, the Comte Henri de Saint-Simon. In 1851 Britain was to mount the first World's Fair at the glittering glass-sheathed Crystal Palace in London, which the French strove to top four years later with their Esposition Universelle, which featured an enormous stone and iron Palais de l'Industrie on the Champs Elysee. The failure of British scientists and technologists to receive any prizes at their own country's exposition was a national humiliation, and they did no better in Paris.

Edmondson's achievement was to have grasped this situation many years earlier, and to translate this emerging national priority into a concrete educational program that eventually would resonate far beyond Hampshire and Britain.

The heart of Queenwood's teaching method in science, and in other fields as well, was the laboratory. Unlike their contemporaries elsewhere in the English-speaking world, students at Queenwood not only studied science in the library but in the laboratory as well. To facilitate this, Edmondson had a laboratory building constructed on the grounds at a point safely distant from the main building. It was among the best equipped laboratories in Britain at the time. Here students and their instructors carried out chemical experiments and also explored problems in physics, which was at that time a new academic subject. Thanks to this pioneering facility, students not only learned science by doing it, but they did so in an atmosphere of research. Edward (later Sir Edward) Frankland, an instructor at Queenwood who discovered helium and laid the foundation for the development of modern chemistry, declared that Queenwood College was the first school to introduce the practical or laboratory teaching of science."[113]

Edward Frankland, chemist, bacteriologist, later discoverer of helium.

Edmondson himself was active as a teacher. Always the innovator, he broadened the concept of "laboratory work" to include field research. Typically, he challenged students to plot out the most direct and efficient routes for future railroad lines. To do this he placed in their hands detailed works on geography and also copies of George Bradshaw's recently published Bradshaw's Descriptive Guide to the London & South Western Railway (London, 1845). He assigned them the task of discovering routes that minimized the number of bridge crossings and tunnels, stayed clear of steep gradients, and avoided congested areas, while at the same time serving England's expanding cities.[114] It is no wonder that more than a few graduates of Queenwood College proved to be pioneers of modern civil engineering.

Beyond extending the teaching of science and technology into the research laboratory and the field, one of Edmondson's prime reasons for moving to Queenwood was the possibility of developing there a training program in agriculture. Prospects were excellent. The College buildings were surrounded by abundant agricultural land and Robert Owen had developed vegetable and fruit gardens and even installed an innovative reservoir for storing liquid manure. But why Edmondson's sudden passion for agriculture?

At one level, it was a return to an old interest. Daniel Wheeler had been a farmer even before going to Russia, and in Russia both he and Edmondson were professionally involved with agriculture for the seven years they worked together. Charged with the development of 50,000 acres by the Emperor of Russia, Edmondson was no amateur in the field of agriculture. Meanwhile, England's soaring population presented a challenge on how the country would feed itself. In 1838 the Royal Agricultural Society was founded with the explicit purpose of advancing the scientific development of agriculture. It is likely that Edmondson attended one or more of the Society's travelling demonstrations. Under any circumstances, its existence signaled the arrival of "scientific agriculture" as a legitimate field of enquiry. Edmondson saw his role as extending this new approach into the sphere of education.

What were the further components of Queenwood's curriculum? In a publication which today would be considered a recruiting brochure, Edmondson laid out an expansive program, the goal of which was "To give an education in harmony with the age, an education that shall combine practice with theory and assimilate, as far as possible, the occupations of a College with those of real business, and thus to fit youth to fill and adorn the position in life he is to achieve and maintain."[115] In other words, Queenwood was conceived from the outset as a kind of business school for the upwardly mobile, where future leaders of various branches of industry would learn those things necessary "to achieve and adorn the position in life he is to achieve and maintain." This statement opened the door to a curriculum far broader than at Tulketh Hall, and broader, in fact, than any other institution in the English-speaking world. In addition to geography, surveying, basic design and draftsmanship, Queenwood offered painting, music (surprising for a Quaker-run institution), and even elocution, not to mention Latin, Greek, French and English.

It was one thing to announce heady educational goals but quite another to develop teaching methods that would enable students to achieve them. Edmondson's main pedagogical commitment was to overcome the split between theory and practice. Learning by doing was his motto, which he applied in every field. As he had done in St. Petersburg, Edmondson also favored the so-called "Lancastrian system," whereby older students instructed the younger ones. Beyond this, he paid tribute to two Swiss educational reformers, the renowned Johann Heinrich Pestalozzi (1746-1827) and Philipp von Fellenburg (1771-1844). Pestalozzi's youthful commitment to Rousseau and the ideal of human perfection never left him, even though he tempered it with a Christian sense of human fallibility. It was Pestalozzi's belief that correct method would enable anyone to learn that prompted Edmondson to open Queenwood's doors to anyone who applied. Such notions had inspired the teachers at Ackworth in Edmondson's youth. Fellenburg added to this his belief that education could overcome differences of class and mentality, which again influenced Edmondson's open-door admissions policy.

Such an approach presented a challenge to traditional systems of grading students. Here again, Edmondson took what was at the time a radical approach. In the College's newspaper, the Queenwood Reporter, he issued an announcement that Queenwood students must have received with rapture, namely, that "Schools and colleges seldom do more than afford opportunities for the acquirement of knowledge' for its right application and lasting retention they scarcely profess to make any provision. A leading object at Queenwood is to remedy this defect. Our pupils' progress will be tested by their ability and not by the amount of their knowledge." (ital. S.F.S.)[116]

One further aspect of Edmondson's educational program bears mentioning. Far more than most schools of the day, Queenwood was deliberately international in character. Foreigners, mainly from continental Europe, were to be found among both the faculty and student body. This was nothing new: Ackworth and William Singleton's school had both welcomed scholars from abroad. What was different was Edmondson's more focused recruitment from those European centers that most nearly shared his educational values. Notable in this regard was von Fellenburg's school at his estate Hofwyl outside Bern, with which Queenwood maintained regular contact and from which Edmondson drew several teachers.

In the last analysis, the quality of an educational institution is defined by the abilities and distinction of its teaching staff. During its dynamic early years, Queenwood's teaching staff was quite fluid, with people coming and going and then coming again. Two of the founding group of faculty went on to became major British scientists: Edward Frankland and John Tyndall. Both taught there only briefly during the school's first decade but thereafter remained loyal to its ideals and gave it much credit for the development of the natural sciences in British education.

John Tyndall, chemist, pioneer of climatology.

Frankland, like Edmondson, hailed from Lancashire. He had spent time as an indentured servant to an apothecary in Lancaster. After a kind of apprenticeship in London he travelled to Marburg in Germany, where he had introductions to the renowned chemist Robert Bunsen (inventor of the Bunsen burner). Edmondson recruited him on his return, obviously indifferent to the fact that the rising chemist was only twenty-two years of age. One must assume that Edmondson learned of this highly talented young man from Lyon Playfair, a Scottish chemist in whose laboratory Frankland had worked and who provided the introduction to Bunsen.

The Irish-born physicist John Tyndall began his career surveying railroad rights-of-ways in England. He met Frankland in London and was inspired by Frankland's conclusion that since Germans led the world in physics and chemistry, the two of them should go there. After meeting Bunsen at his laboratory at Marburg, Tyndall returned to work with Bunsen for another two years, after which he spent three years as a faculty member and researcher at Queenwood. In the College's records he is identified as Professor of Chemistry, an Assistant Master in classics and mathematics, as well as a lecturer on philosophy and field instructor in surveying and engineering.[117] Even at that period the lean and nervous Tyndall was conducting pioneering studies on how infrared radiation absorbs heat. His quest was to discover how oxygen, nitrogen, ozone, methane and other gases absorb heat. As he later confessed, this was at the time "perfectly unbroken ground." Within a few years he had succeeded, and on February 7, 1861, announced his discoveries in a lecture before a packed audience at the Royal Society in London.[118] He explained how the higher the concentration of absorptive gases in the atmosphere, the higher atmospheric temperatures on earth would be. In one stroke Tyndall had detailed the functioning of the "Greenhouse Effect" and laid the theoretical foundations for atmospheric science!

Thanks to Edmondson's keen eye for talent, students at Queenwood College benefited from Tyndall during the most formative phase of his career, as they had also from Frankland. Nor did the link with the University of Marburg end with Tyndall, for mathematician Thomas Archer Hirst renewed it several years later.

Besides Frankland and Tyndall, Queenwood could claim a half dozen other faculty or students who went on to important careers in the sciences and technology. Proximity to London enabled Edmondson to invite scientists and other distinguished figures to visit and speak before the school. Among those who appeared frequently at Queenwood were physicist Michael Faraday (1791-1867), whose picture later hung on the wall of Albert Einstein's study, and comparative anatomist Thomas Huxley 1825-1895), who coined the term "agnosticism" and was known as "Darwin's Bulldog" on account of his impassioned advocacy of Darwin's theory of evolution. Another of Darwin's most effective champions was Henry Fawcett, a blind Queenwood student who went on to a notable career as an economist and politician.

Evening lecture, sketch by Fred Shields, GWE album. S.F. Starr

By no means all of the most renowned graduates of Queenwood College were chemists or physicists. Following a very different course was yet another student from Lancaster, James Mansergh, who distinguished himself as a civil engineer in Britain and America. Ernest Sanson, who ended up in medicine, was the first to diagnose heart disease and to expound the practical and theoretical aspects of anesthesiology, while artist Tristan Ellis, who was a math wizard at Queenwood, gained distinction for his precise yet and evocative paintings of Egypt, Syria, Asia Minor, and Mesopotamia.

There can be no doubt that intellectual life at Queenwood was at a high level and intense. A typical examination in practical chemistry included the following questions:

1. In what form is silicon usually met with, and in what proportion does it combine with other elements?
2. How do silicates contribute to the fertility of soil?
3. To what useful purposes have soluble alkaline silicates been applied?

4. Describe the process employed in the manufacture of glass. What is the composition of flint, crown, bohemian, and bottle glass?

5. Why is a mixture of two silicates necessary for the production of good glass?

6. Describe the process employed in the preparation of chlorine. To what uses has it been applied? Give diagrams.

7. How does chlorine act in destroying noxious effluvia and miasmata?

8. State the processes used in the manufacture of bleaching power. How is it employed in the arts? Give an example of the manner in which the percentage amount of chlorine in any sample of chlorine of lime may be determined.

9. How is muriatic acid procured; what are the properties and by what simple process can its strength be ascertained?

10. How is iodine prepared? What are its properties and how can it be detected?

11. Whence is bromine procured and in what relation does it stand to chlorine, iodine, and oxygen as regards affinity?

12. Give an outline of the processes employed in the production of Daguerreotype images. What is the probable action of light on the prepared plates?[119]

Similar questions were posed for mathematics and all the other fields of study. Is it any wonder that students thus prepared found themselves better trained than even their professors at many institutions they later attended?

Faculty at Queenwood engaged students with bench-level research. Tyndall later reported on some of his research with Queenwood students:

"It was pleasant to prove by mathematics, and verify by experiment, that the angular velocity of a reflected beam is twice that of the mirror which reflects it. From the hum of a bee we were able to determine the number of times the insect flaps its wings in a second. Following up our researches on the pendulum, we learned how Colonel Sabiroff had made it the means for measuring the figure of the earth' and we were also startled by the inference which the pendulum enabled us to draw, that if the diurnal velocity of the earth were 17 times its present amount, the centrifugal force at the equator would be precisely equal to the force of gravitation, so that an inhabitant of those regions would then have the same tendency to fall upwards as downwards."[120]

No less valuable than instruction in the laboratory and classroom were the informal discussions involving students and faculty that took place in the weekly meetings of what was called the "Queenwood Mutual Improvement Society." Here is a list of a few of these weekly topics:

> What are the duties of the Astronomer Royal?
>
> Does the dew rise or fall?
>
> What is the cause of waterspouts?
>
> How is it that a black hat can be moved by forming round it a magnetic circle but a white hat remains stationary?
>
> Is it true that men were once monkeys?
>
> What are those rings that we see round the gas and sun?
>
> If a towel be wetted with water, why does the wet portion before darker than before?
>
> What is the cause of the sensation called "pins and needles"?
>
> What is meant by Lancashire witches? {i.e., the Lancashire trial of Quakers as witches, 1612.[121]

The list of luminaries who emerged from Queenwood might suggest that the Queenwood student body was comprised entirely of earnest and highly motivated young men who were there to fit themselves, in Edmondson's words, "to fill and adorn the position in life [they were] to achieve and maintain." This was not quite the case. Thanks to Edmondson's Pestalozzian belief that anyone could be educated in any field, the school had what today would be called an open admissions policy. But it did not come cheap. Tuition was thirty guineas a year with an additional four guineas for laundress and seamstress. A published list of clothing and equipment each student was to arrive with included three suits, six shirts, twelve collars….and a silver spoon and fork.[122] The wife of John Tyndall, who knew the student body at first hand, described Queenwood as:

> "An odd mixture of an ordinary junior boys' school and a technical college for older boys and young men," "the whole being under one and the same roof…Many of [the students] were verging on manhood, some were failures from the universities, others had disappointed their parents in their vocations, and they combined to form an element of idling and unruly tendency, which would call for strong and judicious handling."[123]

The mixing of ages among the student body may have conformed to Edmondson's Lancastrian belief that older students could teach their younger peers, but it did not always work out as neatly as he might have wished. Older students did indeed teach younger ones, but, as the wife of John Tyndall astutely recalled, "the younger ones arrived at the institution with virtuous habits but leave it initiated in vice.[124] "Vice," of course, is a relative term, and Edmondson defined it in rigorously Quaker terms that today might be considered "politically correct." Being English, the students threw themselves with gusto into Guy Fawkes Night, the annual November 5 celebration of the hanging of the pro-Catholic conspirator, Guy Fawkes, whose gunpowder plot of 1605 had aimed to overthrow the Crown. Edmondson permitted a bonfire and a few firecrackers, but banned the traditional effigy of Guy. As the Queenwood Reporter put it, Edmondson "objected to the honoring of an anniversary which tends to keep alive any feeling of resentment against any party... The pupils were asked not to connect their fun with any commemoration of a gunpowder plot." [125]

Edmondson seems to have responded to this with theory rather than action. In public statements he insisted that Queenwood seeks "to make a home for students and to surround them with the best of educational appliances."[126] But as Mrs. Tyndall's observation confirms, this high-minded approach did not work in every case, nor does it appear that Edmondson was any more deft at the "judicious handling" of wayward students. His own son reported on a major pillow fight, and one of his son's friends left us a drawing of the fracas.[127] That the head of the school rather than some junior teaching master had to intervene to stop it suggests that all authority at Queenwood was concentrated at the top.

Pillow fight at Queenwood College, by student Fred Shields. George William Edmondson album. S.F. Starr

The heyday of Queenwood College extended for a decade after its founding in 1847. By 1857 Edmondson was sixty years old. The arduous work of creating and managing a new institution, coming on the heels of demanding years at Tulketh Hall and, before that, in Volkovo, had taken its toll. A photograph of him in these later years reflects this. He is still standing proudly, but thin, with thinning hair and grey pork-chop side whiskers, looking down (because of being unable to focus on the camera for the length of time needed for an exposure) and looking rather dependently to his wife, Ann, who is serenely reading. Queenwood had been a one-man show. As the British Dictionary of National Biography reports, George Edmondson had had the power of influencing those about him by his own enthusiasms.[128] But by the late 1850s the physical strength that supported such enthusiasms was flagging. There is no evidence of Edmondson's close involvement with Queenwood between the late 1850s and his death in 1863. He was buried in the Quaker cemetery in Southampton, along with his wife and his former pupils, the three sons of Daniel Wheeler.

George Edmondson and his wife Anne Singleton Edmondson, in his later years. S.F. Starr

Under Edmondson's successor, Charles Wilmore, Queenwood College carried on for another thirty-three years. When Wilmore retired, no one stepped forward to run the school and it closed. Wilmore and his family stayed on at the property, watching as the land was turned into a poultry farm. He died in 1902 in the fire that destroyed Harmony Hall. Queenwood farm is now a park. The only physical reminders of this visionary educational institution are several cottages that once served as masters' quarters, the former chapel, the walls of the kitchen garden, and fragments of the grand alley of yew trees planted by Robert Owen.

IV. The American Edmondsons and Their World

George William Edmondson, 1837-1915

The last photograph taken of George Edmondson, the Quaker who labored for God and the Tsar in Russia and the great educational pioneer, commands our respectful attention. He is focused, principled and stern, the epitome of a nineteenth century Quaker educator. By contrast, the last two photographs of his son, George William Edmondson (1837-1915), reveal a starkly different sort of man, good natured, artistic, worldly, and a keen observer. In one, he stands with paintbrush, using oil colors to brighten one of his large photomurals in a public library in Cleveland, Ohio. The other, showing only his head, could be mistaken for a photograph of Sigmund Freud on an unusually good day, with neatly trimmed white goatee and an almost bemused look. If the father saw his life's mission as shaping the young to become moral and competent leaders of the industrial age, the son clearly found his challenge in dealing with people as they are.

George William Edmondson, 1903, by George M. Edmondson. S.F. Starr

George William Edmondson did not start his life this way. He had been born in 1837, when his father's school at Lower Bank in Blackburn, England, was thriving. His entire formal schooling took place in institutions founded and run by his father, first at Tulketh Hall and then at Queenwood College. It is safe to conclude that at both institutions "GW," as we will call him, was treated as neutral putty to be molded into a productive and ethical member of Quaker and English society. How he reacted to this regimen is unknown. The surviving record provides only two hints regarding his personality as a boy and young man. Both of them suggest a certain mischievousness.

George William Edmondson ca. 1900-1905, painting a photomural in Cleveland. S. F. Starr

First, is the pillow fight at Queenwood, mentioned above. That GW preserved throughout his life a drawing of this wild event by artist Frederic Shields and included that drawing in a scrapbook he prepared for one of his own sons sixty years later suggests that he had been more than a passive observer of this raucous event. Second, there exists a small oil painting by young Edmondson himself depicting gypsies who passed through the Salisbury countryside. A family tradition that persisted for a century holds that GW, playing his mandolin, loved to join them in singing.

Gypsies near Queenwood, George William Edmondson, ca.1860. Melissa Edmondson Bausman

In the same scrapbook, dated 1906, he presented a photograph of the yew alley at Queenwood and noted underneath that this was the cryptic inscription "The place where your grandfather [George Edmondson] lectured your father [i.e., GW]."

What was this "lecture" about, and what gave rise to it? GW left no record beyond the laconic note in the scrapbook. However, both of his only grandchildren believed that GW had announced to his father that he wanted to become an artist and that he would not remain a Quaker. Both grandchildren also reported that George Edmondson responded to this declaration by disowning his son. If this was in fact what occurred, then that "lecture" 'neath the yew trees" was less a homily than a bitter parting of ways. Shortly thereafter GW headed to North America. It is no wonder that more than half a century later that meeting with his father was still burned into GW's memory.

The key to this encounter lay not at Queenwood itself but two hundred miles to the North, in Manchester. On numerous occasions GW's granddaughter repeated to the author that he had worked as a draftsman and apprentice architect in the firm of Alfred Waterhouse (1830-1905) at the time Waterhouse was planning the new Houses of Parliament. Since the new Houses of Parliament were designed not by Waterhouse but by Charles Barry, half this recollection must be dismissed out of hand. But the other half? It is significant that Waterhouse was a Quaker. Working from his offices in Manchester, he was rapidly establishing himself as the country's premier practitioner of neo-Gothic architecture. Barry apparently engaged Waterhouse to help in his great London project. Edmondson had studied drafting and measured drawing at Queenwood, so the chance to work under this talented and reliable Quaker architect made solid professional sense. His father, the headmaster, doubtless supported it and probably even proposed it. But the move to Manchester created turmoil in the life of the twenty-one-year-old Quaker, who had lived his entire life under the stern pedagogical eye of his upstanding and austere father.

Frederic Shields, artist and friend of GWE.

Back in Queenwood Edmondson had met the talented young illustrator and artist, Frederic Shields (1833-1911). Shields rose from a background of poverty to become an important member of the British Pre-Raphaelite movement and close friend of artists Dante Gabriel Rossetti and Ford Maddox Brown. In 1860 he was living in Manchester and hard at work on illustrations for Defoe's <u>History of the Plague</u> and for Bunyan's <u>Pilgrim's Progress</u> that were to earn high praise from the critic John Ruskin and launch his career as a pioneer of early <u>art nouveau</u> design. Shields had first visited Queenwood in February, 1859, where he made sketches and watercolors of the college and students, including one of Harmony Hall that his younger friend Edmondson preserved as a wide format photo. It is even possible that it was Shields, not Edmondson's father, who came up with the idea of George's working in the Waterhouse studio. At any rate, the two got together again in the northern city early in 1860.

Freed from his father's tutelage and on his own in Manchester, Edmondson tore up the town. On March 1, 1860, Shields wrote in his diary:

"Rose [at] 7. [Read Thackeray's] 'Vanity Fair' to 3. Dinner. To town to see G. W. Edmondson about a model for Wanton in the Pilgrim's Progress. Saw him and arranged to go with him the whole round of the scenes of Manchester dissipation. Got tea first, and then to the Canterbury Hall, next to the Dog, then the Shakespeare, and at 12 o'clock to the Egyptian Hall, where I staid sketching till 3 A.M. Having had a terrible row with two of the girls about it, I was most mercifully preserved from harm. To the Shakespeare again just as it was closing, and home to Edmondson's by 4.30. Bed. I could not pray, for I have sinned and I fear willfully led both Edmondson and myself into temptation, and though the Lord has preserved us from outward evil, this lessens not my crime.[132]

This was surely not Edmondson's sole night of dissipation in Manchester, for one way or another word got back to his father at Queenwood. Perhaps young

Edmondson's Quaker soul was still sufficiently intact that he himself confessed it all to his father. What is sure is that George was soon back at Queenwood, where his father confronted him in the memorable face-off in the ally of yew trees. Family lore holds that George Edmondson's "lecture" to his son was occasioned by the latter's declaration that he wanted to abandon architecture and turn instead to art. But was this really such a problem? Drafting and drawing were included in the Queenwood curriculum, and at least one well-known future artist studied there. All evidence points to the fact that a furious George Edmondson Sr., shocked and appalled by his son's waywardness, rather than his interest in art, delivered a dressing-down that opened an unbridgeable rupture between them. Within months of that tense meeting George William was in Canada. Over the coming years he occasionally exchanged letters with his mother and sisters, but his father never reversed his decision to disown the young man and cut off all contact with him.

George William Edmondson's movements between 1860 and February, 1863, are a complete mystery. Not one letter from or to him survives, and the most basic information on his movements must be reconstructed from indirect evidence, since he left no accounts, business records, or diaries. Perhaps the gap is the inevitable result of a young man's undocumented Wanderjahren. Or perhaps GW was covering his tracks.

A curious detail regarding GW is that to the end of his life he walked with a limp. The source of this limp is explained by another family story, this one quite colorful, which also explains GW's whereabouts during the first years after 1858. That the report was repeated many times by his granddaughter and grandson indicates that it came to them directly from GW himself. According to this report, GW signed on as a sketcher or photographer with a Royal Geographical Society expedition to the Canadian North. In the course of his work on the Canadian mainland he got separated from his party and broke his leg. Frostbite set in, but a band of Indians found him and brought him to their settlement. There a "medicine man" examined him and announced with a sawing motion accompanied by the sound "Kek-kek-kek" that the frostbitten and broken limb should be amputated. But GW refused, at which point a "squaw" took charge and slowly nursed him back to health. When spring came he found his way to Quebec City.

It should be readily possible to verify this colorful tale by searching the records of the Royal Geographical Society. Exploration of Greenland and Canada's frozen North was a national mania during those years. Driven by the hope of discovering a Northwest Passage to the Pacific, the Society had sent out a well-equipped expedition of two ships under the command of John Franklin in 1845. When Franklin's ships failed to return, the English press was filled with speculation on what had happened. The Royal Navy sent out several ships to rescue Franklin and his 150 men but they returned empty handed. The last effort by the Admiralty to rescue Franklin began in 1852 under the command of Admiral Sir Edward Belcher. Not only did Belcher fail to find evidence of Franklin's party but he had to abandon two of his ships in the ice of Mercy Bay, off Canada's northern coast near Alaska.

Two years after Belcher set out, the Hudson Bay Company sent an expedition under John Rae to explore the islands north of the Hudson Bay. From local Inuits Ray heard of the fate of some thirty-five of Franklin's men, who starved to death near the mouth of the Back River, northwest of the top of Hudson Bay. Another Hudson Bay Company expedition, this time by canoe in 1855, found further relics of Franklin's last days. Meanwhile, Franklin's widow, frustrated at what she considered the Admiralty's indifference, paid for and equipped yet another expedition which set sail from Aberdeen on 2 June 1857 under the seasoned Francis McClintock, this time for the sole purpose of discovering her husband's fate. Members of McClintock's expedition explored thousands of miles by sledge, focusing on the area around King William Island, northwest of Hudson Bay. After being frozen in ice for a winter McClintock's ship, the Fox, returned with detailed information on the Franklin expedition's tragic end.

All of these adventures were widely reported in the English press and could have sparked the imagination of a footloose young man who was bent on escaping his father's austere regimen. But a glance at the map shows that these expeditions all focused on the far North of Canada, 1500 miles from Quebec City. Beyond possibly suggesting a means of escape from his father's plan for him, they are irrelevant to George William Edmondson's purported adventure; indeed, the records of the Royal Society include no mention of him.[133]

However, Sir John McClintock (whose search for Franklin had earned him a knighthood), made one further trip to the Canadian North, this time between July and November 1860 on the paddle-wheeled steamer Bulldog. Unlike the previous expeditions, this one had as its object the definition of the best route for a telegraph cable from England to Canada via the Faroe Islands, Greenland and Labrador. Had Edmondson been on the Bulldog he would have arrived on the coast of Labrador in September or early October. If in fact he was injured and got separated from the crew, and if we allow time for him to recuperate during the winter, he would have been able to make his way to Quebec City by the following spring. In short, both the route and timing are perfect.

The only problem—and a serious one—is that there is no record of Edmondson ever setting foot on the Bulldog. McClintock was by now the leading explorer of the northern waters and prided himself on careful organization and solid scientific work. Yet neither the expedition's technical report nor a book on the expedition make any mention of Edmondson or of losing a member of the crew.[134] This does not mean that Edmondson was not aboard the Bulldog, nor does it exclude the possibility of his having been injured or—and this is a serious possibility—jumping ship. In either case the chronicler would not have been eager to document the event. Finally, there remains the possibility that GW made up the entire story!

We do not pick up his trail again until February 8, 1863. On that day George William Edmondson was baptized and joined the Wesleyan Methodist Church in Montreal. This was a natural move for George, for the original English Methodists and their American counterparts were seeking a warmer, more "enthusiastic" form of faith than Calvinism or Quakerism provided. Even as they embraced singing and impassioned preaching, the Methodists took a hard line on such worldly as drinking, which Edmondson apparently welcomed, being well aware of his own weakness in that department.

Significantly, the witness listed on his baptismal document was Henry "Hy" Sandham (1842-1910), an aspiring Canadian artist who was Edmondson's junior by five years. Sandham had refused to follow his father in the business of house painting and chose instead a career in art. By the time Edmondson met him he had just been promoted to a junior position in the newly established art department of the photographic studio of the Scottish born photographer. William Notman (1826-1891). Notman, by nature a tinkerer and experimenter, had just prepared a photo album for Queen Victoria, who promptly named him "Photographer to the Queen." Sandham, whose artistic ambitions led him to a successful career as an illustrator, was employed at the time to color Notman's photographic prints. It was through Notman and Sandham that Edmondson was introduced to photography, and to the possibility of a career combining technology and art.

William Notman ca. 1863.

En route to Montreal Edmondson had stopped in Quebec City. During the months the Bulldog was cruising the northern waters the historic town had mounted a brilliant reception for the Prince of Wales and future King Edward VII, who was starting an extended tour of North America, the first by an heir to the British throne. Nineteen years old, Edward was genial, charming, and relished parties and dancing with attractive young women. Quebec opened its heart to him, with visits to the Governor, tours of the citadel, meetings with the Catholic bishops, illuminations, and a fireworks display. The Prince's program also included a reception at the Ursuline Convent, the oldest institution for women in North America. The young ladies sang a song for the guest that included allusions to the Prince, and "at each of which the young ladies gracefully curtsied, and the teachers murmured 'Long live the Prince.'" Young Edward, however, made clear that if the locals really wanted to show him favor, let them throw a ball, at which he promised to dance all night and to go home with the ladies ---provided that his father, the Duke of Kensington, would allow it.

The ball, held on 21 August, 1860, proved to be the high point of his visit. The fun-loving Prince danced every dance, changing partners throughout the evening, and stayed through the last waltz. As the New York Times reported,[135] he also took a fall while waltzing with Miss Anderson: "His foot slipped and he fell heavily to the floor, causing her to fall upon him. He struck the funny bone in his knee and brought his royal nose into immediate contact with the floor, but to-day he has been perfectly well, save a slight lameness in the joint, and feeling somewhat abashed."

Mary Jane Mountain, who danced with the future King Edward VII on 21 August 1860. S.F. Starr

Among the many young ladies with whom he danced that evening was Miss Mary Jane Mountain. A half century and many travails later Mary Jane was still recalling the Quebec ball as the magical moment of her life. The oldest of six children, Mary Jane was short, light-hearted, frivolous, and a good singer. She had been born on shipboard when her family was emigrating from Scotland to Ireland. The name Mountain had been changed from Montaigne nearly three centuries earlier when the Huguenot Montaigne family had fled from France to Scotland. After a few years in Ireland the family relocated again to Quebec, where they joined the Episcopal Church. In spite of this, both Mary Jane and two of her younger sisters, Sophie and Anne, were students at the very Catholic Ursuline Convent School. The Mountain family included three sons as well.

Their father, John Mountain,[136] was a successful businessman. So successful, in fact, that he could afford to send his daughters to the best school and a son, John, to McGill University in Montreal, where he studied for the Episcopal priesthood. At a time when few in Quebec could afford to maintain a horse and carriage, Mountain maintained two, which enabled him to loan one of them to the visiting Englishman.[137] His daughters Anne and Sophie later recalled that the family enjoyed "firkins of butter."[138] In contrast was Mountain's wife, apparently a very austere woman whose grave attitude was shown by her decision to pose for a photographic portrait holding a book of the works of the Emperor Julian, "The Apostate." Was this because she had abandoned Calvinism for the Church of England and was sending her girls to a Catholic school?

At some point during the year following the ball in honor of Prince Albert, two momentous events occurred in the Mountain family. First, James Mountain went broke. He had countersigned a loan for a friend and the loan had come due, robbing Mountain of his entire fortune. At nearly the same moment an attractive young Englishman, George William Edmondson, arrived in Quebec City. No sooner did he meet the vivacious Mary Jane Mountain than the two fell in love. But he was bound for Montreal and was not able to return to Quebec City until 1863, by which time he had found a new profession, photography, and joined the Methodist Church.

We don't know which of these events preceded the other. What we do know is that on November 9, 1864, George William Edmondson and Mary Jane Mountain were married at the Methodist Church in Quebec City. GW, Mary Jane, and Mary Jane's entire immediate family all stayed in Quebec City down to 1865. Had it not been for the American Civil War the now impoverished and humiliated Mountain family might well have gone immediately to Norwalk, Ohio, where two of James Mountain's brothers had already settled. But they didn't, and instead stayed in Quebec and tried to recover financially. GW stayed as well. But except for a single photograph of Mary Jane, apparently taken in Quebec, we have scarcely a hint of what he was doing.

Mother of Mary Jane Mountain, b. ca. 1815, with book by Julian the Apostate. S.F. Starr

The town of Norwalk, Ohio, is nearly seven hundred miles distant from Quebec City. At a time when cities like Buffalo, Pittsburgh, Boston, New York, Chicago and Milwaukee were burgeoning, Norwalk was not an obvious choice for young immigrants, let alone for a family accustomed to the city life of Dublin or Quebec. Equidistant from Cleveland and Toledo and near Lake Erie but not itself a port, Norwalk was the heart of the Firelands, a congressionally mandated place of refuge for families whose homes had been burnt by the British navy during the War of 1812. In 1865 its population numbered barely 2,000 souls and did not reach the 4,000 needed for incorporation until 1881.

The sole reason for which both the Mountains and GW and his new wife moved there is that a brother of John Mountain (b. 1820), had settled there before the Civil War. Indeed, one of the sons of this family, William Mountain (b. 1841), had joined the Union Army and had been killed at Antietam on 17 September, 1862. Though only twenty-one at the time, the young man was memorialized by various Norwalk groups of which he had been a part, including the Sons of Temperance.[139] He is one of only two of the numerous Mountain family who ended up with a headstone in the Woodlawn Cemetery.

The Mountains from Quebec reached Ohio in the spring of 1865 and petitioned for U.S. citizenship a few years later.[140] But GW and Mary Jane did not leave Quebec for the United States and Norwalk until May, 1866.[141] He immediately went to work for Byron H. Benham, who had been doing photography in Norwalk since 1861. Within months he had bought out Benham and set up business by himself on Courthouse Square.[142]

But Norwalk was by no means virgin territory for a young photographer. Besides Benham, seven other photographers (two of them women) had tried to set up shop in Norwalk between 1860 and 1865, not to mention other potential competitors in neighboring Port Clinton, Sandusky, and Fremont.[143] Several, notably C.H. Ballou, who opened his shop in 1865, were competent and successful. So GW toiled at his studio long enough for his first son to be born in Norwalk and then decamped for the village of Plymouth, twenty-miles to the South.

Plymouth, Ohio, ca. 1870, by George William Edmondson, whose studio was in the building on the right (still standing). S.F. Starr

At first glance this appears an even stranger choice than Norwalk. The 1870 census recorded only 703 people in the "town," which did not double over the next century and a half. In spite of its having called itself "Paris" before 1825, Plymouth "was founded without design," in the words of Huron County's historian.[144] What he meant is that the county line runs down Main Street, all but guaranteeing that taxes and local finances would be in a permanent state of confusion. Still, it had prospects, which accounts for the fact that three other photographers are known to have worked there in the 1870s, after Edmondson himself returned to Norwalk.[145]

*Carte de visite of unknown man, Plymouth, Ohio, 1870s.
Scores of such portraits by George William Edmondson survive. S.F. Starr*

GW first set up shop behind the Congregational Church and shortly thereafter moved to the new Connell Hall Block, an ample frame building on Main Street that can be seen in one of GW's photographs. His business expanded, but he did not rely solely on the Plymouth market. A new interurban electric trolley reduced the travel time between Plymouth and Norwalk to well under an hour, enabling Edmondson to maintain photographic studios in both towns. To facilitate this he entered into partnerships in Norwalk, first with George Butts and then with a man named Lee. He also seized on a new opportunity by refashioning his own business there into the "Edmondson Photograph Enlarging Company."[146] Cartes de visite were the bread and butter of nineteenth century photographers, but several of Edmondson's early images are nonetheless arresting. These, along with his readiness to dress up his prints with pencil, crayon, or paint, caused his business to boom.

Through sheer hard work the operations in Plymouth and in Norwalk both flourished. The young Edmondsons now had three children and, after 1873, GW found it convenient to focus his efforts entirely in Plymouth. GW's father having died, he was now once again in regular contact with his family in England, who were firmly convinced that George William Edmondson and his family were living in poverty and in need of their charity. Nephews and nieces in England were told not to dirty or tear their clothes since there were to be sent "to the poor little American cousins." GW's young son George Mountain Edmondson hated the English cousins because of the Lord Fauntleroy suit and kid gloves that kept coming from England, and which he had to wear to church in Plymouth and Norwalk.[147]

Meanwhile, GW did everything possible to expand his business. He offered to photograph everything from "farms, residences and machinery" to animals, and of course advertised that "baby pictures are a specialty." In short, he was prepared to "to photograph ANYTHING to order." To enable him to make good on this promise, GW bought a wagon and outfitted it with a complete photographic laboratory. Beginning around 1872 he and his young son George were regularly seen bouncing down country roads heading to some remote farmstead.

Many of GW's clients were farmers who, out of thrift or fear, obstinately refused to have their photographic portraits "taken." So as not to be left without an image of a loved husband or father, relatives of such people waited until the pater familias died, at which point they would summon Edmondson from Plymouth. While he and his photographic wagon were en route, the family would dress the deceased in his best suit and tie and seat him at a reading table. GW's son, George Mountain Edmondson, remembered assisting as his father made portraits of such corpses. Special care had to be taken to bend the head downward and slightly to one side, so the camera would not record the fact that the corpse's eyes were closed. All this had to be done quickly, before rigor mortis set in. Young George M. recalled to his children that more than once he would spend great effort arranging his subject in this manner, only to have a dead arm suddenly shoot out and upset the lamp!

From his earliest days as a photographer, George William Edmondson embraced the artistic side of the new medium as well as its technical challenges. In doing so, he remained loyal to the decision to become an artist. Thus, on the reverse side of images issued from Plymouth and Norwalk he advertised "pictures finished in crayon, ink, oil, and watercolor." Not only did he expand his repertoire from individual portraits to what he called "new style groups" but he used his skill with oils to paint backgrounds for both individual and group portraits. That these are to be seen mainly on larger format pictures indicates that anyone seeking to be portrayed against a background of oriental-looking hills or an abstract design had to pay extra for it.

Edmondson's keen interest in both the artistic and technical sides of photography came together in his enthusiastic embrace of the stereoscope and the stereopticon. Both of these technologies made possible the taking and viewing of three-dimensional images. The stereoscope required a double-lensed camera which, like human eyes, took two images at once. The actual stereoscope was a simple hand-held or table-mounted devise that enabled the viewer to perceive both pictures at once, thus producing a three-dimensional image. Inventions in Germany in the 1840s and Scotland in the 1850s advanced this technology but it was only when two Americans, Oliver Bates and physician and writer Oliver Wendell Holmes Sr., patented a much-simplified version in 1862 that the stereoscope became all the rage worldwide. Subsequent patents in 1867 and 1874 made stereoscopic cameras and inexpensive viewers accessible even to photographers and farmers in Richland County, Ohio.

Among Edmondson's first stereopticon images: Union School, Plymouth, Ohio, 1875, S. F. Starr.

No sooner did Edmondson acquire his stereoptic camera in 1872-3 than he began photographing and printing local scenes for sale to the public. Early efforts included "A View on the Huron River," "Engine No. 172 of the Baltimore and Ohio Railroad," and "Emigrant Train," showing a line of Conestoga wagons heading westward. Then, in keeping with the prevailing sentimentalism if the day, he turned out genre scenes, including "Fast Asleep" and "All Round my Hat" depicting the Edmondsons' kitten in various poses, "Tired of Play" and "Sick Patient" featuring the family dog, "Mutual Friends" showing the two together and, for good measure, a bust of Charles Dickens.

These were purely commercial products, but GW's fascination with both the technological and artistic sides of the new medium found expression in many other projects. From the outset he was intrigued with the possibility of capturing on a glass negative the image of objects in motion. It was to this end that he labored long and hard in Plymouth to catch live stereo pictures of a "Fox from Life," Squirrel from Life," and a "Dog on Horseback." Advertisements printed on the backs of other pictures boasted of all three of these as "instantaneous" photographs." On the artistic side, he explored the possibility of making photographs of photographs, using each stage to add unexpected dimensions to the image. This technique of grouping separate images, which Notman had pioneered, gave rise in 1876 to a pair of stereo images of the competing Republican and Democratic presidential and vice-presidential candidates of that year. Republican Rutherford B. Hayes, Democrat Samuel Tilden and their running mates were jowly and bewhiskered burghers, but through the magic of Edmondson's reconfiguration, they all peep out from large bouquets of flowers, like harbingers of a political springtime.

The pairing of these two scenes reflected another feature of the commercialization of both mono-optical and stereo photography in the 1870s, namely, the production of whole series of related images, to be marketed and sold as a group.

George W. Edmondson, bouquet of presidential candidates, 1876. S.F. Starr

Edmondson's first venture into this took place when he lugged his stereoptic camera and box of glass plates to the belfry of the just completed (and still standing today) Union School in Plymouth. Through the resulting group of eight carefully integrated stereo images he enabled the viewer to experience a 360-degree view of the town and surrounding countryside.

Once GW had mastered the technical aspects of stereo technology and explored its possibility for whole series of images, he used it to indulge his rather quirky imagination. One notably bizarre result of this activity was a ten-image series depicting some of the many words ending with the suffix "-ation." As advertised on the back of stereo images from 1875 and 1876, these included "Multiplication, Equalization, Temptation, Cremation, Flagelation, Consternation, Irritation, Abbreviation. Consolation, and Aggravation." Fortunately, he spared his customers "vexation," "mutilation", and "desecration"! Each of these was presented as a charade or tableau vivant, the kind of acting out that was popular at family home entertainments before the days of radio.

Unfortunately, none of these curious products are known to survive. We can be sure, however, that they included painted backdrops, multiple and sometimes costumed actors, and dramatic and highly theatrical gestures signifying the "-ation" word in question. The fact that GW advertised them over several years suggests they found a good market.

George William Edmondson took the use of tableaux vivants for linked stereoscopic images to its logical conclusion with a twelve-part series entitled "The Drinker's Progress." Unlike his previous stereo series, which were grouped only by their relationship to an organizing subject or theme, these comprised a single narrative, consistently developed from the first image to the last. In light of his own personal experience with alcohol back in Manchester, it is easy to understand Edmondson's commitment to this project. The narrative of The Drinker's Progress" consists of the following scenes:

Satan in His Lab. Making Whiskey.

First Drink at a Fashionable Party.

First Drink at a Public Bar.

First Intoxication. Bachelor's Carouse.

Out for a Night of It.

Caught in the Toils.

Gets into Trouble with Police.

Tries to Retrieve His Fortune at Cards.

He is "Cleaned Out"

Commits Murder for Gain.

Delirium Tremens.

The Bitter End. Pauper coffin and Lone Watcher (which is a stuffed rat)

Each of these <u>tableaux</u> was elaborately staged, with up to five characters per scene. Special costumes and even a full-head mask were needed for Satan, and also for the policeman, but otherwise the actors play their roles in street clothes or formal wear. Furniture and other necessary props like the coffin and stuffed rat who appears as the "Lone Watcher" in the drinker's death, were assembled or constructed and then brought to the studio, but the bar scene was shot at the saloon in Plymouth.

Edmondson also painted three backdrops for his pictorial melodrama: one showing the gloomy interior of Satan's lair, a second presenting a street scene in perspective for the "Out for a Night of It," "Caught in the Toils," and "Gets into Trouble," and a third for "Delirium Tremens," featuring the fearsome monsters that confront the poor drinker in his last stages of degradation. With these exceptions, most of the scenes are framed by curtains. This was a photographic convention of the day, but it also frames the tableaux in a manner recalling the curtains of a theater.

Here is the entire drama:

"Satan in His Laboratory Making Whiskey," The Drinker's Progress, 1875

"First Drink at a Fashionable Party."

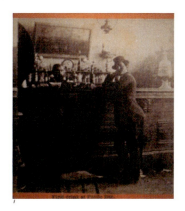 

"First Drink at a Pubic Bar" (left), "First Intoxication. Bachelors Carouse." (right).

"Out for a Night of It.:" (left), "Caught in the Toils." (right).

""Gets Into Trouble" (left), "He Resolves to Retrieve His Fortune at Cards." (right).

 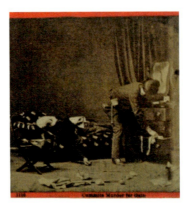

"Cleaned Out." (left), "Commit Murder for Gain."(right).

"Delirium Tremons"

"The Pauper's Coffin and Lone Watcher" (a rat).

Demand for "The Drinker's Progress" was so strong that Edmondson patented the series. It was such a hit that Edmondson told a reporter from the Huron County Chronicle that he "couldn't keep up with orders…."[148] Clearly, his timing could not have been better. For several years Evangelical and Methodist women had been demonstrating outside saloons. Their effort led to the foundation on 23 December 1873 in Hillsboro, Ohio (a town of about the same size as Norwalk just northeast of Cincinnati) of a temperance league. The group attracted so many recruits that it was able to mount a national convention in Cleveland. Northern Ohio was fertile ground for this campaign--when men finally organized a national "Anti-Saloon League" in 1893 they did so in Oberlin, 42 miles from Plymouth and 23 miles from Norwalk. Edmondson was obviously abreast of all this, and of political developments generally. A reporter from the Huron County Chronicle sought him out in Plymouth for an interview and found him in his 'usual good-natured humorous style." After a tour of Edmondson's Art Gallery the reporter found him eager to discuss the main issues of the day: the impending state and national elections and the continuation of paper currency unsupported by gold, which Edmondson, using the slang of the day, called a "Ragbaby." [149]

The success of "The Drinker's Progress" convinced Edmondson that the future lay with the production and sale of large groups of photographs rather than the small, individual cartes de visite that had become the staple of most photographic work since the introduction of photography in Paris in 1854. An ideal opportunity presented itself in 1873 when a group of northern Ohio Methodists purchased a mile square tract of land on the tip of the Marblehead Peninsula on Lake Erie, thirty miles northwest of Norwalk and forty miles east of Toledo. Beginning that summer they held retreats and religious revivals there. When many families began there for much of the summer, the Methodists began offering building sites on ninety-nine year leases. In 1874 they erected a dormitory-style building called "Pilgrims' Rest" and a year later began construction of a large and handsome Hotel Lakeside, which still stands today.

Lakeside is less well-known than its larger contemporary, Chautauqua, but its mission and program were—and are today--identical. Chautauqua was also founded by Methodists, but in 1875, two years after Lakeside. From the outset both were committed to evangelical Christian piety, a high-minded intellectuality, and engagement with the issues of the day. George William Edmondson determined early to become Lakeside's photographic chronicler.

Main hotel, Lakeside Camp Meeting, Ohio, 1875, print from stereopticon image. S.F. Starr

Edmondson's Lakeside series eventually number at least twenty-eight images. This, at least, was the number in the Lakeside archives in 1980, when the Lakeside Association decided to issue a calendar featuring Edmondson photographs. All were originally issued in both stereoscopic format and as "cabinet photographs," a four-by-six-inch format that was gaining wide popularity precisely in the mid-1870s. In the early1880s Edmondson pulled together a large number of his Lakeside images depicting the community's progress from the era of "board tents" to the present, and offered them as a book, entitled Picturesque Lakeside. Eschewing economies of scale yet minimizing his own investment and avoiding problems of excess inventory, he announced that the book was "only printed to order."

The Child Preacher, Lakeside Camp Meeting, Ohio, 1875. S.F. Starr

The Lakeside series is not without some high points. The image of the grand hotel with hundreds of people lining its exterior porches, probably dates from its opening in 1875 and is certainly memorable by any standard. But if "The Child Preacher" draws attention as a curiosity, it fails as a photograph. Similarly, "Our Girls" presents an attractive record of women's informal wear in the 1870s, and is of local interest because it included Anne Mountain, Mary Jane Mountain, and several other members of the Mountain and Edmondson families.[150] But neither in its artistic or technical dimensions is this, or any other picture in the Lakeside series, in any way noteworthy. And that may be what made them attractive to the public at the time. Up to this point nearly all photographs were stiffly posed and painterly studio portraits. Edmondson set out in an entirely different direction. A decade and a half later George Eastman introduced his Kodak camera, which made photography accessible to the masses and made possible a new kind of informal picture-making. Long before Eastman's innovation, Edmondson was striving to achieve the same informal effect as the later snapshots.

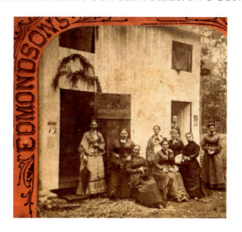

"Our Girls," showing assembled Edmondson and Mountain ladies, from the Lakeside series, 1875. S.F. Starr

After more than a decade spent mainly in Plymouth, GW late in 1878 moved back to Norwalk and set up shop above the First National Bank Building on Main Street in a studio marked with a large sign that read "G.W. Edmondson, Artist and Photographer."[151] There were several reasons for this move. First, as both newspapers reported, Edmondson was already well-known in Norwalk, and his activities in Plymouth had only added to his fame there. Second, he would now become—briefly, at least—the sole photographer in Norwalk. And, third, while Plymouth's population was stagnating, Norwalk's grew. By 1881 its population reached 4,000, the minimum required to become registered as a city,[152] and Norwalk had for several years boasted city-wide gas lighting, a water works, two banks, two newspapers, and twelve churches.

Once established again in Norwalk, Edmondson carried on an active photographic business and continued at the same time to find time to experiment with innovations. Among these, none was more important than his next steps along a decade-long path to capture images of animals and objects in motion. This had been his purpose back in Plymouth in photographing a dog riding horseback. Now, in an advertisement for his new establishment printed on the back of a photograph he boasted that "The instantaneous process [is] used exclusively," and that "*Portraits of animals and objects in motion a specialty.*"

With the benefit of hindsight it is clear that all these efforts by untold numbers of tinkerers, experiments, and inventors were all steps along the wandering path that led to motion pictures. A related consequence is that they gave both artists and engineers a much subtler understanding of all forms of motion, including that of the human body, than ever before. A pioneer in this effort was another English-born American, Edward Muybridge (1830-1905), who began his studies in 1872 when the millionaire Leland Stanford challenged him to establish whether a galloping horse ever had all four feet on the ground at the same time. Using twelve cameras simultaneously,

Muybridge concluded they did, a finding that led the University of Pennsylvania to engage him from 1884 to 1887 to advance the study of <u>Animal Locomotion</u>, which he did in a book by that name published in 1887.

Edmondson was a tinkerer by instinct, having already patented one of his inventions, a washing machine. In the same years that Muybridge was carrying out his experiments, George William Edmondson was exploring the technical problem of a making a photographic shutter work fast enough to capture a bird in flight or speeding freight train. A news story published in the Norwalk Chronicle on 21 August, 1884 announced his success in this endeavor:

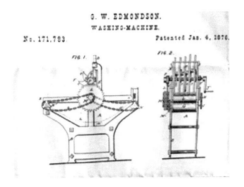

Patent for Edmondson's Washing Machine. S. F. Starr

"Mr. Edmondson of this city has just succeeded in photographing the fast mail train on the Lake Shore Road. The negative was taken while the train was going at the rate of 85 miles per hour. It was by the instantaneous process and the moving parallel bar is distinctly shown. This is said to be the best photograph of the kind yet produced."

By the early 1880s George Edmondson was an established and respected figure in the Norwalk business community. He was known to be reliable and prudent---too cautious, some in his family said. A decade before, when a thirty-three year old from Cleveland named John Rockefeller came through town selling stock in his new Standard Oil Company, Edmondson passed up the opportunity, telling anyone who asked that he was "not a plunger."[153] Edmondson had also become, to all appearances, a staunch churchman. When they reached Norwalk the Mountain family found that the Episcopalians had yet to form a church but that the Methodists had been the cornerstone of the community since its founding. They therefore all joined the 143 other members of the Methodist Church, and participated in the dedication of a new chapel in 1868. Edmondson joined with them and after his return to Norwalk in 1878 began teaching Sunday-School classes. Indeed, by 1880 he was superintendent of the Methodist Sunday School.

Methodist Church, Norwalk, Ohio.

To this point one might assume that the Mountains and Edmondsons were typical hard-working immigrants on the path to financial security and a solid place in the local establishment. But this was not quite the case. Both sides of the Mountain family were in the clothing business, in Norwalk. But soon after they opened their tailoring shop in 1867 the business reached a plateau.[154] Rather than evolve into a general store with its own building on Main Street, as the dry goods store owned by the Benson family had done, the Mountains' outfit remained a tailoring establishment, a top-end one, to be sure, but nothing more. Never during the 1870s or 1880s were any of the Mountains able to afford to purchase a home of their own in Norwalk. Nor, for that matter, could George William Edmondson.

By the time he reached his early forties, GW had reason to think that his life had reached a dead end. His business was solid but prospects for expanding it were slim at best. He now had four children to raise, three of them boys (George, William, and Ernest) who would need to be set up in business or in a profession and the fourth, Ivy, a girl for whom he would have to find a suitable partner. Moreover, there were an additional twelve members of the Mountain family, both the "Quebec" branch and the earlier settlers in Norwalk, with their constant concerns.

Complicating this still further was the fact that his wife Mary Jane had turned out to be anything but the light hearted and fun-loving person he thought he had married, in Quebec. Maybe it was bitterness over the negative turn the Mountains' lives had taken since their father's bankruptcy. Maybe it was disappointment that her husband spent more time photographing speeding mail trains than making money for the family. Maybe it was his unexplained absences and local talk of his philandering. Or maybe it was simply the nature of her personality as she aged. But by common consent, by the time she had reached her forties, Mary Jane Mountain Edmondson, the girl who had gaily danced with the Prince of Wales, and whom her grand-daughter remembered as having a twinkle in her eye, a love for singing, and "still the belle of the ball in her eightieth year,"[155] had never adjusted to the new life that she entered upon after the collapse of her father's fortune. Critical of all those who fell short of her expectations and steeped in Methodist piety, she became demanding of everyone around her, and particularly of her husband.

Edmondson responded to this by escaping from his home on Newton Street. In spite of his "Drinker's Progress" and role at the Methodist Sunday School, he also took to drink, disappearing for days at a time.[156] By the mid-1880s his marriage had collapsed. But Mary Jane refused to grant GW a divorce, then or later.

George W. Edmondson, Tinsmith, Norwalk, Ohio, 1870s.
One of many images of colorful locals and guests. S.F. Starr

Edmondson's split with Quakerism and his father had occurred in part over GW's desire to pursue a career in art. He never abandoned this commitment, and in the 1880s it found new expression in portraiture and scenes from nature. Of the former, a remarkable image of a tinsmith stands out both for the pose and the intense expression of the subject and the dramatic angle from which GW took the picture. In the same spirit but less successful is a portrait of two costumed trapeze artists on their trapeze. Of the latter, his "portraits" of ferns, pumpkins, and quartz crystals are notable.

Another example of Edmondson's interest in colourful figures. S.F. Starr

Edmondson Manufacturing Photographers, Main Street, Norwalk, Ohio, 1880. S.F. Starr

It is revealing that the sign at Edmondson's studio identified him as Artist and Photographer. His interest in art was reflected in the circle of people among whom he moved 18. By 1880 he had met a talented young painter from nearby Sandusky named Wilder Darling.[157] Though only twenty-five at the time, Darling had already established himself as a rising artist with solid European training. Beginning with studies in Cincinnati, probably with Henry Mosler at the McMicken School of Design, he moved on to the Academie Julian in Paris and to Munich, where Cincinnatian Frank Duveneck was offering classes to a growing number of aspiring painters from Europe and America. Now Darling was back in the United States, trying to figure out how to make a living as an artist. Beginning in 1880 Wilder Darling appears in the annual census as a member of the Edmondson household. By 1885 he was back in Europe, never to return.

Self-portrait by Wilder Darling at the time he lived with the Edmondsons.
Rachel Davis Fine Arts, Cleveland.

About this time another new technology entered GW's life, the Stereopticon. The stereopticon was a device for projecting stereopticon slides onto a screen. Powered initially by gaslight and later by electric light bulbs, stereopticons could make a single three-dimensional image simultaneously accessible to an entire seated audience. They invited the production of whole series of pictures on diverse topics, to be supported by a running narrative.

A stereopticon projector, 1880s, (left). A stereopticon hand viewer (right).

Edmondson seized on the stereopticon projector as a vehicle for launching a new career as a photographer-lecturer. He could shoot whole series of pictures on natural, historical, or religious topics or buy them from other photographers and then make money presenting his lecture-shows to paying audiences. His first "Magic Lantern" programs featured his Lakeside series, but these were soon followed by many others all of which, unfortunately, have been lost. Edmondson turned out to be an effective lecturer. He laughed easily and uproariously, so much so that the audience would often take as much pleasure in him as in his slides. From the standpoint of his personal life this new venture offered the additional advantage of providing an excuse for him to travel widely to prepare new stereopticon series or to present them to an expanding public, and thus to absent himself from home.

By 1886 GW faced a triple challenge: what to do with his two eldest sons, George and William, and what to do with himself. Calling on his new interest in the stereopticon, he devised a plan for solving all three problems at once. According to this scheme he would travel to England and Europe to take stereopticon pictures which he could then leverage into a lecturing career for himself back home. His second son, Willie, had already studied painting at home with Wilder Darling. He had shown sufficient promise that Darling suggested to Edmondson that he send Willie to Europe for further study at an appropriate art school there. As to young George, at twenty years of age he could take over the studio back in Norwalk and keep the money flowing to Mary Jane until his father returned.

On 2 August 1886 the Norwalk Chronicle announced that, "On Wednesday of this week George William Edmondson, the photographer, and his son Willie left Norwalk for New York, where they will take steamer for Europe. Mr. Edmondson goes on a photographic tour. Willie will remain in London for about one year and then go to Munich, Germany, to pursue his studies in the art schools of that famous city under Professor Darling, formerly of Norwalk, who has won fame as an American artist, and others." Days later the Norwalk press reported that the Methodist Church presented Edmondson with a silver-headed cane in honor of his years as superintendent of the Sunday-School. Singling out his Magic Lantern lectures for special praise because they had made the material interesting to young people, the report noted in conclusion that "The illustrations last Sunday embraced scenes in and around Jerusalem, where he hopes to visit before his return home."

Other than the fact that Edmondson did not venture as far as the Holy Land, we have no information on his travels in Europe. By 1886 both his parents were long since dead, but he and Willie almost certainly visited those of GW's siblings who remained alive and in England. He definitely visited Queenwood and photographed the site of the "lecture" he received from his father thirty-five years earlier. Assuming that pictures in the folio he gave to his son George Mountain Edmondson in 1907 were made during this trip, they also visited Blackburn and Preston, as well as Ireland, where his sister had moved with her husband. Except for a number of photographs taken in Ireland, there is no surviving evidence of Edmondson taking any series of pictures in either England or France for use in future Magic Lantern shows. The plan to photograph the Holy Land also proved to be a chimera.

It is hard to escape the conclusion that George William Edmondson's trip abroad was simply an excuse to get out of the house and out of Norwalk. However, it had lasting consequences, many of them positive. He succeeded in enrolling son Willie at the Academie Julian, whence he was to emerge a few years later as a competent impressionist. And young George did such a good job of managing the photographic studio on Norwalk's Main Street that he resolved to set out on his own as soon as his father returned from abroad. In 1888 young Edmondson moved to Cleveland and in the same year his father sold his photographic studio to C. W. Parke of Norwalk, a Civil War veteran who had taken up photography because his wounds prevented him from pursuing a more physically demanding career.[158]

In 1889 George William Edmondson and his wife Mary Jane moved to Cleveland.[159] They set up and maintained separate households, for by now, (if not earlier) George William Edmondson had a mistress. Before moving he negotiated to buy a plot of land outside of Norwalk from the Methodist preacher, possibly for a future home for himself and mistress or for his wife, but this came to nothing. At fifty-two years of age, Edmondson was probably too old to launch an entirely new venture but he managed to continue along his former lines, printing large mural scenes and tinting them with watercolor (this is what he was doing in the photograph in the Cleveland Library mentioned at the start of this essay), enlarging or copying old pictures, and offering Magic Lantern lectures. At the age of seventy-three he was still practicing his craft, "doing excellent work in unexplored fields of the photographic profession," as a 1910 <u>History of Cleveland</u> put it.[160] He maintained a studio on the top floor of a building on Euclid Avenue at 105th Street, where he held court for an unlikely coterie of old friends, artists, and the merely curious. Charming and lively to the end, he developed a friendship with the anarchist and socialist Elbert Hubbard (1856-1915), founder of the arts and crafts Roycroft colony in East Aurora, New York, and with many other people who shared his lifelong penchant for art, technology, and life on the fringes of polite society.[161]

In GW's later years it fell to his son, George Mountain Edmondson, to support both him and his wife, Mary Jane, as well as the Misses Sophie and Anne Mountain.

William John Edmondson (1868-1967)

George William and Mary Jane Edmondson had four children: George, William Ivy, and Ernest. George Mountain Edmondson, the eldest son, merits and will receive special treatment here, not only because of his position as the father of Ivy Jane Edmondson Starr, but in his own right. A second son, Ernest, was boisterous and outgoing. He was infamous in Norwalk for having instigated a classroom brawl at the high school that included his teacher, a Mr. Mitchell.[162] Ernest left Norwalk for Baltimore and Philadelphia in the late 1880s. There he married, had no children, but pursued a successful career in advertising and then in journalism at the Philadelphia Ledger. Ivy Jane Edmondson Starr, his niece, met him during his occasional visits to Cleveland and remembered him as high-spirited and eager to poke fun at his mid-western relatives for being overly restrained and, well, mid-western. But since he did not figure in the lives of the next two generations, he can be passed over here. Thus, it remains here to say a word about William and Ivy Edmondson.

William, Willie, or Will Edmondson (1868- 1946), as he was later known, was physically far the most fragile of the four Edmondson children. This can be detected in childhood photos and was sufficient clear to his father that he designated Will for a career as a painter, in contrast to his older brother George, whom he guided into the photography business, or his younger brother Ernest, who became a successful businessman. At a time in life when most artists would have been focusing on their careers, Will spent more than a year at death's door with tuberculosis. Yet he outlived all his siblings by decades.

Though shy and somewhat withdrawn, Will Edmondson was no pushover. As a boy he earned fifty cents each Sunday by pumping a local church organ. When the church's treasurer refused to pay, Willie persisted. Knowing that the treasurer owned the local hardware store with a gleaming new Columbia "high wheel" bicycle in the window, he proposed payment in kind. And then a year later he asked for and received a newer, larger model.[163]

Will Edmondson of Norwalk, Ohio, dressed for the Academie Julian in Paris. S.F. Starr

Willie's father instructed all his children in drawing and painting. The arrival of Wilder Darling in the Edmondson household when Willie was thirteen brought more focused instruction. When Darling returned to Europe, he proposed that the Edmondsons send the young man to continue his studies with him in Munich. But Darling's plans changed, which forced George Edmondson to improvise. In the end he enrolled nineteen-year-old Willie at the continent's fastest rising art school, the Academie Julian in Paris.

The Academie Julian was a private institution that welcomed students from abroad. Both foreign and French students flocked there, in part because of the distinguished artists who taught there and in part because there was no examination for admission. This contrasted sharply with the Ecole des Beaux Arts, which required applicants to pass a rigorous examination conducted in French. The American John Singer Sargent succeeded at this but few other foreigners even tried. Most went instead to the twenty-year old Academie Julian and hoped then to move on to the Ecole des Beaux Arts and to a crack at the prestigious Prix de Rome.

When Will Edmondson arrived at the Academie Julian in 1886-1887, there were already six Americans there, all of whom went on to notable careers as painters. Edmund Tarbell became a competent impressionist; John Henry Twachtman, also a future impressionist and notable landscape painter; William Metcalf, a budding portrait painter and landscapist; Arthur Wesley Dow, who became a printmaker and photographer as well as painter; and Childe Hassam, whose career spanned impressionism and several currents of post-impressionism.

Two stark differences divided Will Edmondson from all these future masters. First, with the exception of Twachtman, who hailed from cosmopolitan Cincinnati, all the others were from Massachusetts. The split between the Midwest and East represented a cultural divide that was at least as important in the 1880s as it was a half century later, when F. Scott Fitzgerald put it on America's cultural map. Second, Edmondson was much younger than the other Americans at the Academie Julian. Tarbell, who was closest to Edmondson's age, was five years older. Exhibitions in Europe and America had already featured the works of Hassam and Twachtman. On average, the others were just short of a decade more senior than the nineteen-year-old neophyte from Norwalk, Ohio. No wonder that the retiring Will Edmondson is barely visible amidst a of group photographs of Academie Julian students.

Students at the Academie Julian, 1886, with Will Edmondson barely visible in the upper left.

Of all the artists teaching at the Academie Julian in the 1880s there were two in whose studios the Americans all the Americans sought to gain a place: Gustave Boulanger (1824-1888} and Jules Joseph Lefebvre {1834-1912}. Boulanger was best known for his paintings of "oriental" (i.e. North African) subjects but he was also a master of the waning French tradition of classicism; Lefebvre was a figure painter who was best known for his canvasses depicting women. Both were worthy pedagogues and both engendered a high level of technical competence among their students. But there is some truth to Childe Hassam's complaint that "the Julian Academy is the personification of routine. [It] crushes all originality out of growing men."[164]

For years Will Edmondson toiled in the studios of Gustave Boulanger and Jules Lefebvre. He appears in several group photographs of Academie Julian students, usually the short, neatly dressed figure with stylish goatee standing on one side or somewhere near the back. He shared a studio with a fellow Clevelander, Lou Rorimer, born Rohrheimer, who later opened a fancy antiques and furnishings shop on Euclid Avenue and remained Will's lifelong friend. Rorimer's son later directed the Metropolitan Museum in New York. Over his time in Paris Will gaining a solid mastery of classical technique, figural painting, and landscape painting. Like most of his contemporaries, he did not emerge with a fixed technique or style. Instead, his studies in Paris exposed him to classicism, realism in the spirit of Corot, <u>plein-air</u> impressionism, symbolism, and various styles of portrait painting. Over the next sixty years he was to revert again and again to what he had acquired during his studies, shifting from one current to another but venturing only rarely into entirely new territory.

How many nineteenth century novels and operas conclude with the hero or heroine succumbing to tuberculosis? Will Edmondson, never strong, got this disease of the century while in Paris and had to be carried off the ship in New York on a pallet. Family lore records that he was not expected to live. His elder brother George met him at the boat and took him directly to Asheville, North Carolina. Thanks to its altitude, climate, and access by railroad, Asheville had become America's leading center for the treatment of what had become the leading cause of death in the United States. Some 130 sanitariums and boarding houses catered to those suffering of "the White Plague."[165]

Pan and dancers, William Edmondson, ca. 1895. Brad Edmondson

After a period of convalescence in Asheville, Will Edmondson went to New York to continue his studies under the painter William Merritt Chase. Indiana-born Chase had studied in New York but settled in St. Louis, where he so impressed local aficionados that they made a collection to send him to Munich for further study and to purchase art for them. Further periods of travel in Italy and England and study in Germany and France encouraged Chase to develop a style that was a fruitful cross-fertilization of the dark and loosely brushed figurative painting of Munich with the brighter and more impressionistic landscapes of Paris.

Just before the time Edmondson showed up in his studio, Chase had married a wealthy Manhattanite whose portrait he had painted, and opened a studio on Tenth Street in the same quarters where the western painter Albert Bierstadt had once reigned. The heretofore modest Chase lavishly decorated his new lair, furnished it with exotica from distant lands, and conducted himself like a Victorian caricature of an artiste---until he went broke a few years later. But Chase was not only a fine and diversely gifted painter but also a dedicated pedagogue who taught at all the best American art schools of the day and founded what became the Parsons School of Design. Chase became Edmondson's main teacher and influence. His influence can readily be detected in some of Edmondson's best portraits and also in the many plein air paintings he produced over the decades. William Merritt Chase and William Edmondson were to remain good friends down to Chase's death in 1916.

With his skills as a painter honed in Paris and burnished in New York, Will Edmondson returned to Ohio in 1890. In some respects this was a step backwards. In the same year Edmondson had gone to Paris the innovative French art dealer Paul Ruland-Ruel had mounted a show of 289 Impressionist paintings at the American Art Galleries in New York and effectively commercialized the art Edmondson had studied in Paris. During the decade after Edmondson's return, ten members of the rising generation, including three of his fellow students from Paris, along with Chase, quit the Society of American Artists in a successful effort to bring notice to Impressionism and the other more contemporary currents. By returning to Ohio, Edmondson placed himself outside these and other subsequent developments, and on the eve of an era of great ferment and change.

William J. and George M. Edmondson, ca 1898, ArtNEO, Cleveland.

Will Edmondson returned not to Norwalk but to Cleveland. His older brother George had moved there three years before and was achieving success as a photographer. George had entered into partnership with an established Cleveland photographer but he had a further plan that involved Will. His idea was for his brother to join him in a joint enterprise, so that clients who wanted to be photographed could go to him but those who wanted a painted portrait could turn to Will. In other words, the two sons of George William Edmondson would divide their father's two interests between them and set themselves up in such a way that both brothers would benefit.

In practice, George was far the stronger of the two. A large pastel that Will did at this time shows Will from the back, sitting at his easel and drawing a female figure. Frowning at the scene from the upper left of the picture is brother George, as if admonishing Will to get back to serious work. At first there were few portraits to be painted, so Will indulged his own interests. A number of his paintings from the 1890s are fantasies depicting wispily clad females moving in rhythmic patterns amidst classically sylvan settings. Suggesting symbolism or some form of allegory, these works reveal his knowledge of, and interest in, the work of Pierre Puvis de Chavannes (1824-1898). In later years he was to present many women in a manner that was both decorative and suggestive of symbolic meaning.

*Pastel sketch by William Edmondson showing himself,
the artist, and a stern brother George, upper left, looking on. S. F. Starr*

Will Edmondson's life as a portrait painter for those Clevelanders who didn't want portrait photographs done by his brother was productive and uneventful. Even today the city is festooned with Edmondson oil portraits of the grave titans of industry who made the Cleveland America's economic capital in the generation before the First World War. Several, like the canvasses of dour personages hanging in Cleveland's Union Club and in the Allen Memorial, call to mind his father's photographic portraits of corpses. Perhaps it was the subjects' own desire, but few of these portraits reveal any kind of sentiment or human emotion. But there are wonderful exceptions. A study of a young woman examining a blue feather ("The Blue Feather," 1917)[166], shows his skill at depicting stylized females and his mastery of the decorative elements of the day.

William Edmondson, ca. 1900. Self Portrait (ArtNEO, Cleveland).

Fragment of lost work by Will Edmondson, 1915. Brad Edmondson

1919 he garnered a first prize for figural painting from the Cleveland Museum of Art. A portrait from the late 1920s of his artist friend water colorist Ora Coltman (1858-1940) sitting next to an easel and painting, is as warm as the "official" portraits are cold. Around 1935 Edmondson did a stunning portrait of Cleveland's dapper man-about-town, Winsor French. French (1905-1973). A wealthy journalist born in Saratoga, New York, French parlayed newspaper features on Cleveland's night life into a nationally syndicated column on night life, both high and low and from New York to Los Angeles, with stops in Palm Beach, Miami and Havana.[167] Edmondson's lively portrait recalls the bold, broad brush strokes and undiluted colors of the American Robert Henri. It became the feature of "Winsor's" restaurant at the Wyndham Hotel on Playhouse Square but disappeared when that facility was remodeled around 2000.

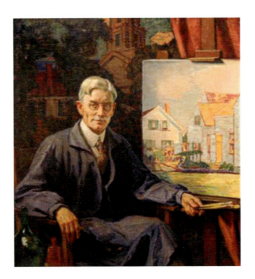

Portrait of Artist Ora Coltman, 1925, ArtNeo, Cleveland.

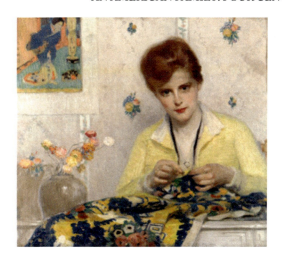 

Portraits of unknown girls, ca. 1923.
Widely reproduced, the locations of the originals of both works are now unknown.

It is not belittling to acknowledge the decorative element in some of Will Edmondson's art around the time of the First World War. Both photography and painting at the time had come under the strong influence of mass magazines and of the sophisticated new advertising art they contained. Edmondson was very much in step with these developments and explored the new genres effectively and, in all probability, profitably. Thus, around 1913 he did a charming group portrait of dolls belonging to his niece, Ivy Jane. Arranged as if watching a clown doll dance, the dolls are represented in a frankly sentimental manner. The portrait was reproduced in several national magazines. In a closely related spirit is a poster promoting patriotism, which Edmondson turned out for the YMCA in 1919. Realism and sentimentalism once more link arms, this time with images of beaming young men gazing into the future in a manner that anticipates later Soviet and German propaganda posters.

Poster of American Youth 1921.

There is no reason to think that Will Edmondson turned out these stylish and popular works simply for the income they produced. For in spite of his brother's exhortations, he was under no pressure to earn money, nor had he been since his marriage. An undated and highly accomplished self-portrait of Will Edmondson from around 1900, now at the ArtNEO Museum in Cleveland, reveals him back then as sandy-haired, with neatly trimmed goatee and an expression that is at once intelligent and also polite---all in all an attractive and highly civilized man in his early thirties. This is how he must have looked when he married Florence Holloway, whom he had met while he was in New York studying under William Merritt Chase. The Holloways had money and strong ideas about what is right and wrong. Her mother, whom Ivy Jane Edmondson Starr described as "a Henry James New Yorker,"[168] had sent her to Miss Bennett's Finishing School in New York. When a brother went off to Hawaii and married a Hawaiian princess of color his picture was turned to the wall. Years later Ivy Jane Starr recalled staying at "Uncle Will's and Auntie Florence's" house and seeing a faded photograph of the Hawaiian royal family on the bedroom wall. Florence Holloway lived only a few blocks from Chase's Tenth Street studio and probably met the young artist from Norwalk there. The money this gracious young woman brought to her new life in Cleveland enabled the couple to buy a spacious home in Shaker Heights and a sailboat which they kept at the Mentor Harbor Yacht Club. More important, it freed Will Edmondson from the need to do further hackwork of any kind and to concentrate on his first love, which was painting en plein air. The fact that the Edmondsons had no children meant that he had ample time to pursue this passion.

Plein air painting was for Edmondson an excuse to travel, a form of escape from the formal and highly structured Cleveland society. With the coming of spring, he and his wife would head to the Berkshires in Massachusetts or, later, to the Shenandoah Valley in Virginia, for extended periods of painting. Favorite sites, notably a small Virginia river and adjacent farmland, he would paint again and again, in early spring, deep summer and in the autumn with piled cornstalks. The couple travelled also to Maine, but only one Edmondson seascape is known to exist. The densely-populated art world of Winslow Homer and his followers was not for him.

Untitled, ca 1920, ArtNEO, Cleveland, gift of Ivy Jane Edmondson Starr.

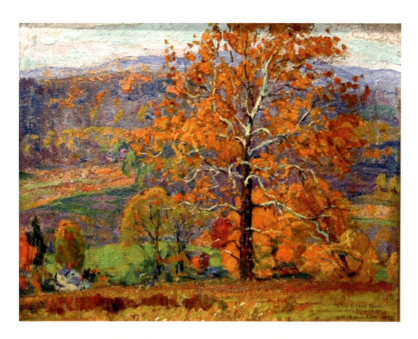

Berkshire scene, ca 1925. S.F. Starr

Scene in Berkshires, ca. 1925. S.F. Starr

Virginia Meadow, 1947, May Show, Cleveland. S.F. Starr

When San Francisco mounted the Panama-Pacific International Exposition in 1915 it stimulated a growing interest in California among landscape painters. The exposition's Palace of the Arts raised the state's status in the art world and inspired more than a few eastern and Midwestern artists to relocate there. Article's like "California for the Landscape Painter," which appeared in the American Magazine of Art in 1920[169] reinforced the impression of the Golden State as a new Mecca for painters.

Beginning in the 1920s Edmondson responded to this call. With easel and palette he travelled widely through the state, painting grandly wooded hills under towering clouds, peaceful missions, and the rocky coastline along Route One. On at least one of these western trips he also visited Taos, New Mexico, where he painted the ancient Taos pueblo, using a broad brush to stress the cubic grid of the facade.

Detail from oil painting of Taos Pueblo, late 1920s. S. F. Starr

Edmondson was one of several dozen painters from the East and Midwest who were drawn to California in those years. It is striking that most of them belonged to the single generation of which Edmondson was a part. Thus, William Ritchel was born in 1864, William Wend in 1865, Guy Rose in 1867, Granville Redmore in 1871, Alan Clark in 1876, and Maurice Braun in 1877. Edmondson, born in 1868, was squarely part of this generational movement. Like many of the others, he joined the California Art Club in San Marino, founded in 1909 to advance painting in southern California, and steadily earned for himself an honorable place among California impressionists and plein air painters.[170] Then in 1950 he and Florence moved from Cleveland to Monrovia, only seven miles from the Club. His new home was also just east of Pasadena, where Will's sister, Ivy, had settled after her husband Fred Colson's death.

Carmel Mission, S.F. Starr

California Coastal Scene. Rachel Davis Fine Arts, Cleveland.

California landscape, George A. Starr, Berkeley, Ca.

California landscape, George. A. Starr.

Our knowledge of the art of William John Edmondson is extremely fragmentary. Since he sold his paintings and drawings directly from his studio we cannot consult exhibition catalogues to identify and date his works. Nor did he put dates on his paintings or keep a register of his oeuvres. And for some unknown reason he destroyed all his sketches and drawings. To date, no scholar has attempted to gather more detailed information on his life and works. Thus, nearly all we know of him as an artist derives from the reminiscences of his niece, Ivy Jane Edmondson Starr, the handful of paintings preserved in the families of his niece and nephew and the few pieces that have turned up at auction in recent years.

Acknowledging these impediments, it is nonetheless readily possible to identify four different poles, between which nearly every one of Will Edmondson's landscapes can be placed. First, there is the careful and highly studied realism of a type that traces to Corot. Preceded by careful oil sketches, these paintings show meticulous organization and invariably focus on a narrow range of carefully modulated darker colors. Second, there are a handful of paintings in which he used a bold impressionism, with dramatic brush strokes and strong contrasts in color. Third, there was a new realism that appeared especially in the 1920s and early 1930s, these large canvases present rural scenes bathed in sunlight and presented with meticulous detail. And, fourth, there was the rather academic variant of Impressionism that he employed in a number of paintings from Virginia and the Berkshires and which he used extensively, almost exclusively, in California. At one level this places him squarely within the then-emerging regional school in southern California. But in contrast to most of the other plein air painters in the southern part of the state, Edmondson did not indulge in bright colors and stunning chromatic effects, preferring instead a more restrained pallet. But otherwise he stands squarely within the tradition of southern California Impressionism.

Landscape, S.F. Starr.

The world of William John Edmondson was one of moderation and harmony. Free of the professional pressures and personal dramas that plagued his father and brother George, he retained the openness and innocence evident in his early self-portrait. It shines forth clearly in a group portrait with his other siblings done at the time of George's eightieth birthday party. His utter disengagement from the world of everyday toil is clearly evident in the dry and bloodless "official" portraits he did of the titans of Cleveland business and cultural life. That he did not have his heart in these paintings is painfully obvious, yet they clearly met some standard that demanded symbols of probity, responsibility, and honor. By contrast, his most successful portraits show his ability to identify, appreciate, and communicate the distinctive qualities of others. It is no accident that every one of his best portraits depict the subject at leisure or play, and definitely not at work.

In the end, Will Edmondson abandoned people for nature. His earlier landscapes often include farm buildings, hay stacks, roads, or other signs of human activity. Over time these fade away, leaving the viewer to contemplate an untouched natural world of rivers, ponds, seashores, or wooded mountains. Edmondson's nature is a friendly place. If he ever contemplated the West's high mountains or barren deserts, they certainly did not move him to reach for brush and paint. His world is serene, not sublime. His choice of places to set up his easel was not dictated by a quest for that which is awe-inspiring or majestic, let alone by a desire to impress his viewer with the physical risk he endured to get there. Rather, one senses that he was always seeking a place to picnic, or to build a quiet retreat with a porch opening on the vista.

Considering what appears to have been the artist's frame of mind, one must conclude that Edmondson was very successful in his art. His best portraits depict people at ease or at play, and he presents them with strong colors and vivacity of line that attest to an artist in command of a broad range of skills and techniques. As to his landscapes, not only did he find those serene and bucolic sites, but for each one he chose a technique or style that was eminently suited to communicate its essence to the viewer. In the end, William John Edmondson's life and art were all of a piece, which cannot be said for many artists in any era.

Ivy Edmondson and Frederick W. Colson

Ivy Edmondson was as lively and engaging as her mother had been during her young days in Quebec but, unlike her mother, continued that way throughout her life. Tall and statuesque, with golden hair and dignified in the manner of the day, she invariably appears in portrait photographs as if she had just stepped off the pages of an Edwardian fashion magazine. And well she might have, since Ivy, as they say, had "married well."

Frederick W. Colson was born in Kent Ohio, but his family was from Norwalk. Since their department store on Main Street provided just about everything needed to set up a household, it flourished in the newly incorporated city. Nor were the Norwalk Colsons and Edmondson strangers to one another, as the wife of Mr. Colson was the daughter of GW's first employer, photographer Byron Benham.

On paper, the life of Fred Colson's father might seem to presage his son's becoming a professional musician or perhaps a professor. The dignified and respected organist, bald headed and rarely without a cigar, served for thirty-seven years at the venerable Old Stone Church on Public Square in Cleveland. "Professor" Colson was a founding member of the American Guild of Organists and the Musicians' Club of Cleveland and a co-founder of the Cleveland School of Music. His vespers recitals at the Old Stone Church drew an appreciate audience of serious music lovers, of which there were many in Cleveland.[171]

The only complication in this otherwise earnest and proper picture is that Colson Sr. had a mistress who maintained a piano studio in the Cleveland Arcade, a five minutes' walk from the Old Stone Church. Both their names were painted in gold lettering on the door, and rightly so, because the two of them would organize performances such as one at the Academy of Music, in which 125 of their students performed such immortal classics as "Say a Kind Word When You Can" and "Take Me Home Again." Their joint venture was no gold mine, however, and behind the scene Colson's son Fred helped support the studio of Colson and Ms. Brubaker.

Young Fred Colson's first job was as a national salesman for A. L. Garford, an Englishman who was producing bicycle saddles at a factory he had set up in nearby Elyria, Ohio.[172] Colson spent several years selling Garford's saddles as far afield as Chicago and New York. Garford meanwhile bought up a bicycle company and then went on to take over the Worthington Machine Parts Company, which was manufacturing wheelchairs for use by the half million wounded Civil War veterans, tens of thousands of whom were amputees.[173] The resourceful Englishman who had started this firm, George Worthington, conceived the idea of offering both "Lee" and "Grant" models of wheelchairs for sale in the North and South. He also gave reality to an idea spawned by Garford and a Cleveland investor over a game of golf in Akron, Ohio, home of Goodrich Rubber. Garford's friend was shown a spool of rubber thread and immediately proposed that it be used for golf balls. Worthington promptly designed a ball winding machine that made Garford's firm the country's third largest producer of golf balls, after Goodrich and Spalding.

By this process Garford ended up with a diversified company producing each year a million patented bicycle seats with springs, modern "safety" bicycles, chain-driven tricycles for children, wheel chairs, and wheeled hospital beds. Moving with the times, Garford in 1902 decided also to produce automobiles and trucks. He took personal charge of the new enterprise, which he called the Garford Manufacturing Company, and promoted Colson to run the bicycle and wheelchair business. Colson threw himself into this new challenge, improving both the bicycle and wheelchair lines and expanding sales by setting up showrooms in seventeen cities. By 1917 he was able to buy out Garford and rename the firm the Colson Company.

Advertisement for Fred Colson's "Fairy" line of bicycles, with niece Ivy Jane Edmondson. Photo by George M. Edmondson. S.F. Starr

Colson designed and manufactured bicycles under Garford's name beginning in 1900 and then under his own name from 1918 to the 1940s. His "skip toothed" chains were somewhat old fashioned but otherwise both his designs and construction earned his machines a respected place in the upper tier of American bicycles. Especially popular (and still sought after by collectors today) were his tandems with a chain connecting the rear handle bars with the front. These had been invented in around 1897 by the Patee bicycle company of Peoria, Illinois, but had never gained popularity, largely because the rear steering was so obviously designed to enable the woman to sit fore but for the man to override her steering whenever he wished. Colson's rear-steering tandems were more equitable, leaving it to each couple whether the man or women sat in front.

It was during this time that a near contemporary of Colson's, Sherwood Anderson from Clyde, Ohio, showed up in Elyria. Anderson, who had failed in business in Cleveland and suffered a nervous breakdown, took a job as Colson's book-keeper while working evenings to set up his own retail paint company. The paint company was moderately successful but Anderson hated Elyria, not least because his marriage collapsed there. In what was probably a faked second nervous breakdown in December, 1912, he abandoned his wife, business, and Elyria and headed to New Orleans, where he launched his career as a writer. His dislike for small-town Ohio found expression in his Winesburg Ohio. Colson reciprocated by calling Anderson "nothing but a bum."[174]

Fred Colson's marriage to Ivy Edmondson was childless but otherwise very happy. They travelled the country in grand style and moved about the Cleveland area in a chauffeur-driven Packard or a sporty 1920 Buick roadster. The same year he founded the company bearing his name Fred Colson bought a stately antebellum home with square columns on 324 Washington Avenue in Elyria, Ohio, across the street from the U.S. ambassador to France, which he and Ivy proceeded to fill with antiques picked up during buying trips to the East.

Frederick W. and Ivy Edmondson Colson, by George M. Edmondson, ca 1920, S.F. Starr

Ivy Colson (left), S.F. Starr and Fred Colson's 1920 Buick, with the author at the wheel.

Fred Colson was a simple, whimsical man, with undeniable charm. While on a visit to Chautauqua in New York he penned the following humorous poem, which he read over a dinner with friends:

> Never spent so little money in my dog-done life.
> What? I owe the inconvenience to my charming wife;
> For she likes the sound of silver and she likes the glint of gold,
> And she says we've got to save, because we're getting pretty old.
> So to fill her heart with gladness make her mind content,
> I began to keep a record of the odds and ends I spent—
> All the really necessaries don't amount to very much,
> It's the little incidentals that run up so like the Dutch.
>
> Well, of all the sad remorses one experiences when
> One discovers what is gone and isn't coming back for one to spend—
> Say of all the mental anguish and real genuine distress—
> To arrive when one discovers one's worth nothing—and some less!
> Friends, I'm stricken with a stringency that changed my mode of life.
> And I owe that reformation to my lady love—my wife.

With no children of their own, the Colsons lavished parental love on their niece, Ivy Jane Edmondson (later Starr) for whom Ivy Colson became, in the words of the young girl, a "fairy godmother." Colson had good reason to spoil his young niece, for in the 1890s his beloved younger sister, Elsa, had died. Besides a single photograph of her, the only surviving memento of her life is a note from her to her brother, when he was already "on the road" for Garford:

15 November 1891

Dear brother Fred,

I thought I would write to you this Sunday afternoon. It has been raining all day today. And this morning it snowed, but it all melted away afterwards and then began to rain. I went to dancing school yesterday. It met at Mrs. Adkins' and next week it will meet at Mrs. Gray's. My teacher's name is Mrs. Standish. Mama knows her. I went down to visit the sewing school before the dancing school commenced with Lillian yesterday and liked it very much. Lillian lost one of her mittens, never to return. Well, I must stop, for papa is going to take this letter over town with him.

Good bye, your loving sister, Elsa.[175]

Colson himself was tall, rotund, and drank more than he should. His niece recalled him as "affecting a stern, morose air that scared a lot of people." Next to nothing is known of his views on either politics or religion. The fact that he had in his library a copy of Thomas Paine's irreverent Age of Reason: Being an Investigation of True and Fabulous Theology, with its spirited denunciation of "the three frauds, *mystery*, *miracle* and *prophesy*," invites speculation. He spoke and wrote in a platitudinous but colorful language that recalled no one so much as George Babbitt, the hard-working and guileless booster who gave his name to Sinclair Lewis' 1922 novel, Babbitt. A "Dear Willie" letter to his brother-in-law, artist William Edmondson, is full of bantering complaints against "my woman" for pushing him to write, and good-natured-grousing over being so full of food that he could not bear to sit at his desk. Clearly, Fred Colson was a "good ole' boy" who loved the thigh-slapping humor of the Babbitt era. As a young man he published a number of tiny booklets with titles like "Deacon Dictum's Bull" or simply "Wit and Humor." But like Babbitt, Colson was also deeply sentimental, the one who could be counted on to pen brotherly, highfalutin, low-browed, dainty, or lugubrious verse for every occasion.

It is appropriate to end this biographical sketch with a characteristic poem in the form of a toast to his twenty-one year old niece Ivy Jane Edmondson, delivered at Thanksgiving dinner, 1930:

> She used to be so cunning when we gathered to partake
> Of turkey wings and gizzards, in the city by the Lake.

Her cheeks were like to peaches, her hair a tawny tow

And her neck--where she had washed it—was as white as driven snow.

Her eyes we0re blue as sunlight on an agitated sea,

And always she was busy as the busy little bee.

A rugged little blossom, is what she was, I think,

A rosy bloom—a rose bud—and always very pink.

Now time has ravaged all of these. She is no more a kid.

She deals in high-brow knowledge stuff, as old Athenians did.

This pedagogic tension makes a furrow in her brow,

Of course, you cannot see it, but it's there, you must allow.

She is, in fact, a school-marm, sedate as she can be

The agitated blur of eye now seeks tranquility—

But don't think this transition engenders any pain.

For after all she's just the same old lovely Ivy-Jane.

The Colson Company thrived down to the Depression, was reorganized in the late 1930s, and revived briefly during World War II. In 1953 it was sold to thirty-year-old Jay Pritzker of Chicago, who used it as the first building block in a real estate and hotel empire that would make him one of the richest men on earth. Meanwhile, Frederick W. Colson died in 1941 and his wife Ivy Edmondson Colson in 1954.

George Mountain Edmondson (1867-1948)

It was not easy to be a son of George William Edmondson. Not only was George Mountain Edmondson his father's oldest son and namesake, but he was early enlisted as his assistant at the photographic studio and designated to be his father's successor and heir in that profession. Unlike his father, who had run away from home, GME, as we shall call him, remained a loyal and hardworking son to the end.

Born in 1866 in Plymouth, Ohio, a young GME watched wounded Union soldiers returning on crutches from wartime captivity at Andersonville, Georgia, as well as Confederate soldiers returning home from incarceration at nearby Johnson Island in Sandusky Bay. Even before he began his formal apprenticeship in photography under his father in 1880, he assisted him. Every morning he was responsible for cleaning the studio before work began and preparing glass plates. He accompanied his father on his photographic wagon to nearby farms, where sometimes his task was to help arrange the corpses of farmers attired in their Sunday best so that they could sit for pictures they refused to have taken while living.[176]

George M. Edmondson, rt., with Ohio reservists 1886, S.F. Starr

GME's father, following the custom of the day, channeled each of his three sons into what he thought was the most appropriate career. Even though GME may have had more artistic talent than his younger brother, Will, it was the more fragile and less practical Will who was assigned to a painting career, while the more practical GME was designated to carry on the photographic business. Accordingly, when his father and Will left for Paris in the autumn of 1886, the twenty-year old GME was left in sole charge of the photographic studio on Main Street in Norwalk. When Will returned on a stretcher with tuberculosis, it was GME who was assigned to pick him up in New York and deliver him to a sanitarium in Asheville.[177]

GME did such a good job at managing the Edmondson photographic studio that he came to the attention of an established Cleveland photographer, James F. Ryder (1826-1904), who invited him to join him as an associate. Ryder was known for his interest in both the artistic and technical sides of photography. Edmondson, realizing that booming Cleveland offered far more prospects to a photographer than Norwalk, jumped at the offer, which had the added advantage of taking him out from under his father's tutelage. It was Ryder who discovered the Wellington, Ohio, wagon painter Archibald Willard (1836-1918) and used the new chromolithograph technique to publish his humorous genre paintings, even before Willard gained national fame for his painting "The Spirit of '76." Ryder was also expert at large-scale enlargements and the use of the new bromide paper.

Ryder was already well over sixty and on the lip of retirement when GME arrived in his studio, so when another practitioner, Edgar Decker (1833-1905), was in need of a younger partner GME seized the opportunity. Decker had practiced photography in Cleveland since 1856 and had gained fame for his group portraits of local Civil War regiments. Separated in age by more than three decades, Decker and Edmondson became close friends, taking photographic expeditions together to points in and around Cleveland. On one of these Decker took a portrait of Edmondson with his camera that marvelously captures the young man at the moment his career was taking off.

Ryder portrait of George M Edmondson on Lake Erie, sold on Ebay to unknown buyer.

For more than a decade the two practiced together, during which time Edmondson advanced to the forefront of photographers in Cleveland and then in America. By 1900, when Decker retired and GME put his own name on the studio, the thirty-four-year-old photographer from Norwalk had already been elected president of the Photographers' Association of Ohio and vice-president of the Photographers' Association of America, the main professional organization in the field. In 1902 the latter group named him president and a year later bestowed on him honorary life membership.

Accounting for Edmondson's rapid rise, a local journalist noted that he "combines artistic skills of rare quality with a vigorous, aggressive nature in a way that compels success."[178] This was certainly true, but only part of the story. For over the previous generation Clevelanders had transformed the formerly quiet mid-western town into an institutional and financial center of America's new industrial economy. Huge ships owned by Cleveland entrepreneurs like Samuel Mather carried iron ore from Minnesota to sprawling furnaces along the Cuyahoga River, or for transshipment by rail from Cleveland to Pittsburgh. Cleveland's John D. Rockefeller was now the richest man on earth, thanks to the Standard Oil Company which he founded in Cleveland in 1870. Jeptha Wade founded and headed the Western Union Telegraph Company in Cleveland; the van Sweringen brothers parlayed a few regional interurban rail lines into a national railroad empire; while inventor Charles Brush made a fortune by bringing electric lighting to America's cities and developing the world's most efficient electric generators.

These and many other innovators and entrepreneurs all built grand residences along Cleveland's grand thoroughfare, Euclid Avenue.[179] Varying in style from Gothic and Norman to neo-classical and Second Empire, these palaces equaled or surpassed in size and opulence anything in America at the time. For decades the design and construction of these palaces had preoccupied the industrial titans who built them. Once completed, the builders turned their attention to immortalizing themselves, their wives, and families through portraits. Painters like Will Edmondson toiled to depict the self-made owners of new wealth as solid and responsible burghers and their wives as ladies of grace and sophisticated. But no painter and no other photographer came close to George Mountain Edmondson in portraying the captains of Cleveland industry, their families, and even their palazzos as they wanted to be and as they actually were. Just as Diego Velasquez captured the human face of the Spanish court in the Golden Age and Anthony van Dyck did for Stuart England, George Mountain Edmondson became the visual chronicler and leading artist of Cleveland during its most opulent decades.

Edmondson's output was phenomenal. The Edmondson archive at the Cleveland Public Library numbers more than 2,000 images, but hundreds of others are preserved at the Western Reserve Historical Society, the Cuyahoga County Archives, and in untold numbers of private collections. Virtually every leader of local life came to his studio at 2362 Euclid Avenue or, later, to his studio in his London-plan town house on East 97th Street, to have their portraits taken. Many returned again and again: Samuel Mather and John D. Rockefeller commissioned twenty-five Edmondson portraits each, the latter both before and after he began wearing a wig. Edmondson did a total of fifty-two portraits of other members of the Rockefeller family, not counting the scores of pictures of their residences. Former Senator and political king-maker Marcus Alonzo Hanna alone commissioned forty-nine portraits. Lawyers, bishops, and manufacturers all crystalized their status by commissioning Edmondson to do portraits of themselves.

Dinner at Mr. and Mrs. Mark Hannah's, with president and Mrs. William McKinley, John Hay, etc., Cleveland, ca. 1899.

Most, but not all Edmondson portraits were of Clevelanders, but he also did national and international figures. Among these were Presidents William McKinley and Teddy Roosevelt and his wife, Alice. John Hay, a member of the Cleveland Establishment who had served both as Lincoln's secretary and Secretary of State under McKinley and Roosevelt, also sat for him. While still with Decker, Edmondson was summoned to composer Richard Strauss' private railroad car to do his portrait and later did several portraits of pianist and composer Sergei Rachmaninoff.

John D. Rockefeller, 1910, one of scores of portraits of the magnate by George Edmondson, Cleveland Public Library.

Edmondson owed some of his success to his open and engaging personality. His first studio at 2362 Euclid Avenue at Fortieth Street was the only commercial building on the most elegant part of the avenue. Nearby stood the lordly mansion of Secretary of State John Hay. There, and at his later studio on East 96th Street, he held court for two generations of Cleveland society. He was both a lively and humorous talker and a sympathetic listener and easily broke out with uproarious laughter. It did not hurt that he kept a good liquor cabinet, even during Prohibition. Cleveland's newspaper editors, cultural leaders, and philanthropists dropped by Edmondson's simply to chat with someone they considered one of the city's most engaging and best-loved citizens. The Catholic bishop was a regular, and said of his friend Edmondson that "If there were more like him there would be no need for a Church."[180]

But beyond all the bonhomie, George Edmondson was a deeply committed artist and master practitioner of a technologically sophisticated craft. Had this not been the case he would never had achieved the professional success he did. Portrait photography had been practiced since the moment painter and portraitist Louis Daguerre presented his new invention to the French Academie des Sciences in 1839. From the outset, the presentation of human subjects in the new medium was pulled between literal documentation and prevailing trends in painted portraits. To the extent that photography altered portraiture in its early years it was to introduce a greater element of spontaneity.

George Mountain Edmondson's approach to portraiture, unlike that of his father, was firmly rooted in the world of painting. In portrait after portrait one immediately detects the presence of painterly methods and techniques. For example, his seated portrait of the elderly Cleveland businessman and philanthropist John L. Severance, who donated the money to build Severance Hall for the Cleveland Orchestra, is taken from waist height, looking up. By this simple ploy Edmondson made the diminutive Severance appear like a Roman senator in a frock coat. His portrait of Severance's wife reveals every glint and fold of her stiff silk dress. The slight backlight coming through her grey, curly hair frames the face in a way that enables every feature to stand forth as if it is sculpted out of marble. When he posed the two of them together he indicated their inter-dependence without sacrificing formality, presenting the couple as stern yet thoughtful, dignified but humane, and above all as a timeless image of Prosperity in the service of Civic Responsibility.

The same could be said of Edmondson's portrait of philanthropist and feminist Alice Wade Everett. Elegantly posed and wearing an informal skirt and white blouse that is backlit from a window, Mrs. Wade sits at her desk and looks intently at the camera, as if evaluating some civic project. This is a far cry from his many portraits of women in luxurious evening dresses, painted in the grand manner and exuding the opulence of the Edwardian era. Yet the method is the same, namely, to pay careful attention to every detail of the meticulously posed subject, yet at the same time capturing the personality to the fullest extent possible. Here is how a contemporary critic described his approach:

> Mr. Edmondson was more concerned with his sitter than on equipment. Using little more than an eight-tube studio portrait skylight, the photographer established a genuine rapport with his subject. In one of his speeches before members of the Photographers' Association of America, Mr. Edmondson urged, "Do not give the impression of being fussy. It tends only to annoy the sitter and to prevent spontaneity of expression." He further relied heavily upon inspiration, and his approach to portraiture mirrored that of an improvisational musician. The results were stunning and uniquely original portraits that revealed the spiritual and emotional essence of Mr. Edmondson's sitters.[181]

This could have been a description of the working method of the American painter John Singer Sargent (1856-1915), the most renowned portrait painter of the era. Raised in France and a graduate of the prestigious Ecole des Beaux Arts, Sargent attained such mastery that he could sketch directly on canvas with the brush. This enabled him to infuse his subjects with remarkable spontaneity and individuality. His decision to focus on portraiture was a natural one in the 1880s, for it offered the best avenue to an art career. When he arrived back in New York in 1887, he secured commissions from precisely the same kind of newly enriched American grandees who were to become Edmondson's patrons a decade later.

Sargent was at the height of his fame in the same years that Edmondson was launching his own career in Cleveland. Thanks to his brother Will, Edmondson was closely attuned to the world of painting and was quick to seize on Sargent as the best model for what he aspired to achieve in photography. He studied Sargent's technique closely and sensed that it would be possible to achieve as much or more individuality and spontaneity with the photographic camera as Sargent did with the brush. Indeed, many of Edmondson's portraits of women directly call to mind prototypes from Sargent's oeuvre. Edmondson became the John Singer Sargent of American photographers.

George M. Edmondson's studio and home, East 96th Street, Cleveland, about 1920.

In one area Edmondson went beyond his master. That he was a "society" photographer meant that many of his commissions were of women and children. However, Cleveland society was defined above all by self-made men, powerful personalities who were literally transforming the world about them. It is in these portraits that Edmonson achieved particular distinction. Time after time he captured the sheer force of personality that accounted for his sitters' worldly success. Thus, his head-and-shoulders portrait of inventor and entrepreneur Charles Brush depicts the subject as if he had just been presented with a new idea, which he was weighing carefully and with a touch of skepticism. John D. Rockefeller, by contrast, emerges in a 1910 portrait as shrewd, wily, and enigmatic, a far cry from the oil portrait Sargent himself did seven year, in which Rockefeller seems lax and disengaged, in fact, as if sitting for his portrait.

Alice Wade Everett, by George M./ Edmondson (Cleveland Public Library).

Mark Hanna, by George M. Edmondson (Cleveland Public Library).

Edmondson's most lasting achievement was as an artist in the realm of portraiture. However, this rested on his solid mastery of the technical aspects of photography as they existed in the early twentieth century. So important were his skills in this area that contemporaries immediately recognized that this was a second area in which he achieved lasting distinction. Following in his father's footsteps, George Mountain Edmondson was fascinated by the challenge of making precise and evenly textured enlargements from the small-format glass plates that emerged from his camera. His large format prints of portraits and architectural subjects are remarkable for their precision and consistency of tone.

This in turn arose from his absolute mastery of the printing process. He considered printing to be fully as important as shooting the image and devoted endless hours to achieving just the right finish for each print. The combination of precision and painterly softness that characterize Edmondson's prints was the fruit of immense effort on his part, involving complex chemical processes that he developed on his own through experiments extending over decades. Contemporary photographers understood that this was the very essence of his art and urged him to write a book on the subject. Charles Abel, editor of The Professional Photographer, went so far as to volunteer to ghost write such a book. But Edmondson was unwilling to share his secrets with anyone and he took them to his grave.

After his death, thousands of his glass photographic plates from a lifetime of work ended up in the Cleveland Public Library. Unable to store them all, the Library ordered glossy and crude contact prints to be made of each plate, after which the plates themselves were destroyed. Due to this foolish act, it will never be possible fully to understand the chemistry and technology of Edmondson's darkroom work, by which he transformed plain images on glass into magically evocative prints. The best that can be done today is to study the few original prints preserved by descendants of his patrons.

George M. Edmondson in 1905, self-portrait. S.F. Starr

A third area in which George M. Edmondson achieved distinction was in the realm of architectural photography. Today this is a large and developed field in its own right, supported by a diversity of wide-angle lenses, highly sensitive cameras, and sophisticated lighting systems. A hundred years ago anyone venturing into the world of architectural and interior photography had to adapt the same equipment he used for studio portraits. Many before Edmondson had taken architecture as their subject, but most of his predecessors were interested more in achieving painterly effects than in creating a precise yet evocative image of the scene. Thus, when Edward Steichen did his renowned portrait of "The Flatiron Building at Night" (1904) his challenge, as he defined it, was to translate the mood of Whistler's nocturnal paintings into the new medium of photography. Edmondson's mission was different: to document buildings and interiors in a manner that was both accurate and evocative of the way of life to which the owner aspired. For a civic building or bank this became a glorification of dignified and responsible government or commerce; for the homes of Cleveland's scores of self-made business magnates it became a celebration of wealth, good taste, and gentility.

The commissioning of an album of portraits of one's home was a serious matter in the first three decades of the twentieth century. For Edmondson, it meant transporting a mass of equipment to the site, which, as in the case of John D. Rockefeller's winter residence "The Casements" at Ormond Beach, Florida, could mean long-distance travel. Waiting for the right seasonal light, he would then produce up to three dozen images, the best of which he would print in large format and in such a way as to produce a soft and velvety effect. These would then be bound in tooled and embossed leather albums specially ordered from Florence, Italy, through Edmondson's friend Lou Rorimer. After the 1929 stock market crash, which took the swagger out of many former titans of industry, such albums were a means of reminding close friends and associates of vanished glory.[182] So successful was Edmondson in this specialized field that his approach set the tone for several generations of American architectural photographers.

A fourth field in which Edmondson became a pioneering practitioner was color photography. From the earliest days of photography this had been the Holy Grail that inventors and experimenters labored to discover. When Edmondson's father advertised that he could tint any photograph with watercolors or oil paints he was merely responding in a low-tech way to what everyone who commissioned a photograph from him really wanted. The path to color photography began back in the 1860s when the Scottish physicist James Clerk Maxwell demonstrated how all hues could be derived from only three basic colors. But research to develop true color photography did not gain momentum until the turn of the century. Chemist Adolf Miethe in Germany began manufacturing a high-quality color camera in 1903 and within five years his Russian disciple, Sergei Prokudin-Gorsky, was doing a color portrait of novelist Lev Tolstoy. The American pioneer in color photography was Frederick Ives (1856-1937), who in 1898 began producing what he called "Kromskop" color photography in the U.S. And in 1903 the Lumiere brothers patented their "Autochrome Lumiere" system in France and began producing it in 1907.

Thus, the years of most intensive development of color photography began at the end of Edmondson's apprenticeship with Decker and the start of his own studio. It is all the more astonishing that he was making a name for himself in color photography as early as 1900--- three years before the German or French systems became commercially available and when Ives' inferior system remained unknown even in America. Edmondson's activity in this nascent field was so well known that the press could tout that "One of his latest achievements is color photography, of which art he is now one of the three American masters.[183]

George Edmondson used color photography for both portraits and architectural images. He employed it in his album on Rockefeller's Florida estate and many other major commissions. Though he used mainly the Lumiere brothers' system, he continued over several decades to experiment with new techniques. His daughter remembered hauling to outdoor shoots boxes containing inks of the three basic colors. Unfortunately, if any glass negatives for color photographs remained when his studio was disbanded they were destroyed after low quality black-and-white prints were made from them. No other color photographs by George M. Edmondson have yet come to light.

By 1900 newspapers regularly reported that "competent critics acknowledge that [George M. Edmondson] is one of the America's foremost photographers."[184] After being elected president of the Photographers Association of America, the Association granted him honorary life membership three years later. Numerous other honors were showered on him over the following years. But in the end, he was nudged to one side and was denied the place he had earned in the history of his art and his profession. It is worth asking why this occurred.

In one case, it can be traced to personal relations. In 1927 a young woman from New Jersey named Margaret Bourke-White settled in Cleveland. She had been briefly married but was now divorced and intent on a career in photography. She therefore presented herself to Edmondson, who gladly took her on as a student and assistant and even invited her to live with the family in the Edmondson household on East 96th Street. Over several months she worked closely with Edmondson, so closely, in fact, that Minnie Edmondson came to the conclusion that she was flirting with her husband. This led to the immediate termination of Margaret Bourke-White's apprenticeship.

Launched on her own, Bourke-White tried to gain commissions for portraits. Failing at that, she turned to the photographing stately homes and gardens in Cleveland and Cincinnati, in other words, to making inroads on Edmondson's business. This work dried up with the Depression so she turned next to photographing Cleveland's dramatic bridges and industrial structures, which earned her an invitation from Henry Luce to become a photo-journalist for <u>Time</u>.[185] She went on to a brilliant career documenting the gritty America of the 1930s but never mentioned her debt to Edmondson in anything she wrote or said.

A deeper reason for the later neglect of Edmondson's contribution to his art is that the nature of photography itself was changing profoundly just as his career reached its zenith. Neither George M. Edmondson nor his father doubted for a minute that photography was an art, and a high one at that. But throughout the late nineteenth century photography, like painting, was struggling to break free of the traditional forms of art patronage, i.e., official institutions, major museums, and wealthy Maecenases. Rallying under the French banner of "l'art pour l'art," many American photographers after 1900 championed a break with traditional patrons and traditional subject matter. Many others embraced the idea that photography could find a great and innovative new field in the commercial realm, freed from the demands of rich patrons.

The person who did most to propound an "l'art pour l'art" approach to photography was the Japanese-German born art critic, Karl Sadakichi Hartmann (1867-1944). An early fan of Alfred Stieglitz, Hartmann in 1903 started his own journal Camera Work, which quickly faded. The next year he played a role in mounting the first American Photographic Salon, in imitation of the French Impressionists salons. This, too, failed, but the vain and hard-drinking Bohemian had launched a career that took him eventually to Hollywood. At some point before 1915 Hartmann discovered the work of George Edmondson at an exhibition in Europe and came to Cleveland to study with him. But the two contemporaries were on totally different wave lengths and the relationship quickly ended. Edmondson, according to his daughter, considered Hartmann "a wild kid."[186] Hartmann went on to write many volumes on modern American photographers but never mentioned Edmondson.

Whatever personal differences may have existed, it is natural that neither Bourke-White nor Hartmann gave Edmondson his due. Edmondson was over sixty when Bourke-White arrived at his door and Hartmann, though a contemporary, belonged culturally to a younger generation as well. Edmondson was a working photographer who had developed his own public and market, working entirely on his own. In terms of both technological skill and artistry he stood at the top of the field. But the niche he had created, and upon which he depended for his livelihood and his family's welfare was tied up with a single generation of industrialists, bankers, and politicians who had made Cleveland a center of America's economic life. However innovative these industrial barons were in their working life, they were quite traditional when they came to spending their money. Their self-image and way of life had more in common with Londoners or Parisians in the Belle Époque than with those in Europe or America who were already rebelling against it. Portraiture is inherently a conservative art, and Edmondson, for better or worse, was the photographic master of that art as it existed in the years 1895-1920.

Edmondson was *the* artist-photographer of choice for the denizens of Cleveland's Euclid Avenue, not Paris' Left Bank, London's Bloomsbury, or Greenwich Village. He was a master at what he did, just as John Singer Sargent had been in his day. Edmondson translated Sargent's world onto the shores of Lake Erie, and with impressive success. But just as Sargent was considered passé when he closed his studio in 1907, so was Edmondson by the time of the Wall Street Crash in 1929. But both remain brilliant artists who created enduring links between their patrons and posterity.

To this point our focus has been on George Mountain Edmondson's professional life as a photographer and artist. However, his personal life warrants at least as much attention, for over a decade it was marked by such giddy high points and such wrenching tragedies that it is a wonder that he survived it all. Any fair appreciation of the man should begin and end with a close focus on his private world. For reasons that will become clear, the dramatic story of his life between his move to Cleveland in 1887 and the establishment of Edmondson Studios in 1902 was largely unknown even to his own children. Fortunately, it can now be reconstructed in some detail.

Even though George Edmondson was from boyhood a gregarious and good-natured person, the demands placed upon him by his father's wayward existence and by his decision that his son follow him into the field of photography were onerous.

While in Norwalk the family survived on a pittance, and when young George became its sole source of support after his father departed for Paris with brother Will, the burden on him increased further. Nonetheless, he was able to buy a printing press, through which he earned enough money to enable him to hire carriages and sleighs for outings with young ladies from Norwalk.

When his father returned from Paris, young George announced his decision to move to Cleveland. No sooner had he settled in a rented apartment in Cleveland than he appeared before Norwalk's Probate Judge Henry Kennan (a great uncle of diplomat George F. Kennan) to obtain a marriage license.[187] On 18 October, 1888 the <u>Norwalk Daily Reflector</u> announced the marriage of George Mountain Edmondson and Jane Adelaide ("Daisy") Williams in an Episcopal service. The home wedding was "informal," and the bride wore a dark blue travelling dress. "The newspaper confided that "Miss Daisy, the bride, had always been voted one of Norwalk's most beautiful and attractive young ladies." while the groom, "well, he looked as if he had drawn a capital prize, and he had." Immediately following the ceremony the couple took the evening train to Cleveland.

The next notice of the young couple appeared in the Norwalk Weekly Reflector on 29 July 1890, with the announcement of the funeral of "little baby Edmondson." Two preachers presided over the infant's interment in Woodlawn Cemetery.

Then on 25 May, 1893 the Norwalk Chronicle, in a report headlined "A Sad Incident," reported on the death of Gertrude, a second daughter of George and Daisy Edmondson. Gertrude was buried next to her sister in Woodlawn Cemetery.

Two years later, on 24 October, 1895, the Norwalk Chronicle announced that a third Edmondson daughter, Margaret, had died at the home of Daisy Edmondson's parents on Bank Street in Norwalk.

George and Daisy had known each other since infancy. She was born in Plymouth, Ohio, in 1866, in other words, in the same place and year as her future husband. In 1882, at the age of sixteen, she had "contracted a severe cold."[188] For half a decade before her marriage Daisy suffered from poor health. Only some years later was her "severe cold" diagnosed as the onset of tuberculosis, by which time she had lost three children.

As the local paper reported, "During all these years she resisted with a most marvelous will power the encroachment of the dread disease, and year by year warded off the final summons."[189] Daisy Williams Edmondson died at the Bank Street home of her parents on 18 February, 1899. The obituary took note of her "quiet, unassuming life." "Possessed of a sweet, loving disposition, always cheerful and uncomplaining, her life, instead of being a deep shadow, was perpetual sunshine, filled with a divine fragrance."

Daisy's father, a Civil War veteran who had suffered a severe leg wound at the Battle of Chancellorsville, was the treasurer of Huron County and "a man of invincible character and disposition."[190] Upon his daughter' death Captain Oliver Williams published a poem:

> Rest, darling one, so many years
> The bitterest sufferings have pursued thee;
> Now all our hopes and all our fears
> Are stilled, for rest has wood thee.
> Rest peacefully.

A few years later Captain Williams, facing paralysis and mourning the loss of his daughter, used his 32-caliber revolver to commit suicide.[191]

These terrible events, extending over eleven years, took place in the very period in which Edmondson was establishing himself as a photographer in Cleveland, carrying out his experiments with color photography, and gaining regional and national recognition as a photographer. We can only imagine how he dealt with them on a day-to-day basis, cared for his wife, and then commuted to Norwalk when she became too ill for him to care for her in Cleveland. Members of his family doubtless did what they could. His elder colleague Decker also tried to look out for him, as that was the apparent purpose of the several informal photographic trips they made together to Wade Park and to the Cleveland waterfront during these years. But in facing the suffering and death of three daughters and his wife he was essentially alone.

Edmondson showed formidable resilience in the face of devastating blows. He remained outgoing and gregarious, so much so that, as Minnie later confided to her daughter, fashionable young women in Cleveland began arranging to sit for their portraits in hopes of making contact with the young widower. But after a year spent pretending all was well, his will to go on collapsed. Wracked with pain and completely paralyzed with what was then called "inflammatory rheumatism," he was taken to St. Vincent's Catholic Charity Hospital in Cleveland. It was a modern hospital where the doctors "believed in the germ theory," as Edmondson's nursing nun later reported. And since germs resided in the mouth, they pulled all his teeth. But this remedy did nothing for him and his condition worsened.

Since he could not even hold a book to read, Edmondson's only diversion in that pre-electronic was to whistle, which he managed to do with gusto, even without teeth. The attending nurse noticed this and was impressed, not least because Edmondson was her very first patient. When other nurses asked why this obviously healthy person was in the hospital she replied defensively that he was the sickest patient in the ward. As she began reading to him he took notice of this handsome, vigorous, and serious young nurse in the wimple and habit of a postulant nun. Under her care his health gradually improved and with it his spirits. By the time he left the hospital he was set on marrying her.

Wilhelmina Niesen Edmondson (1876_-1958)

The aspiring nun whom George M. Edmondson met and fell in love with was named Wilhelmina Regina Niesen. Friends called her Minnie. She was a full decade younger than her first patient. As they began to converse she told him that she, too, was a second-generation immigrant and that she, too, came from a sophisticated small town, in her case Oberlin, only eighteen miles from Norwalk, and had come to Cleveland to seek her fortune. But the similarities ended there, for they came in fact from starkly different worlds, separated from each other by a cultural chasm.

Minnie may have been living in Oberlin but she was actually from Amherst, Ohio, just south of Lake Erie and twenty-eight miles from Norwalk. If Norwalk was a solidly Yankee and Protestant town, Amherst, where the Niesens lived, was just as solidly German and Catholic. Norwalk's main street was, and is, lined with handsome Greek revival homes and churches in the chaste Western Reserve style; Amherst's with modest wooden houses, some of them with gable-ends facing the street, German style. Norwalk was a cultivated town with its own Gardener Concert Hall and a theater frequently visited by touring Shakespearian companies. Even a young photographer who grew up there would be able to spout lines from the Bard that were appropriate for any occasion. Amherst had a single school, and its cultural life was defined mainly by the Catholic Church.

Peter Niesen and Regina Kracht, Minnie's parents, had arrived by separate ships from Germany in 1867, he on 17 June and she on August 12, from Bremen.[192] They went immediately to Amherst, obtained a marriage contract from the local Probate Court on November 3, and were married immediately thereafter.[193] Peter was twenty-six and his wife seventeen. His age is important for it sheds light on his reasons for coming to America.

Niesen had been born in the farming village of Wallersheim in what is now the German state of Rhineland-Palatinate. Alois Niesen, a descendent, now lives across the street in Wallersheim from the house in which Peter grew up. Roger Huss, an American descendent of a Niesen who emigrated to Wisconsin a decade before Peter Niesen went to Ohio, sought out these modern members of the Niesen family and learned that the earliest known Niesens had moved to Wallersheim early in the nineteenth century.[194] Wallersheim is situated on rolling land amidst the low Eifel Mountains close by the German borders with France, Luxemburg, and Belgium. Forty-five miles due north of the ancient Roman city of Trier and about the same distance from Luxemburg, it is, fifty miles from the wine center of Bernkastel, sixty miles from Coblenz, and seventy-eight miles from Aachen. Even today its population is a mere 742.

A curious family tradition tracing to Minnie herself maintains that Peter Niesen had been drafted into the French army during the Franco-Prussian War, was injured and then captured, that he ran off with his nurse and was disowned by his parents for marrying beneath his station. The same tradition portrays Niesen as well educated, even a university graduate.

Where did he meet Regina Kracht? Niesen's wife was born in 1850, making her only seventeen at the time of her marriage to Niesen. Her home town was Seeburg, a tiny hamlet fourteen miles east of Gottingen on an attractive lake in what is today Lower Saxony. Birth records from this village of 1200 indicate that her mother's maiden name had been Plothe, that her godparents both bore that name, and that by the time she met Peter Niesen she was an orphan.[195] Several members of the Plothe family emigrated to America before the Civil War and ended up in Amherst, Ohio. American immigration officers recorded their name phonetically, transforming it into the more recognizable "Plato." While still a child Regina was left an orphan, to be raised by her Plothe/Plato relatives.

Since Wallersheim and Seeburg are 250 miles apart, the couple would have to have met while one or both of them were traveling. It is also clear that the Niesen family disapproved of the union--their daughter Minnie considered it a fact that the Krachts stood far below the Niesens in terms of wealth and education—and that this may have prompted the young couple to run off to America to marry. The Niesens may also have objected to Peter's move to Ohio, as his older sister had already married in Germany and emigrated with another brother to Wisconsin, where both families were living happily.[196] Either version would explain the story of Peter being disinherited, and of his later return trip to Wallersheim in an attempt to make amends with his father. The young couple chose to settle in Amherst, Ohio, because several members of the Plothe/Plato family had already put down roots there.

The problem with this is that after the fall of Napoleon the Rhineland reverted to Prussian rule. If Niesen had either served in the army or fled to avoid service, the army in question would have been Prussian, not French. It is possible that Niesen served in the Prussian army and then fled, or that he fled to avoid service in the first place. That he had his picture taken in the fortress town of Saarlouis wearing what appears to be a cadet's uniform suggests that he did indeed serve and either finished his service before 1866 or, less likely, that he went AWOL.

Over the next nine years the Niesens had five children, the youngest of whom was Wilhelmina (Minnie), born in 1878. Peter Niesen was listed in the U.S. Census for 1870 as running a boarding house, but this venture soon failed and he took employment with what was rapidly becoming Amherst's main enterprise, the enormous sandstone quarries. When Germans founded Amherst, Ohio back in 1811, farming and viticulture were the main occupations. But beneath the town and throughout the surrounding countryside were some of the best deposits of architectural sandstone in North America. By the 1870s nine quarries had been opened there, and the largest of them—the immense Buckeye Quarry— stretched to a cavernous depth of 240 feet and was already reputed to be the largest sandstone quarry on earth. As this and other local quarries came to look like Grand Canyon, the town began promoting itself as "The Sandstone Capital of the World." The only local industry to rival sandstone was the production of wine, which was consumed mainly by the Alsatians and other Germans who worked there.

Carte de visite of Peter Niesen, Saarlouis, France, ca. 1866. S. F. Starr

Peter Niesen was said by his descendants to have been a bookish sort; some even claimed –with no supporting evidence--that he had attended the University at Strasburg and spoke seven languages. His granddaughter, presumably on the basis of reports from her mother, Minnie Niesen Edmondson, even said that he wrote poetry. But if he had been so well educated, one wonders why he was not employed at the quarry offices, perhaps as a bookkeeper? Unfortunately, the quarry records have been lost so we don't know what his actual job was. One of his daughters, who assumed he worked in the quarries themselves, handed down the blunt judgment that "he didn't know what physical work meant."[197] His daughter Minnie wrote to relatives in Wallersheim in 1897 that he had saved little and drank much.[198] He never became a U.S. citizen. His family believed that he contracted "Stone Consumption."

Buckeye Quarry, where Minnie's father, Peter Niesen, labored.

What is clear is that Peter Niesen could not support his family of seven. In 1878 he therefore swallowed his pride and returned to Germany in hopes of gaining his father's forgiveness and receiving his inheritance. He failed, and by 1880 the family in Amherst concluded from his silence that he was dead. Since no record of his death has yet turned up in Germany (or in Ohio, for that matter) this cannot be confirmed, but their word was sufficient for the Lorain County Probate Court in 1881 to name Regina Niesen the head of the family and Henry Plato of Amherst as his executor. Niesen's estate consisted of "zero dollars" and his modest frame house on Middle Street.[199]

Regina Niesen found herself in a dreadful situation, stranded in "an ugly place which she hated,"[200] with five children and no source of income. Her daughter Minnie later recalled her sobbing, "Why did we ever come to this awful country?" Worse, she had extremely poor eyesight, the result of having accepted a dare from other children in Seeheim to stare at the sun. The "blue vitriol" (copper sulfate) that an Amherst doctor applied in a failed attempt to recover her vision left her functionally blind. Her granddaughter, Ivy Jane Edmondson Starr, remembered seeing a photograph of her hanging above a bed in her Aunt Elizabeth's home in Amherst: "I shall always remember it for her square jaw and determined look. My mother (Minnie) must have looked like her." [201]

But a square jaw and determination did not suffice. Faced with a dire situation, Regina Niesen did what nineteenth century Americans always did when facing hardship: she turned to her relatives. Her first step was to "farm out" her middle daughter Elizabeth to a kinsman of her Plato relative in Amherst.²⁰² Her uncle Henry A. Plato Sr., who had emigrated in 1856, had done well in Amherst, first as a dry goods merchant and then as a founder and director of the Savings Deposit Bank. His son, Henry Plato Jr., had also prospered, marrying into the family of Wesbeckers from Baden, who owned the local hardware store and furniture factory and directed the Amherst German Bank.²⁰³ Both stores, solid brick buildings, appear in early postcards of Amherst. It was to various Westbeckers that Regina Niesen farmed out her other children. From 1881 until her death in 1897 Regina Niesen lived on handouts from these relatives and from the Catholic Church.

Church Street, Amherst, with Plato stores to right and left, ca. 1915.

One of Minnie Niesen's earliest memories was of helping her blind mother harvest potatoes in their garden while the older children were in school. As Minnie dug, her mother would rummage around in the loosened earth for the potatoes; Minnie guided her mother's hands from mound to mound. It was clear that Regina's ability to manage the household was slipping, so her oldest child, John, increasingly functioned as head of the family. Seventeen years old in 1885, he was by nature a strong leader. In later years he became a master stonemason and respected civic leader who was responsible for building Amherst's City Hall and St. Joseph's Catholic Church, as well as most of the courthouses and official buildings throughout the region. Several pamphlets published by the town, and also the county history, said of him that "His work is first class, having assisted in the erection of most of the public buildings of the village. He is interested in the improvement of the town and is a highly-respected citizen." The solid house he built for himself still stands at the corner of Middle Street and Cross Avenue in Amherst and many descendant with names like Niesen, Stumphauser, Gil, and Wohlever still live nearby.

John Niesen was a born leader but he could not manage his youngest sister, Minnie. Though she and the family were all devout Catholics, as a young girl she would sneak into the Methodist Church at night and sing hymns with them.²⁰⁴ When the older children took wagons to collect kindling wood to sell, Minnie, then age seven, wanted to do the same. So she went to Plato's Hardware and charged a wagon to her brother. When John received the bill a terrible quarrel ensued. Realizing he could not tame his youngest sibling, he sent her off to live with an aunt related to the Niesens by marriage.

Amherst, Ohio City Hall, one of many buildings built by Minnie's brother, John Niesen.

"Grandma Westbecker,"[205] as Minnie called her, was a widow and the harassed mother of a large brood who lived on a farm outside Brownhelm, Ohio. Had Minnie Edmondson been consistent in her general silence about her relatives, "Grandma Westbecker" would have been a candidate for total oblivion. But this uneducated farm wife from Brownhelm Township came to occupy a special place in Minnie Edmondson's cosmology, not for the saintliness of her character but because Minnie considered hershe was the embodiment of evil.

Brownhelm Township, where Grandma Westbecker farmed, is a rural area adjoining Lake Erie and the site of many vineyards established by immigrants from the Rhineland. For many years she and her husband had run a bar in Amherst. She had become notorious for encouraging quarry workers (like Peter Niesen) to drink to oblivion, running up large tabs in the process. She would then empty their pockets. According to one of Minnie's sisters, the women of Amherst declared that "If by accident the gates of Heaven would open to her the Devil would hang onto her feet and pull her back."[206]

Her husband was now dead and Grandma Westbecker lived solely off the vineyard that had earlier produced wine for the bar. To keep track of her children as she prepared breakfast each day Grandma Plato would order them to shout their prayers at the top of their lungs. Not surprisingly, they were a crude and hardened lot, and missed no chance to torment the new town girl in their midst. Minnie's daughter recalled that fifty years later her mother would rock in her chair and say with satisfaction of Grandma Westbecker that "She lived to see retribution. All her children died violent deaths. One threw himself in front of a train. One got drunk and drowned in a ditch. One drowned herself in Lake Kissimee, Florida, and there were two others who ended just as badly."[207]

At about age twelve Minnie responded to this dreadful regimen by running away to Cleveland, following the tracks of the interurban railroad. Along the way she encountered bums camping in the nearby woods. Whenever she sensed that she was nearing such a group she would speak loudly, as if conversing with a group of fellow hikers. This succeeded, but in the end she was hauled back to Bornholm and duly punished. Her next attempt to run away came a year later, when she was thirteen. This time she headed south by foot to the town of Oberlin, eighteen miles away. The next thing we know of her is that she was taken in as a maid by Professor John Demuth of the Oberlin Conservatory of Music. How she met th forty-one year old Demuth is unknown, but it is most likely that she simply went from door to door offering her services as a house girl.

The duties of a maid or house girl were simple: to clean, sweep, do the washing, and help in the kitchen—seven days a week. By the time she finally left the Demuth household a decade later Minnie was receiving twelve dollars a month for these services, plus room and board.[208] In earlier years she received much less. An unskilled Ohio farm hand received twenty-two dollars a month in those years.[209]

Minnie Niesen moved into an attic room in the Demuth's comfortable Queen Anne style house at 183 Elm Street in Oberlin and spent her pre-teen and teenage years in the Demuth household. Her mother was by now slipping into dementia, and Minnie's relations with her older brother Peter had not improved since she ran away from home. It was therefore natural for Minnie to look on the Demuths as family, or as much a family as she had. The Demuths had three children of their own, but treated Minnie kindly. Professor Demuth became "Uncle John" and his wife was "Aunt Lotte."

Demuth was in equal parts a talented musician and an eccentric. A graduate of West Point, he had turned to music and by the time Minnie showed up on his doorstep he had become the Conservatory's first professor of clarinet and its one-man woodwind department. He led both the College and town bands, which held forth at a Victorian bandstand that he had had erected on the southeast of the Square. Demuth's eccentricity revealed itself in his endless experiments with clocks and timekeeping systems. By the turn of the century he had equipped the entire College with his patented system of synchronized clocks, a useful tool in a school dedicated to the orderly and efficient ideal of human perfection. But Uncle John's grand system did not endure. Arriving late for a Conservatory faculty meeting in the 1980s, the author of this sketch, who was by then Oberlin's President, glanced at the clock on the wall and noted that it was twenty minutes slow.

Mrs. Demuth was later described by Minnie's daughter as "the sweetest, spunkiest old lady I ever knew." She dressed Minnie like one of her own daughters and gave her motherly advice. A pianist, she also participated in the many chamber music evenings her husband organized on Oak Street. Her daughter Charlotte (later Charlotte Williams) was a violinist who went on to Leipzig to study under Brahms' favorite violinist and friend, Josef Joachim, after which she became a founding member of the famed Cleveland Quartet. A son, Fred, also studied at Leipzig before joining the Cleveland Orchestra and then conducting orchestras as far afield as Honolulu.

In light of the regard the Demuths showed towards their maid-runaway, it is all the more surprising that they did nothing to advance her education. A careful review of both graduation and attendance records of Oberlin High School failed to turn up her name. Indeed, there is not a shred of evidence that Minnie's education continued beyond the fifth grade. Professor and Mrs. Demuth, in other words, thought it was quite acceptable to exploit young Minnie's desperate plight without making any provisions whatsoever for her education or later career, and to sustain this for nearly a decade. When Minnie eventually found a path forward for herself as a nursing nun she did so without any help or assistance from her employers, the Demuths, who stood passively aside. It is worth noting that in these same years Oberlin College bent over backwards assisting young African-Americans to gain a college education and prided itself on this important educational mission.

Clearly, Demuth and his wife were comfortably blind to this hypocrisy, and so was the Oberlin community. The results were predictable. Aside from the Demuth children, Minnie formed no lasting friendships among her contemporaries or students in Oberlin. And even though the Demuth children were of roughly the same age as their "house girl," it never occurred to Professor and Mrs. Demuth that their German housemaid might also want to sing or play the music of Bach or Schumann.

However, thanks to the Demuths Minnie would always believe that music is somehow Important. And thanks to the community of which the Demuths were a part, she believed that serious people do serious things in the world. Her informal education began with their next-door neighbor, Sarah Bradley, daughter of Dan Beech Bradley (1804-1873), the American medical missionary who brought the first surgery, printing press, and newspaper to Siam (Thailand) and befriended the Buddhist monk who later became Mongkut, the reformist king and the subject of "The King and I." Two doors away lived ambitious widower Chauncey Williams, who came each weekend from Chicago, bringing candy and liquor. After his wife died he was to marry violinist Lottie Demuth and commission his Oak Park neighbor and friend, Frank Lloyd Wright, to design a landmark home for him.

Beyond her "family" and immediate neighbors, Minnie Niesen encountered a college and town founded on the Evangelical doctrine of Perfectionism. Forget about Original Sin, its founder, Charles Grandison Finney, had proclaimed in 1833. Human beings fulfilled God's design by striving to perfect themselves and the society around them. Charged up by this ideal, Oberlinians of the late nineteenth century led the country in the number and commitment of its graduates whom it sent into life-long missionary work abroad. Such an environment generated in Minnie Niesen a lifelong respect for self-improvement and learning. She read everything, and with formidable earnestness searched out the Deep Thoughts contained in the books that passed her way. Though a devout Catholic, Minnie Niesen somehow absorbed this Perfectionism, and to the end of her days considered any deviation from the path to perfection as the sign of a weak will.

By the time she reached age sixteen Minnie realized she needed an education and that she could not get one in Oberlin. So she once more took fate into her own hands. Oberlin was solidly Evangelical, Methodist, and Baptist, but Father McGuire of Amherst came from time to time to offer Mass to the few local Catholics. He told Minnie about the Sisters of Charity in Cleveland, and about the new Charity Hospital at which the nuns all worked as nurses. The Sisters of Charity were known to be highly skilled nurses and effective managers who were running a foundling home, hospital, and home for unmarried mothers. Word was out that they intended soon to open a school of practical nursing at St. Vincent Charity Hospital. Minnie saw her chance. Knowing that the Demuths would not approve her leaving, let alone for the purpose of becoming a nun, for the second time in her life she ran away.

Minnie knew she could not simply go the Oberlin station and get the inter-urban electric railroad, for everyone in town would soon know of it. So she set out for the next station, Elyria, on foot, following the tracks for eight miles. Along the right-of-way she encountered vagrants who eyed her suspiciously, so she whistled to keep up her spirits. She eventually reached Lake Avenue in Cleveland and the newly built Motherhouse of the Sisters of Charity, where she presented herself to the Mother Superior. Sister Marcellin received her very kindly, told her she was much too young, and suggested she return to Oberlin and present herself once again in a few years' time. Minnie swallowed her pride and returned to the Demuths.

Sister Marcellin, by Ivy Jane Starr, ca. 1930, St. Vincent's Hospital, Cleveland.

But she was not to be deterred. With her usual determination, Minnie pored through old copies of The Ladies Home Journal to find out what she needed in order to be a well-dressed young lady in the big city. She then sewed or knitted twelve sweaters, twelve skirts, twelve petticoats, and twelve of everything else, embroidering each article with her initials. So successfully did she prepare her trunks of clothes that when eventually she showed up again on Lake Avenue the other nursing students concluded she came from a rich family. What Minnie had not realized was that the Sisters of Charity and Hospital provided nursing students and candidates for the monastic veil with all the garb their calling required.

Minnie also faced more practical problems. In February, 1896, she received word that relatives had submitted an application for her mother to be committed to the "Infirmary for the Incurably Insane" in Amherst.[210] In its judgment on the application the Probate Court referred to the Widow Niesen as "an alleged lunatic." What we don't know is whether her mental condition was simply the result of being abandoned by her husband and despair over her blindness and inability to care for her family, or if it arose from more deep-seated psychological or physiological causes, i.e. genetic factors. Under any circumstances, it did not endure long. On February 11, 1897, Regina Kracht Niesen died.[211] Aside from a half interest in the Amherst house, valued at $250, she owned no personal property. Minnie reported this sad news to a cousin, Johann Niesen, in Wallersheim. Written in folksy but confident German, the letter showed impressive tact.[212] There was no mention of her mother's blindness, let alone of her mental state during her last years, or that she had died in an "Infirmary for the Incurably Insane." Instead, Minnie staunchly reported that her mother "had been in ill health for years," that she had "suffered much," and that she simply fell and died.

A few months later Minnie wrote again in her rustic German to Johann, this time to report that she was soon moving to Cleveland to "go to a hospital and pursue my education":

Minnie Niesen, 41 Eichen (Elm) St., Oberlin, Ohio, North America.
15 Jan 1899

Dear Cousin Johann,

I received your letter of December 4 and was happy to hear from you again. If all goes well I will be here for four more weeks. Then I'll be going to Cleveland, which is two hours away from here. It is a city of 100,000 people but does not resemble any European cities, according to the daughter of my people [i.e., Charlotte "Lottie" Demuth] who still lives in Leipzig. There I will go to school and work in a hospital to pursue my education. I must stay there for 2 ½ yrs. If you stay 3 ½ years you are as good as a doctor for many illnesses. I've prepared myself to go there.

I would gladly go to Germany but first I want to go to school. Then I will have a "business." I would not remain forever in Germany. The daughter of these people [i.e., Lottie Demuth] writes that if her people [were to come] there they [wouldn't] want to return to America. But they are very wealthy and have seen everything and don't need to work any longer. She is of the opinion that Prague is the most beautiful city in the world. She writes that the poor people in Germany have it very hard. They must work long and hard for their meager wages. When I finish school I will earn 10 to 20 dollars a week. That is 40-80 marks. Now I earn 12 dollars or 48 marks per month. Here in America the food is a lot cheaper than in Germany, but clothing costs 2 to 3 times as much as in Germany, we've heard little about the war here, only what is in the papers.

As it is, I can't really say if it is better here than for you in Germany. But I can say this: a poor man is worth as much as a rich man. If he wants to work, he can always find employment and earn a good wage if he does what is right. Right now we would be very rich if my father hadn't drunk so much and saved more. If people want to make something of themselves they must always do what is right in all things.

I'll send you my address when I am in Cleveland and then I will write to the other relatives. I hope that you are all healthy and that I will see you all again. The time will pass quickly while I am in Cleveland.²¹³

When Minnie presented herself for the second time in Cleveland Sister Marcellin welcomed her back and accepted her into the training program for nurses and as a postulant nun. The trainees were worked hard. Minnie reported to her sister that the nurses washed the linens of their patients and sometimes had to work all night after a full day's work. But as she said, "I was young, and could stand it." She survived the full program and by 1900 was allowed to enter the wards of St. Vincent's Charity Hospital as a fully-fledged nurse. George M. Edmondson was her first patient.

As the young widower's health improved he opened his eyes to the nurse who had watched over his recovery. Ivy Jane Edmondson Starr later observed that "her fresh country good looks and vigor appealed to him."²¹⁴ As the weeks passed he realized he was in love with her. Minnie Niesen was deeply attracted to him as well, not least because she had never had the experience of caring for another person and having that person return to life under her ministrations. But Minnie had planned her life carefully and the plan did not include marriage, so she turned him down. Only after several months, during which she took counsel from Sister Marcellin, did she allow herself to accept his proposal.

Wilhelmina Niesen at the time of her marriage to George M. Edmondson, 1903, by G.M. Edmondson. S.F. Starr

George Mountain Edmondson and Wilhelmina Regina Niesen were married on April 10, 1901, in the parlor of the Demuth's house on Oak Street in Oberlin. The Oberlin News carried a detailed report of the event:²¹⁵

"A very pretty wedding occurred at the home of Professor and Mrs. Demuth, on Wednesday afternoon, April 10, the contracting parties being Mr. George Mountain Edmondson of Cleveland and Miss Wilhelmina Rejeau (sic.) Neason (sic.) of Oberlin. Miss Neason has been since her girlhood a member of the household of Professor Demuth and possesses the charms and accomplishments which eminently fit her for her new station in life. Mr. Edmondson is a young man of excellent habits and business qualifications and is one of the leading photographic artists in Cleveland.

Several years ago Miss Neason began studies at St. Vincent Hospital in Cleveland with the purpose of becoming a trained nurse. Her first patient after assuming the practical duties of her new calling was Mr. Edmondson, who went to the hospital with a severe case of rheumatism. As the excruciating pains of this disease subsided it became evident that a new malady had set in, caused by the tender ministrations of the young nurse. As this latter was beyond the power of the hospital authorities to treat with any hope of a cure the young man was dismissed, despite his willingness to undergo longer treatment. The new malady grew apace and the wedding on last Wednesday was the result.

"The bride was prettily attired in white, and the groom wore a black frock suit with white waistcoat. The presents were numerous and embraced many articles of utility as well as beauty. The ceremony was performed according to the rites of the Roman Catholic Church, of which the bride is a member, by Father T. F. McGuire. Among the guests from out of town were the following: Mr. and Mrs. Edmondson, parents of the groom; Miss Mountain; the Misses O' Neill; Miss Shield; Miss Adams; and Mr. Bateman of Norwalk.

The carriage which conveyed the bridal couple to the station was elaborately decorated, regardless of expense, with placards and old shoes, the work of a number of young women who are known to have special talent in this line.

After a short tour to New York and other cities in the East the young people will go to housekeeping in Cleveland, a handsome flat being furnished and ready for their occupation."

Three details of this account are worth noting. First, Minnie's maiden name appears not as "Niesen" but as "Neason." This was probably an effort by Minnie to Anglicize her name, but it could also have been the result of simple ignorance, for she had misspelled her mother's maiden name on the marriage license writing "Kraft" instead of "Kracht." Second, not one member of the Niesen family was present, nor anyone else from Amherst besides Father McGuire. Third, neither of the two was presented as having had any kind of life prior to their wedding day. Everyone understood without being told that, for both, it was a new beginning.

George and Minnie Edmondson shortly after their marriage, 1903. S.F. Starr

The Edmondson-Niesen marriage lasted until George's death forty-seven years later. Two children, George and Ivy Jane, were born in 1906 and 1909, respectively. For more than thirty years George Edmondson maintained his standing as one of the country's leading portraitist and the photographer of choice for the Cleveland elite. Success brought its own challenges, however, beginning with the fact that commissions were more numerous than lucrative and many patrons were casual about paying. More than once Edmondson had to rush about town on Christmas Eve to collect outstanding bills. To help meet their budget, in 1921 Minnie organized a tour of Europe for her twelve-year-old daughter Ivy Jane and eight of her friends, with fees from the other girls' families covering the costs for Minnie and her daughter. It is typical that Minnie, who spoke German but had almost no formal education and had travelled beyond northern Ohio only on her wedding trip and on a visit to the St. Louis World's Fair, would venture across England and Europe with the daughters of eight of Cleveland's elite in a state of unwavering self-assurance. Her daughter recalled their running out of money in Florence but this did not deter the intrepid daughter of a stone¬cutter.

Ivy Jane and George Edmondson, Jr., 1912 by G.M. Edmondson. S.F. Starr

The Edmondsons' family budget was complicated by the fact that George had also to cover the housing and living expenses of both his parents, who by this time were living separately, as well as his two maiden aunts. His father continued to hold court at his studio down to his death in 1916, but young George paid his bills too. His mother, Mary Jane Mountain Edmondson, still conducted herself as if she were the belle she had been in 1860. Her sister Anne took in sewing but she was a bad seamstress who found work only because wealthy Cleveland ladies valued her lively and somewhat bawdy conversation and her companionship. George's uncle, John Mountain, who had never married because of the need to support his mother and sisters, used all his savings to build a house near the Edmondsons on East 97th Street, where he and the Mountain ladies resided. On Sundays he and his three sisters made up the core of the choir at the Methodist Episcopal Church in University Circle, dubbed the "Holy Oil Can" on account of its needle-like spire. After church John would visit his former sweetheart, who lived nearby, and recount to her the day's sermon.

Minnie's pampered mother-in-law treated her as a country bumpkin from a boarding house background. One day Minnie's daughter, overhearing her grandmother comment that "Minnie's from the countryside and is used to hard work," gave the elderly and impoverished grande dame a tongue lashing, accompanied by many tears. By contrast, Minnie's husband George deliberately sheltered her from the belle monde of the Cleveland elite in whose company he spent his working life. He would come home from evenings at the great houses with tales of Euclid Avenue princesses so drunk that they had to be helped into their cars. It did not occur to him to bring his wife into such society, but he also knew that it was for her an alien world. Yet he did not hesitate to cast himself as part of the scene, keeping his hair short rather than affecting the longer hair that "artistes" were expected to sport. From time to time his involvement with his patrons led to serious missteps, however, as when several times he lost money on investments promoted to him by wealthy friends, among them former Senator Mark Hanna.

After her marriage Minnie Niesen Edmondson grew ashamed of her background. Old resentments caused her to have no contact with her brother John, who had become a pillar of the Amherst community and whose devotion to hard work and sense of responsibility so closely resembled her own. Only once did she take her son and daughter to meet her sister Elizabeth, whom Ivy Jane recalled as living in a tiny house in Amherst and weaving rag rugs on a loom that completely filled the living room; Aunt Lizzie gave them all to St. Joseph's Catholic Church to help support the congregation. Minnie maintained closer contact with her older sister Mathilda (Tillie), who married early and had a daughter, Mae, who in turn married a Yankee farmer and sometimes spiritualist from nearby La Grange, Ohio, named John Rockwood. This marriage was the first between a Niesen and a Yankee. Rockwood's grandparents had fought in the Revolution before settling in Ohio. They bought their farm on Diagonal Road in preference to the land that is now Public Square in Cleveland, and built the Western Reserve house that still stands today, near the family cemetery.

Even though Minnie shared the local Germans' contempt for Yankee farmers as dirty and uncouth, she admired them as hard workers. The Rockwoods were to become Ivy Jane's "country cousins," to be visited on weekend trips in a 1909 Ford with brass lamps and radiator. A number of times Ivy Jane attended classes at the country school, to which the children travelled by horse drawn wagon. Rarely, if ever, did the Edmondsons receive their country cousins in the big city.

Minnie Edmondson remained a Catholic for the first five years of her marriage. By this time her husband had joined the Unitarian Church and was teaching in the Sunday School, bringing home the textbooks to study at night. Finding the books on his table, she read through his entire syllabus and forthwith became a Unitarian. Cleveland's Unitarians at this time came largely from New England and remained faithful to their highly intellectual, austere, and high minded New England roots. This appealed strongly to Minnie, whose self-assurance and confidence in her own views soared. She became a voracious reader, began attending political tent meetings and, in her daughter's recollection, "became an ardent feminist, a kind of Mrs. Roosevelt." Her husband teased her by saying he married her because of her firm square jaw.[216]

George's politics were more conservative. After supporting Teddy Roosevelt in 1904 and again in 1912, when TR launched the Progressive "Bull Moose" Party, Edmondson voted against Woodrow Wilson and remained a staunch Republican throughout the 1920s. Meanwhile, Minnie's ardor waned over time. As her daughter put it, "devotion to [her husband] cut short her career. Smart and strong willed, her self-confidence nonetheless dwindled under life's pressures and she turned to living out her ambitions through [her daughter]."[217]

The marriage of George and Minnie Edmondson was a happy one, but was founded on the bedrock of their very difficult lives prior to 1901. Both recognized this, but neither wanted to dwell on it. In fact, over time their lives prior to marriage were very rarely mentioned and then only with difficulty. For Minnie, the world of Peter and Regina Niesen, their German relatives, and Grandma Westbecker and her savage brood remained a closed book, taboo subjects that Minnie would never discuss with her own children and of which they were largely ignorant.

George Edmondson triumphant. Self-portrait with his two children, 1914. S. F. Starr

George Edmondson covered his entire prior marriage with Daisy Williams and the death of his wife and three children with a similar blanket of silence. Only once was the corner of that blanket lifted, and then only partially. One Sunday in 1914 he loaded his wife and children into his brassy Ford for an outing to Norwalk. Along the way he pointed out spots connected with his childhood, telling amusing stories. Passing through the shady streets he came to a certain house and said, "That's the old Williams place. I wonder if there is still anyone living there. Come on, Minnie, let's go in." But Minnie protested, so he and five-year-old Ivy Jane proceeded alone.

Ivy Jane was dressed in shiny patent leather boots with white kid tops and lots of buttons. Inside the Victorian parlor a little old lady and George Edmondson whispered together, and then they kissed and wept together. The elderly lady hugged Ivy Jane, saying "After all, I'm your grandmother, too, in a way." Edmondson stiffened, struck his gauntlets against his thigh, and announced that they must leave immediately if they were to reach Cleveland by nightfall. Outside the house, as Ivy Jane recalled eighty years later, he put on his goggles and cap and turned aside her questions.

The Edmondson family visits Norwalk, O., ca. 1911. S.F. Starr

Minnie Edmondson approached the raising of children with the same earnestness with which she had planned her own career. Thus, while she herself had received practically no schooling in Oberlin, she had met several Accomplished People, beginning with Sarah Bradley back on Elm Street. During the First World War Minnie Niesen Edmondson took her daughter to visit this great lady, who lived behind lace curtains with a parrot. Dressed in white gloves and hat, young Ivy Jane listened to stories of Siam and of the Boxer Rebellion in China, her mother reminding her all the while that she was meeting a historic figure.

Thanks to the years she had spent as a house girl in the musical Demuth family, Minnie considered musical accomplishment to be the very pinnacle of human achievement. Following the model she knew best, Minnie decided that Ivy Jane would be a great pianist, so great, in fact, that if anything ever happened to George Edmondson she could support her mother from concert earnings. Naturally, there was no place in Minnie's plan for her daughter to marry.

Minnie sent Ivy Jane for lessons to Miss Brubaker, Fred Colson's mistress, in the upmost tier of Cleveland's old Arcade. This fleshy and rouged lady reminded Ivy Jane of a Japanese doll. She had once been the most gifted protégée of the great Russian virtuoso Josef Lhevinne (1874-1944), but arthritis had ended had put an end to her performing career and forced her return to Cleveland. Now she shared a music studio and an intimate relationship with Fred Colson's father, "Professor" William Colson.

This arrangement greatly embarrassed the Edmondson family, but it was not the cause of Ivy Jane's eventual defection from music. Rather, it was the draconian regimen of practicing that her mother imposed on her. It was clear to Ivy Jane that she was approaching a crisis over piano playing but it took something close to divine intervention to resolve the issue. Professor Colson, it seems, was in the habit of taking lunch at the Masonic Hall and then hanging around through the early afternoon for a few racks of billiards. Some years earlier the Russian pianist and composer Rachmaninoff had performed in Cleveland. George Edmondson did his portrait and in the course of his visit Rachmaninoff and Colson also became acquainted. On a later visit, after lunch and billiards, Colson, asked if the virtuoso would consent to meet his young grand-niece, an aspiring pianist.

Ivy Jane found the renowned Russian to be spectral and forbidding. To make matters worse, before deigning to shake the hands of this twelve–year old girl he slowly drew on long white gloves, finger by finger, as if he was facing in this young aspiring pianist some kind of contagion. This, at any rate, is how she interpreted the event. Within weeks Rachmaninoff's implied judgment was echoed by her own teacher, who mercifully informed her mother that the girl's talents lay elsewhere than in playing the piano. Ivy Jane promptly ceased to practice the piano and, in a youthful act of rebellion, took up drawing and painting instead. Over the next eighty-five years she made art the center of her world.

The piano lessons were but one manifestation of the fact that Ivy Jane Edmondson was raised under what she later called her mother's "terrifyingly threatening German discipline." As an orphan, she had not herself received a mother's love and didn't know how to express her own love to her daughter. Of her mother's kisses Ivy Jane wrote that, "They were preceded by a tightening of the lips, which were pressed firmly, almost painfully, to my cheek, then opened with a resounding smack and quick withdrawal, as if from something unpleasant."

In spite of this, Ivy Jane came to appreciate her mother as an early feminist whose career had been cut short only by her devotion to her father. "Smart and strong-willed," Ivy Jane continues, "her self-confidence dwindled under life's pressures and she turned to living out her ambitions through me." And as to those kisses, she went on to say that, "sometimes I noticed there were tears in her eyes."[218]

Fortunately, her irrepressible father would often sweep Ivy Jane away from the piano and away from her studies in order to see the latest Charlie Chaplin film at the Alhambra Theater, just around the corner from their home. And when Marshall Foch visited Cleveland in 1921 George Edmondson brought his daughter to his studio on Euclid Avenue to watch the parade from the steps. Doing even more to balance Minnie's stern discipline was Ivy Jane's fairy godmother, Ivy Colson, who did not miss a chance to indulge her niece, whether through fancy clothes, trips to the East Coast, or party-filled weekends in Elyria.

When young George was ready for school his father arranged for him to be enrolled at the prestigious University School in Shaker Heights. A few years later he made similar arrangements for Ivy Jane to study at the elite Hathaway Brown School, conveniently located just across the street from the Edmondsons' house on East 97th Street but socially a world away from Norwalk and Amherst. In both cases Edmondson did portrait photographs of the schools' buildings, their faculty and students, in lieu of tuition. Even then, the Edmondsons' finances were strained. While other girls were delivered to school in limousines, Ivy Jane often had to run across the street to get lunch money, which her father would dig out of the safe.[219]

Hathaway Brown School brought unexpected pleasures of a sort normally reserved for the children of robber barons like the van Sweringen brothers, railroad magnates who built Cleveland's Terminal Tower and developed Shaker Heights. Each Christmas Davidson Jencks, the adopted son of one of these bachelors, invited his schoolmates and young ladies from Hathaway Brown for sleigh rides around the estate in Hunting Valley, followed by oyster stew and hot chocolate. The girls giggled that their friend Jencks looked just like the elder "Van" brother.

Of more lasting value were the excellent art classes offered by Miss Raymond. Ivy Jane had been interested in art since she was five and her Uncle Will, on long walks, would ask her to describe the color of the hills. Miss Raymon, thrilled at the girl's progress in drawing, arranged for her to attend Saturday drawing classes at the Cleveland Art Institute. One summer Miss Raymond even took Ivy Jane to Provincetown on Cape Cod for yet more instruction.

Ivy Jane Edmondson, age 17, 1926 by her father. S.F. Starr

William J. Edmondson, "Uncle Will," took Ivy Jane under his wing and introduced her to watercolor landscape painting and also to the art of portraiture, which was to prove useful as a source of income during the Depression years. Her studies with Will Edmondson were the most important and nearly the only formal training in art she ever received. However, her Uncle Will also introduced her to his young friend Charles Burchfield (1893-1967) from Salem, Ohio, even then gaining national fame as a watercolorist focusing on regional subjects. Birchfield moved to Buffalo in 1921 but continued to visit Cleveland and his friend Will Edmondson. Birchfield's ecstatic views of nature, including fence rows, blossoming fields, and gathering storms, evoked such interest that the newly opened Museum of Modern Art in New York devoted its first one-man show to him and his work. Only in her later years did Ivy Jane acknowledge the deep impact of what she called Birchfield's "wild" view of nature on her own water colors.

Classes at the Cleveland Art Institute were also important, but mainly for reasons other than art. Ivy Jane had thrived at the proper Hathaway Brown School. She was accustomed to the earnest and practical ways of the Cleveland establishment, and was completely at ease in her Aunt Ivy's world of Victorian luxury. Yet she yearned for romance and color and found it in the very world of Hungarian Cleveland that Steve Starr was straining to escape. Art classes at the Cleveland Art Institute put her into studios with a group of aspiring Hungarian-American artists, men with names like Ambrosy Palwoda, Kuli Bela, and Kalman Kubinyi. Here were contemporaries who shared her intense interest in art but were also quick to laugh, young men with whom she could enjoy wine-filled picnics on Lake Erie and evenings at smoke-filled Hungarian restaurants, where gypsy violinists bent low over the guests. Although these gatherings arose from a shared love of art, Ivy Jane found them excitingly déclassé, mildly dangerous, and certainly attractive.

Hungarian art students and friends of Ivy Jane Edmondson, Cleveland, ca. 1931. S.F. Starr

Art, and the company of her Hungarian friends, became Ivy Jane's s alter orbis, her safety valve. Meanwhile, her Aunt Ivy was organizing polite parties at her grand home on Washington Avenue in Elyria, where her niece might meet nice boys from the Ely family (descended from the town's founder) and the Fauvers (attorney's for the Colson Company), all of them upstanding alternatives to the "artsy" crowd Ivy Jane was running with in Cleveland.[220] Still living in both worlds, she invited to her school dance harmless Arthur Demuth, a member of the musical Demuth family from Oberlin and practically a cousin, rather than one of her exotic eastern European friends.

Ivy Jane Edmondson during a picnic on Lake Erie with Art student friends, ca. 1929. S.F. Starr

Ivy Jane came gradually came to realize, as she said later, "that my parents were pushing me in a direction I didn't want to go. I had to be a lady, you see. That was what girls were supposed to be in my time." When in her ninetieth year she was asked what she had wanted to be at age sixteen she replied emphatically, "Well, I just wanted to be a real person!"[221] As her grand-nephew Brad Edmondson put it after conducting a long interview with her, art had become her safety valve, her therapy, her profession, and her fountain of youth. Inevitably, she wanted to go to art school, but her parents insisted instead on a proper College. She eventually spent two years at Smith before graduating from Barnard. As a result, she had to acquire on her own much that she would have learned in art school. "If I had gone to art school, I would have [mastered all that] at an early stage. I think I have been struggling all my life."[222]

Concluding his interview with her, Brad Edmondson asked whether she had ever thought of resisting her mother's will. Just as he was shutting off the tape machine she replied that, "I wish that I had had what it took to have a fight with my mother when I was young, the way my brother did," she said. "But I just couldn't do it."

Ivy Jane Edmondson's years at Smith and Barnard were beneficial, for they broadened still further the base in classical civilization and European culture that had been laid down at Hathaway Brown. Following her graduation from Barnard Ivy Jane thought briefly that she would stay in New York and freelance. She quickly learned that in the New York art world "You had to sleep with someone if you wanted the job." Recoiling from this discovery, she decided to return to Cleveland to teach at Hathaway Brown and pick up portrait commissions that her Uncle Will didn't want. This was the moment when another young Hungarian, Stephen Zoltan Starr, appeared on the scene and turned her life in a very different direction.

Let us close this history of the American Edmondsons with a brief look at the later years of George Mountain and Minnie Edmondson. Both continued patterns they had set during their earlier life together. He continued to be feted by professional photographers, who turned his eightieth birthday party in Cincinnati into a celebration of his life and era, and Minnie took an active interest in raising their eight grandchildren, all the while continuing her life-long quest for education and useful knowledge by reading voraciously. In 1947 Edmondson sold his photographic studio and all its contents, including thousands of glass plates. As noted above, the Cleveland Public Library eventually acquired this horde, made crude contact prints from them, and then destroyed the plates themselves, a tragic mistake.

After living briefly with their son, George Jr., and his family at their farm in Virginia, Edmondson that same years gave his son $12,500 to enable him to buy 300 acres of land and start dairy farming in Nakomis, near Venice, Florida. Neither George nor Minnie thrived in that pioneering farm environment, which was foreign to them both. George Mountain Edmondson died on November 8, 1948 and Minnie Niesen Edmondson moved in with her daughter's family in Cincinnati. There she helped with the housework and cooking, and travelled by the No.4. streetcar to the main Public Library downtown, attended lectures on culture and politics, and drew out books on subjects as unlikely as arctic exploration and Genghis Khan. Thus she lived to 1959.

In the 1940s that daughter, Ivy Jane Edmondson Starr, painted an oil portrait of "My Old Parents." He is sitting comfortably and she very erect and both, even in old age, exude the fortitude and dignity that had enabled them to thrive amidst very demanding circumstances. Later, this dual portrait filled the artist herself with deep sadness as she remembered all her parents had lived through. Yet George and Minnie Edmondson, in their starkly different ways, set a standard of responsibility, hard work, and creativity that still inspires their heirs, three generations later.

V. Two Lives: Work and Days.

In Chapters I and Chapter IV we met Stephen Zoltan Starr and Ivy Jane Edmondson. It is their marriage in 1933 that brings these two very different family histories together. They were the parents of the present author and, as such, his main reason and inspiration for producing this detailed family chronicle.

In the last pages of Chapters I and IV we followed the lives of both members of this unlikely couple down to the end of their college years. This chapter picks up their story at the time they met, courted, married, and stated a family. But it does not pretend to cover the history of Stephen and Ivy Jane Starr's life as a married couple. This central element of their story *can* be written, and in great detail, for at various times they both kept detailed diaries and even at times a joint diary. And whenever they were apart they exchanged letters, which they carefully preserved in labelled bundles tied with blue strings. Nearing her hundredth birthday, Ivy Jane thought of destroying them as being "too personal," but was dissuaded from doing so by her children.

These diaries and hundreds of letters between "Ivy Jane" and "Etienne," as she often called her husband, doubtless contain essential insights on their parents and siblings, their children, and above all on their relationship with each other. This relationship was often strained. Steve had wanted seven children, and Ivy Jane chaffed under familial demands that at one point became so burdensome that she considered divorce. But these and other important subjects are best left to others, who have the perspective brought by the passage of time. It is no surprise that not one of their four children evinced the slightest interest in perusing those diaries and letters. For my part, I have no desire to explore or make public my parents' intimacies. Because of this, those bundles of letters and diaries remain unread and have not been utilized for this memoir. Let new generations of descendants turn to the archives of the Western Reserve Historical Society to read and understand these documents of a complex, devoted, and enduring marriage.

Let us then start with the courtship, marriage, and early married life of Steve and Ivy Jane Starr. Having done so, we can then turn to the careers which as young people they each hoped to pursue but which they were unable to take up seriously until they were fifty years old: Stephen Starr's historical writings and Ivy Jane Starr's paintings and sculpture. Neither considered this their main life's work; raising their family always took first place with both of them. But their dearest dream was to write and to paint or sculpt. Any picture of them, either as individuals or as a couple would therefore be woefully incomplete without noting what each accomplished in their respective realms. Such an assessment will also provide an answer to the question of whether it is possible to launch a professional career at age fifty and achieve anything of lasting value. More important, it will provide an essential element of our picture of their lives as a whole.

What follows treats only the "professional" lives of our two subjects, history for Stephen Starr and art for Ivy Jane Edmondson Starr. It does so because both husband and wife were passionate about their chosen fields, which they held to be second in importance only to the family. Both gladly gave up many pleasures to toil away at desk or easel, which they did throughout their marriage, cramming such activity into late night hours and occasional moments of respite. And both, the minute their children were out of the house, reorganized their lives to devote full time to their passions. Both were fortunate to live long enough to complete many, but by no means all, of the tasks to which they had dedicated themselves. As a result, we have at hand a formidable stack of books and articles by Stephen Z. Starr and some four hundred paintings, drawings, and works of sculpture in several mediums by Ivy Jane Edmondson Starr.

Why focus on these works? Family members and the dwindling number of their old friends should be interested and, indeed, they are. Future generations may also find them interesting and of value. Indeed, they may, through contacts with these books and works of art, better understand themselves and that part of their own world that came down to them from the past.

Are the respective achievements of Ivy Jane and Steve Starr of significance in their own right? I am deeply convinced that they are. My strong prejudice on this important point is obvious. Equally obvious is the fact that countless historians and art historians are more qualified than me to carry out such a survey and evaluation. First among these would be my surviving siblings, George A. Starr and Diana Starr Cooper. I defer to their judgments on everything in this chapter. Fortunately, both are patiently indulgent towards me…most of the time. I shall therefore charge ahead, and assert bluntly at the outset that the accomplishments of this couple in their respective fields of endeavor merit the attention, respect, and admiration of future generations.

We last encountered young Csillag Istvan, now reminted as Steve Starr, as he timidly courted Miss Kate Messick, the daughter of the lordly Homer Dwight Messick, president of the Union Trust Bank in Cleveland and, for young Istvan, the embodiment of the successful and solidly American world to which he aspired. For her part,

Kate had firmly resolved that Stephen Starr would be her husband. But in the end it turned out that he was attracted to her more as a symbol than as a reality.

Ivy Jane's attentions meanwhile focused on the leader of her group of Hungarian artist friends, the talented etcher and emerging painter of the "Ash Can School," Kalman Kubinyi (1906-1973). This lean, mustachioed, and high-strung young artist came from an aristocratic Protestant family that had resided at their castle in eastern Hungary until the collapse of the ancien regime forced them into exile and eventually to Cleveland. Photographs from his early days show this young Cleveland artist in various dramatic and often costumed poses, usually with a smile. After a number years spent painting and picnicking together, Kubnyi assumed he and Ivy Jane Edmondson would marry. When George Edmondson moved his studio from Euclid Avenue, Kubinyi even made sure that he took over the old one, as if it were already a family matter.

Kalman Kubinyi (left), and Castle Kubinyi, Hungary (right).

Both Steve Starr and Ivy Jane Edmondson had been searching for a life that embodied not what they were but what they dreamed of becoming. And, it should be noted, their aspirations lay in diametrically opposite directions. These two very different lines of development eventually crossed when Steve met Kate Messick's friend, Ivy Jane Edmondson. Even though her father was a portrait photographer and not a titan of business, Steve could see that Ivy Jane was thoroughly assimilated into the ways of the Cleveland establishment. Her lively manner and golden curly hair attracted him, and he wrongly assumed that her painting was merely a polite accomplishment, not a vocation. On her side, Ivy Jane found the earnest Western Reserve student pleasantly attractive, but over the first four months of their acquaintance she failed to detect that he was, in fact, a Hungarian. Only when this suppressed information came out did she place him anywhere near that charmed circle of foreign-born free spirits in which she longed to move. She wrongly assumed that he was more of a free-spirited Hungarian than was in fact the case.

Steve Starr at the time he was courting Ivy Jane, by his friend John Mills. S.F. Starr

With the help of Ivy Jane's yellow Model A Ford roadster, the couple could reach places like Cuyahoga Falls and Nelson's Ledges (now Nelson Kennedy State Park) in Portage County, Ohio). In the course of long picnics they grew closer, and eventually Steve proposed to her. But the Edmondsons strongly opposed the marriage. This stemmed not from Steve being either Hungarian or Catholic but because they considered him arrogant and spoiled. And his father was worse yet. Readers will recall that Alexander Starr (Csillag Sandor), over dinner at the Edmondsons, had snobbishly belittled the famed Cleveland Museum of Art, comparing it unfavorably with the museums of Europe. Pointedly linking the son with his father, the Edmondsons thereafter referred to Stephen Starr as "The Crown Prince." As a dutiful daughter, Ivy Jane broke with Steve…for a while.

During the year following their graduations from college, Ivy Jane returned to Hathaway Brown to teach art and paint portraits and Steve took various minor jobs in Cleveland. After her parents ruled against her marriage to Steve, she decided to apply for a National Scholarship to the Arts Students League in New York. Working at her Uncle Will's studio on Euclid Avenue, she carefully prepared her portfolio. To her astonishment, she won one of the coveted prizes. Her mother didn't want her living in Bohemian Greenwich Village and installed her instead in an apartment on West 62nd Street, which turned out to be in the heart of Hell's Kitchen and a block full of prostitutes. In order to renew her contact with Steve, Ivy Jane took out a post office box under the name of Jane Mountain.

Eventually Steve and Ivy Jane married. More precisely, they eloped. Steve hitchhiked to New York during a raging snow-storm and they presented themselves at the Unitarian Church on Lexington Avenue to be married. The preacher there turned out to be none other than Ivy Jane's old minister from Cleveland, Minot Simon who, with her father, had founded the Unitarian Church in Cleveland and had baptized Ivy Jane. This prudent divine hesitated to marry a couple that had in fact eloped, and yielded only when they assured him the alternative would be a City Hall ceremony.

Minot Simon then wrote to Ivy Jane's father, George Edmondson, who at once wrote back to his daughter. He reported that her mother was calling down doom upon the arrogant Steve Starr, that she was nearly hysterical, and that if she, Ivy Jane, cared at all about her family she should return at once and deal with her mother directly. This she did, staying two weeks at her parents' new home in Shaker Heights. Only on the last day did her mother bring up the marriage, and then as if it had been the most normal event in the world. Grandma Starr sent her daughter back to Manhattan with rugs, chairs, and many bits of advice.

When her other suitor, Kalman Kubinyi, learned of Ivy Jane's marriage, and to a fellow Hungarian at that, he locked himself in his room and refused to eat for three days. But the marriage lasted for more than a half century and, in spite of many hardships, strains, and frustrated dreams, was a happy one. And Kubinyi went on to a distinguished career as an honored member of the Ash Can School and as a nationally admired engraver.

The gulf between the two young partners was broad. Steve was a determinedly assimilating immigrant in an age when Horatio Alger's novels were still proclaiming a "strive and succeed" philosophy to a vast and diverse American audience. Viewed in this rather clinical light, his young wife represented success. She was, after all, a graduate of the most exclusive schools and colleges and her father was on close terms with virtually the entire Cleveland establishment. She, by contrast, accepted all this as being the normal course of things. For her, the frontier to be conquered was in the spirit, to break out of all she had grown up with and enter the exciting world of art and foreign cultures. Seen in this light, it is clear that each entered into marriage under an illusion. Each idealized the other as an embodiment of what they themselves were reaching for, without realizing that the other was moving in precisely the opposite direction.

Contemporary portraits of the two reflect precisely these qualities. Stephen Starr as photographed by his new wife's father, appears as a self-contained, brooding, yet proper young American, a twenty-one-year-old banker without a bank. His portrait of Ivy Jane Edmondson taken about the same time shows her to have been beautiful, self-assured, a charter member in the Roaring Twenties, yet at the same time intense and thoughtful. When one of their friends, John Mills, a photographer with Eastman, made a portrait of the two of them together the result was an arresting document. Here, in 1930, Ivy Jane and Steve Starr emerge as a beautiful couple who, for all their differences, are standing close together and looking in the same direction.

Ivy Jane and Steve Starr, 1934, photo by John Mills. S.F. Starr

Acknowledging this, it is important also to note that both Steve and Ivy Jane had rejected other possible partners who more truly represented the world to which they thought they aspired than did their actual spouse. Steve may have idealized solid bourgeois values but rejected Ms. Messick, who truly embodied them; Ivy Jane may have idealized Central European art and spontaneity, but in the end rejected the artist Kalman Kubinyi. In some unconscious way, both acknowledged and acted upon who they actually were, and not just their aspirations.

In spite of this, the deep differences between Ivy Jane and Steve Starr produced dissonance. The first manifestation of this arose not from Steve's drive to find his place in American life or from Ivy Jane's passion as an artist but from the old-fashioned ideas about the role of women that Steve had inherited from his father. Seventy years later Ivy Jane wrote that "[Steve] came a long way. When we were married he was ashamed that I was an artist. But I was actually earning much more than he did. By the end, he had changed completely." Ivy Jane also changed fundamentally, especially as she came to appreciate her husband's steadiness, his devotion to her and their family, and his dedication to hard work in their behalf. These were in fact her own parents' values, and over time she embraced them as virtues in a way that had earlier been impossible for her to imagine. The start of this fragile bridging of two worlds marks the point at which their real marriage began. The responsibilities of raising a large family provided the glue that held them together through this sustained and often difficult process of discovery and self-definition.

The young couple lived first at 54 Morton Street in the Village. Ivy Jane promptly began practicing her art by painting a large mural covering an entire wall. Next door lived Stephen Vincent Benet, who only a couple of years earlier had published his long narrative poem John Brown's Body, a work that fed Steve's growing curiosity about the American Civil War. Steve's version of his wife's large mural was a twenty-two-page scholarly study of "Louis

Kossuth and the War of 1859," which he completed shortly after their marriage. Meticulously researched in Hungarian and English sources, the essay delves into the complex yet superficial diplomacy preceding the war] that led to Italy's independence. Starr considered this episode to be "an amazing commentary upon the dilettantism, the frondeur spirit, which underlies so much of what has been called, perhaps in irony, "Grand Diplomacy."[223] No less striking than the ironic distance between Starr and his hero, Kossuth is his deiberate and elegant writing style. For this young businessman, the vocation of historian was no casual matter.

Even as he was typing up this scholarly article, Steve Starr was consumed by his new job with Schenley Distillers Co. With the lifting of Prohibition in 1930 this solid old firm, with offices in New York and distilleries in Kentucky and Indiana, was once again producing bourbon whiskey. Steve was lucky to have any job. As the Depression deepened, there were fewer and fewer people who could afford the luxury of having their portrait painted. By 1930 Ivy Jane's portrait business was flagging, and a pensive self-portrait from that period reflects it (reproduced below, "Gallery") Ivy Jane's portrait of her husband presents a similarly thoughtful, even pensive mood:

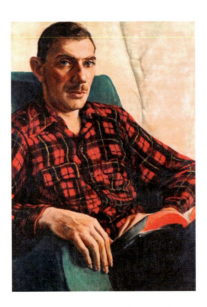

Stephen Z. Starr in 1936, by Ivy Jane Edmondson Starr, S.Z. Starr II.

The birth of a son, George, in 1934, and then of a daughter, Ivy Elizabeth in 1937, meant that the young couple now had to devote their full energies to the children. They found a new apartment at 261 Seaman Avenue, on the northern tip of Manhattan. By the mid-1930s they were so poor that Ivy Jane was reduced to collecting milk bottles in her son George's baby carriage in order to earn the pennies to be gained from redeeming them. Steve, meanwhile, in hopes of professional advancement in a field that had once richly rewarded his father, enrolled in night courses at the New York University Law School, graduating in 1937. As an immigrant from Europe he had missed most of the childhood diseases common in America. Now a severe bout of mumps prevented him from taking his law boards. And by the time he was able to retake them the family was already in Ohio.

Thus, the claims of parenthood during the Depression era forced both Steve and Ivy Jane to suspend their career dreams. Both accepted this reality and neither could conceive of another path. When members of later generations faced the same choice, many sacrificed family to careers, abandoning children to their own devices. Steve and Ivy Jane Starr were among those who made a commitment to family life and stuck by it.

Yet neither of them had forgotten their earlier dreams. As her children grew up and left home, Ivy Jane was able to turn once more to painting, at first confining herself to landscapes hastily painted during family vacations. Meanwhile, Steve's work in Cincinnati also began to leave corners of time in which to read, and he focused his attention increasingly on American history. He joined the Historical and Philosophical Society of Ohio (later the Cincinnati Historical Society) and began collecting material on several Civil War topics that had captured his interest.

By 1960 both Ivy Jane and Steve had celebrated their fifty-first birthdays. Two of their four children had graduated from college and the third would receive his diploma within two years. Their youngest daughter, Diana, was in private school in Cincinnati. To pay for all this Steve had moved on to a more remunerative job as treasurer of the Clopay Corporation and Ivy Jane had continued to exchange portraits for sides of beef or legs of lamb. Now this was no longer necessary. Even though Steve continued his day job, he increasingly focused his main energies on writing history. Ivy Jane, who still regretted that she had been sent to college rather than directly to art school, now enrolled in sculpture classes at the Cincinnati Art Museum.

In short, as they entered their sixth decade both Steve and Ivy Jane Starr finally saw the possibility of returning to what they had earlier hoped would be their life's work, art and history. Circumstances had prevented both of them from receiving the training that would have been desirable but they compensated for this shortcoming with passion, energy, and hard work. In the end, Steve devoted a quarter century to the writing of history and Ivy Jane almost half a century to her art.

Let us therefore turn to what each was able to accomplish in their postponed vocations.

S.Z. Starr as Historian

It is doubtful that any twenty-five-year-old graduate student ever set about his or her scholarly career with the focus and dedication that Stephen Z. Starr showed at age fifty, when he began his career as a historian. He was entering familiar territory. At Western Reserve College the Hungarian playwright and journalist Joseph Remenyi had introduced him to European history. It was probably due to Remenyi's influence that he conceived the idea of writing a biography of the Hungarian revolutionary and reformer, Lajos Kossuth. And in long conversations with Cleveland banker Homer Messick he had developed an interest in, and respect for, American history, which his own father had dismissed as a rude and uncultivated footnote to European history. We have seen that these conversations in Messick's paneled library had occurred because Steve had been dating Messick's daughter, Kate. Nothing came of this romance, but Mr. Messick had sealed Starr's vocation as an American historian.

Down to his fiftieth year Steve Starr had no time to pursue his passion for history. He kept reading, however, and ran up sizable bills at Blackwell's in Oxford, England, stocking high the paneled library he built for himself on Langdon Farm Road in Cincinnati. With his oldest son in graduate school, his oldest daughter at Smith, his younger son at Yale, and his youngest daughter in private school in Cincinnati, 1959 would not appear to have been the best time for Steve Starr to launch his life as a historian. Yet he could clearly see the end of his child-rearing duties and the financial demands they placed on him, and therefore allowed himself, while still working as treasurer of the Clopay Corporation, to research and publish an article on the Astor Place Riot of May 10, 1849.

In this confrontation outside the Astor Theater in New York, partisans of the two leading Shakespearian actors of the day, Englishman Charles Macready and American-born Edwin Forrest, fought a bloody pitched battle, leaving several dozen fans from both sides dead on the sidewalk. Starr traced the history of this thespian feud, marveling at the fact that Shakespearean tragedies could have been the focus of so much passion on the part of nineteenth century American males, who were generally depicted as crude frontiersmen. He also demonstrated that the confrontation had come to a head some weeks earlier at a theater in Cincinnati, when champions of the American, Forrest, pitched the bloody carcass of a sheep onto the stage while Macready was performing his memorable interpretation of Hamlet.[224]

When he and Ivy Jane and their three children arrived in Cincinnati sixteen years earlier they were on alien territory, temporary (or so they thought) exiles from Cleveland, where both had grown up, and from New York, where they had begun their family and careers. Now they put down roots. Steve's deepening interest in American history had already focused on the Civil War, the Centennial of which was being marked at the time. As his connection to his new home deepened, it was a natural step to ask how Cincinnati had figured in the Civil War. His answer came in the form of an article on Camp Dennison, the sprawling Union Army camp outside Cincinnati where tens of thousands of raw farm boys were hastily banded into infantry units and sent off to die at the front.[225]

Starr took delight in each new scrap of information linking Cincinnati to the War. In the process he explored the thirty-three members of the Cincinnati Literary Club (of which he himself was now a member) who had enlisted together as the "Burnet Rifles," and the hundreds of Cincinnati Germans who formed the 9th Ohio Volunteer Infantry, or the "Neuner," as they were called, and marched behind the brass band of the local Turnverein.

What particularly impressed Starr was the fact that the training of these raw recruits was left in the hands of newly appointed officers, "the great majority of [whom] were just as ignorant of tactics as the men they had to teach." With nothing more than an abridged handbook to guide them, the army's instructors had barely begun their own self-training, let alone that of their soldiers, before they were all shipped off to the South to fight. The fact that American soldiers were traditionally allowed to elect their officers only deepened the chaos.

That same year Starr presented a long and carefully researched paper at the Cincinnati Civil War Roundtable.[226] This was a time when Ohio-born General Ulysses S. Grant was everywhere being praised for his brilliant leadership of the Union forces that led to the surrender at Appomattox Court House on April 9, 1865. Starr disagreed. Taking on by name all the leading scholars in the field, including Allan Nevins, Bruce Catton, and T. Harry Williams, he argued that "as a strategist, as a commander of armies, and above all, as a human being, Grant had shortcomings so fundamental as to negate his right to occupy the very highest place his modern-day admirers have sought to award him."[227] Starr accused Grant of trying to micromanage the actions of generals who in most cases were more competent than he.

The core of his argument was that Grant deliberately ignored the pressing need to prevent Confederate General John Bell Hood from crossing Tennessee to Kentucky and then to Ohio. He asserted that Grant should have sent General Sherman against Hood *before* allowing the latter to begin his March to the Sea. Had it not been for a brilliant Virginia-born Union cavalry general, Henry Thomas, the War might have turned out very differently. Woefully understaffed, gravely underequipped, and deliberately ignored by Grant, who threatened at this key juncture to sack him, Thomas miraculously destroyed Hood's army at the decisive Battle of Nashville in 1864, saving Grant's reputation in the process. In a strikingly insightful but profoundly revisionist conclusion, Starr called Thomas triumph at Nashville "the most complete, the most smashing, victory of the war."

This important study should have appeared in a major national journal, where it would have received the attention it deserves. The reason it did not is that Starr himself had only recently organized the Cincinnati Civil War Roundtable and saw his article as a means of jump-starting the fledgling organization. It was never reprinted in one of the major journals and remains bibliographically unknown to the larger historical community. But word got around nonetheless, and soon the best professionals in the field were acknowledging that the Cincinnatian had demonstrated not only a detailed knowledge of the complex flow of the military events and of the diverse materials that constitute the historical record but, more important, a deep understanding of the fundamental strategic issues that were at stake at each phase of America's great conflict.

The fateful confrontation at Nashville between generals Hood and Thomas had of course involved the infantry, but it was above all the different tactical approaches adopted by these two seasoned cavalrymen that informed their actions on the field of battle and which decided the day's outcome.

This struck Starr as quite peculiar. For while the knew there had been plenty of swashbuckling and dashing cavalrymen in the war, he joined most historians in believing that the American Civil War was in many respects the "first modern war" and a prelude to World War I. Were the Civil War cavalrymen, North and South. merely a throwback to an earlier age, or had they evolved with the times in ways that later students of the conflict had failed to understand?

This led Starr to pen a study on "The Saber and the Union Cavalry," in which he argued that while the traditional and symbolically important cavalry saber had still played an important role in the Civil War, it was at that moment being supplanted by the new technology of the repeater percussion rifle. And while many battles still involved mounted troops, more often than not the cavalrymen used their horses simply to get them quickly to the crucial point of battle, where they then dismounted and began shooting their modern rifles.[228]

Starr did not easily or quickly jettison the old romantic view of mounted cavalry. It was probably relevant that his own father had served briefly in the Hungarian cavalry at the start of World War I. And he doubtless felt more than a little nostalgia for the more civil and ritualized practice of war that lingered in memory, if not in practice, down to 1914. In such a mood he came across an extraordinary Confederate cavalryman who epitomized the vanished world of cavalry warfare, the English-born soldier of fortune Colonel George St. Leger Grenfell. A veteran of French battles against the Berbers in North Africa and of the Crimean War, Grenfell arrived in the summer of 1862 at the camp of the Confederate cavalryman John Hunt Morgan in northern Tennessee. Confederate officials in Richmond had granted him the rank of colonel. Over the next year Grenfell and "Morgan's Raiders" conducted bold cavalry sallies across the neutral state of Kentucky with the goal of reaching southern Indiana and Cincinnati, both of which were known to harbor many Confederate sympathizers.

> Morgan, affable and beloved by his men, was, in Starr's memorable description, "an incurable romantic, unstable, moody, erratic, unpredictable and, it must be said, neither very shrewd nor very intelligent. Morgan operated as if he had been a solitary knight errant on the lookout for cross-roads adventure. If he ever thought of the Civil War as something more than a gaudy tournament, he gave no indication of it." [229]

Under the circumstances, it was Grenfell, not Morgan, who gave Morgan's Raiders whatever discipline and tactical skill they possessed and who accounts for their lasting place in history.

Grenfell's extraordinary career ended when he took part in a quixotic effort by a group of Confederate sympathizers in the North to attack a large Union prisoner-of-war camp near Chicago. Their plan was to free the Confederate soldiers incarcerated there and thereby foment an uprising of northern opponents of the war, called "Copperheads," throughout the Mid-West. Unfortunately for them, the conspirators were arrested before they could spring their plot. Grenfell, tried and found guilty in a trial in Cincinnati, ended his days at Dry Tortugas, a miserable Federal fort off the Florida coast.

In 1964 Starr published an article on Grenfell's colorful pre-Civil War career and followed it with a full biography of the man in 1971.[230] This volume, whose author was identified as "a businessman and curator at the Cincinnati Historical Society," received much praise in the scholarly press and went into several paperback editions for the general public. In addition to providing an engrossing tale of derring-do by colorful but doomed adventurers, Starr's biography of Grenfell raised two points of significance to the study of the Civil War. Both were to figure large in his later writings.

First, through its detailed analysis of the life of a single cavalry regiment, <u>Colonel Grenfell's Wars</u> gave a far more sober and realistic account of the daily life of Americans at war than what is provided in the standard histories or even in the regimental histories, more than eight hundred of which were issued by veterans in the era 1870-1900. Starr, drawing on a mass of documents in the U.S. National Archives, a host of state archives, and personal letters, including many preserved by Grenfell's family in England, drew a picture of almost photographic veracity of the war as it as was actually lived. Second, his account of the activities of Morgan's Raiders in Kentucky and southern Indiana and of the bizarre Chicago conspiracy revealed the extent of pro-southern sympathy across much of the Mid-West.

He questioned the image of a Civil War pitting ideologically united forces on both sides against each other. Indeed, there were those who dreamt of a fresh succession by the Midwestern states, to be followed by the creation of a second Confederacy in that region.

During the centennial of the end of the Civil War in 1965 Steve Starr wrote a paper on the war as a whole, which he read before several Civil War Roundtable groups. In it he took the traditional Northern view that the chief cause of the conflict was the refusal by a generation of southern leaders to make any concessions to the northern states on slavery, and the intemperate moves by Southern hotheads following the election of Lincoln in 1860. If he was aware of how the British government (and the state of New Jersey) had peacefully abolished slavery by recompensing slave owners for what had been legal property, he considered it irrelevant. He did not even touch on the possibility that this failure left the way open for northern abolitionists to define the conflict in moral rather than economic terms, and thus cause them to treat it as a war to the death. Ignoring the implications of his own study of the Copperhead movement in Ohio and Indiana, Starr here presented the traditional view of a unified and moral North facing an immoral but stubborn and resolute "slaveocracy."[231]

These comfortable assumptions began seriously to erode as Starr took up the story of another cavalry unit, this time from the North, the Seventh Kansas Regiment, known everywhere as "Jennison's Jayhawkers." Formed before the war at the time of "Bleeding Kansas" and deeply influenced by one of its early members, John Brown, Jr., Colonel Charles R. Jennison's band of 10,000 brigands and murderers believed, in Starr's words, that "anyone in a civil war that was not an active ally was an enemy, whose will to fight had to be destroyed by robbing him of his means of livelihood, and by turning his country into a desert. They believed that both the robbery and destruction were defensible when committed in the service of the great cause: to free the slave, smash the Slave Power, and preserve the Union." [232]

Fanatics, Jennison and his band lived by John Brown's scriptural injunction that "without the shedding of blood [there] is no remission [from sin]." (Hebrews 9:22). "No other regiment in the Union army had so bad a reputation or had worked so diligently to deserve it," wrote Starr. Their grim story had never been written, he added, nor could it have been, for at war's ends its surviving members became normal citizens again and were in no mood to brag about their wartime crimes. Most were all to glad to forget about their earlier barbarity, and for society to do so as well.

After amassing a formidable array of largely unknown or neglected archival data from state and local archives in Kansas and Missouri and from the U.S. National Archives, Starr reconstructed the life of Jennison's Jayhawkers in chilling detail. With clinical precision he recounted the appalling story of their frequent resort to mass lynching and murder, and showed how easy it was to continue along this path once members of the regiment had launched themselves on it. These passages are virtuoso examples of dramatic historical events that have been rescued from formulaic clichés and presented in vivid and precise colors.

Without these gory depictions drawn from neglected archives, the historical and moral challenge posed by Jennison's Jayhawkers would never have come fully into focus. But Starr was not content simply to "tell the story," which in very general terms had been told before. From first to last, he argued, the Seventh Kansas Regiment was ahead of its time. While Lincoln was ready to fight to preserve the Union with or without slavery, Jennison was a thoroughgoing and uncompromising Abolitionist from day one, and so were the hundreds of wild and uncontrollable roughnecks who rushed to his regiment's colors. Unlike George B. McClellan, whom Lincoln named to head the Union's forces and who declared that he fought solely to save the Union and not to abolish slavery, Jennison saw the war purely through John Brown's moral lens. Jennison and his men were not philosophers, but if asked, they would happily have embraced all forms of brutality as necessary and acceptable tools of the abolitionist crusade.

If Grenfell and Morgan were backwards-looking both in the ends they pursued and the means they were willing to employ to achieve them, Jennison, for better or worse, was the future. In that role, this savage and ruthless man showed both Lincoln and the South what the war was really about, torching whole towns that stood in his way. Even though Jennison spent little time reflecting on his actions, Starr insisted there was something eerily prescient about him: long before Lincoln was prepared to issue his Emancipation Proclamation, Jennison was noisily claiming royalties on the future document on the grounds that he was its true author.

With Jennison's Jayhawkers, Stephen Starr had come to recognize the moral complexities of the American Civil War. His studies of Grenfell, Morgan, and Jennison had shown him that most Civil War leaders on both sides were military amateurs impelled more by their personal dreams and hatreds than by any sober knowledge of strategy or tactics, let alone of how to train and deploy raw recruits. Starr was to undertake only one further biographical investigation, this time of a Confederate cavalryman and politician from Kentucky, John T. Pickett.[233]

But what to do with the conclusions he had reached on the existence of a pro-southern "Copperhead" fifth column in the Midwest and of fanatical and brutal abolitionists in Kansas and elsewhere? He might well have chosen to draw out the implications of these findings for our understanding of the Civil War as a whole. True, they would have been unpopular in some quarters, but that is not the reason for which Starr held back. Such speculations would have landed him squarely in the middle of numerous and bitter debates in which both scholars and politicians were deeply engaged. He had no stomach for this, and may well have hesitated also on the grounds that he was a relative newcomer to the world of high scholarship, held no endowed professorship, and was an immigrant to boot.

This is all pure speculation. What is crystal clear is that his work on Morgan's Raiders and Jennison's Jayhawkers had left Starr with a deep and in many respects unparalleled knowledge of the largely forgotten documents that contain records of the day-to-day lives of ordinary soldiers on both sides, and a profound sympathy for the ordinary men and boys who actually fought the Civil War.

Over the half decade following the publication of Jennison's Jayhawkers Stephen Starr published carefully-researched papers on Northern cavalry units from Massachusetts, Vermont, Ohio, Wisconsin, and Michigan.[234] He chose his subjects carefully. Thus, with the First Massachusetts Cavalry he was dealing with one of the best-known units of the war, the subject of studies by well-known veteran-writers Charles Francis Adams and Henry Lee Higginson. In this study and in others on Vermont and Michigan units, Starr demonstrated that the oft-cited regimental histories were mainly the work of self-serving memoirists, who distorted the evidence and completely ignored the life of the regiments "as living human organisms." He also demonstrated how the "voluminous and dull" official records drawn up after the war largely failed to account for either military or human developments that shaped the outcome.

It would have been an easy matter to add a couple more of these regimental histories to the literature and then to bring them all together in a volume embodying the new type of bottom-up military history that the use of heretofore neglected sources made possible. It would have been the kind of book that would have earned tenure at any major university. But rather than take this easy road, Starr looked beyond such a presentation to a broader, deeper, grander, and far more challenging prospect.

In all five of his separate regimental histories, and in many book reviews he wrote in the same period, Starr contrasted the memoirs, official histories, and official records to evidence gleaned from the "Order and Letter Books." This vast compendium of documents drafted on a day-to-day basis and preserved in the U.S. National Archives, offers by far the most concrete, detailed, and unvarnished record of battles and camp life during the American Civil War. Largely neglected by historians until Starr began prowling into them, the Order and Letter Books make possible a reconstruction of the war as it was actually lived. After exhausting the Order and Record Books of five cavalry regiments of the Grand Army of the Republic and presenting his findings in a book and six articles, Stephen Starr resolved to use them, along with other published and published sources, to write the first comprehensive history of the entire Civil War focusing on what he perceived as the decisive military force on the victorious side, the Northern Cavalry.

Through his friend Professor T. Harry Williams in Baton Rouge, Starr arranged for the Louisiana State University press to publish a massive three-volume History of the Union Cavalry. The first volume, published in 1979, covers the story from the formation of cavalry units down through Gettysburg; the second, issued in 1981, recounts the history from Gettysburg to Appomattox; and the third, released in 1986, focuses on the war in the West, including the momentous confrontation between Generals Hood and Thomas about which Starr had written earlier. All three were to be honored with prizes, among them the Fletcher Pratt Literary Award in New York and the American Civil War Museum's Jefferson Davis Award. For the former, Starr was enrolled on a list of past recipients that included the renowned scholars Allan Nevins and David Donald. The volumes went into numerous printings in hard cover and paperback and remained in print for three decades.

Stephen Z. Starr's 3 volume history of Union cavalry.

Why a history of the cavalry in the American Civil War? First, because they were everywhere in the very thick of combat. Starr pointed out that while cavalry numbered only 8% of fighting men, they sustained 15% of all losses. Second, because cavalry units, far from being romantic throw-backs to an earlier era, had so modernized their tactics and weaponry that they offered a level of maneuverability, speed, and modern firepower that was far beyond any of the other branches of the military. Third, because it was above all cavalry that were responsible for the great and decisive battle at Nashville that opened the way to the final Union victory. And, finally, because, as Starr put it in Volume II (p. 486), "There was at the time, and there can be now, little question that the four divisions of cavalry [that were centrally involved in the decisive fighting [on the eve of Lee's surrender to Grant] were entitled to the lion's share of the credit for forcing the surrender of the Army of Northern Virginia at Appomattox Court House." The role of the infantry and artillery cannot be minimized, he concluded, but it was above all the Union Cavalry that won the day.

In undertaking this vast project, Stephen Starr made clear that he was motivated above all by deep respect and sympathy for the ordinary fighting men, as opposed to their officers or generals in the high command. To be sure, there were heroes aplenty among the officers, with men like "Little Phil" Sheridan from Somerset Ohio and George

Custer from New Rumney, Ohio, playing larger-than life roles. But Starr's heroes are the ordinary fighting men. Most were completely untrained. Troopers had to be coaxed and badgered to look after themselves and not to straggle on march, wander away from camp, accumulate masses of personal baggage, or mix uniforms and civilian clothing. With constant turnover. dismissals, resignations, and injuries among their officers, the men had to fend for themselves. Not surprisingly, they exhibited serious shortcomings as soldiers. But on the whole, Starr's conclusion is very positive.

When the war broke the very word "cavalry" had about it a romantic glamor. As Starr wrote in his introduction, "The middle years of the nineteenth century were a time of overripe romanticism:"

> "Otherwise sober men, a generation or two removed from an utterly unromantic frontier, saw the cavalry through the eyes of Sir Walter Scott and themselves in the role of the mailed knight wielding a saber, with its fine sounding French name, the "arme blanche", the true weapon for man-to-man combat…Beyond argument was the immense superiority of a man riding a steed—not a mere horse—into battle, over the heavily laden foot soldier, slogging his dreary way through ankle-deep, viscous mud."

This romanticism quickly evaporated amidst the chaos into which untrained cavalrymen plunged headlong. What was left were bands of tens of thousands of ordinary American men and boys whom fate had thrown together and who, over time, formed enduring links with one another that enabled them to become a very effective fighting force. Their wartime lives were for the most part miserable, and more than a few of them acted badly. Starr had no illusions on that score. "Not all of them were heroes, by any means," he wrote. "The cavalry had its share of deserters, cowards, malingerers, thieves, misfits, the stupid, the drunkards, and the shirkers, and they were to be found in every rank." Yet somehow they and their officers managed in the end to collaborate effectively, and to show remarkable resourcefulness and tenacity on the field of battle. As Starr put in his article on the First Massachusetts Cavalry, the rank and file were "poor soldiers but good fighting men."[235]

Stephen Starr was closely acquainted with the various deterministic theories that traced the outcome of the Civil War directly to large and impersonal economic forces, i.e., Northern manufacturers who far out-produced their South rivals, or to demographic factors that took into count the disproportionate number of males of fighting age on each side and traced the South's inevitable defeat to this one deficiency. Because he was so intimately familiar with the actual actions that took place on the field of battle, Starr would have none of this. His account fully acknowledges the various impersonal forces at play but in the end comes down squarely on the view that the unfolding scene on the war front determined everything. And at that level, it was the Union cavalry that played the most decisive role.

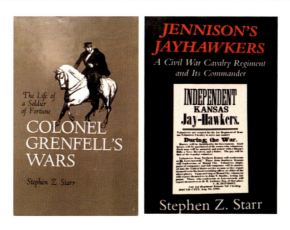

Books by Stephen Z. Starr.

The Union Cavalry accords due attention to the strategic moves of the top generals on both sides, especially McClellan, Grant, and Lee. But even in the first volume it is clear that Starr was intent on highlighting the decisive impact of generals and officers of the second rank, many of whom he considers to have been unjustly neglected. Hence his close attention to Thomas, Sheridan, Custer, and many others who were not part of the senior command. There were strategic mistakes aplenty, but good field commanders were able to offset them, just as bad decisions in the field could neutralize the best of strategies. But these middle-rank leaders were only as good as their fighting men. To present and evaluate the effort by these countless thousands of anonymous cavalrymen was Starr's main purpose in writing The Union Cavalry.

"Stephen Starr writing The Union Cavalry," Underhill Center, Vt., 1972. S.F. Starr

Over 1,649 closely argued and meticulously documented pages Starr presents the wartime world of that branch of the U.S. military to whose efforts above all the Union owed its ultimate victory. It is a sustained analysis of how the most unlikely aggregations of men are capable of banding together to pursue a common goal and of sustaining that effort through some of the most miserable circumstances imaginable. Leadership was important, not least at the middle and lower ranks, but in the end it was organization and will at the bench level that determined the outcome. This conclusion is so deeply woven into the fabric of The Union Cavalry that there was no need for Starr to spell it out in detail. Yet as early as the Introduction to Volume I he showed his hand, and in an uncharacteristically personal way:

> "it is impossible to live with these men in spirit without an ever-growing respect for their hardihood and dedication." (II, p. xiii)

When a historian conducts research in archives and libraries he invariably turns up unknown documents that are potentially of interest both to the general public and to fellow scholars. Steve Starr's kept a whole file of xeroxed copies of such letters and papers that he intended to publish one day. One of the few of these that actually saw the light of day was an account by a Cincinnati soldier of his experiences during the last weeks before Appomattox. "The Last Days of Rebellion" appeared in the Bulletin of the Cincinnati Historical Society.[236] The other such documents remained untouched in the file.

This is not surprising, given the immensity of the task that Starr had assigned himself. The Union Cavalry would have been a lifetime's work for a diligent and productive scholar working full-time in the field from his mid-twenties down to retirement. Starr did not begin his scholarly career until he was fifty. Even then, he had to research and write two lengthy archive-based books and a score of articles before he conceived the idea of writing The Union Cavalry. Moreover, at age sixty-four--in other words, at about the age most men of his generation were retiring—he took over the directorship of the Cincinnati Historical Society, a role he continued down to his sixty-ninth year. In this capacity he wrote long and interesting Director's Reports, penned numerous reviews of scholarly books, and raised money in order to place that distinguished old society (dating to 1844) on a solid footing.

It is tempting to conclude that Stephen Z. Starr was frantically working to make up for lost time. Maybe so. But he loved the *process* of research and writing and constructed a comfortable and satisfying life based upon it. In order to indulge in its pleasures, he and his wife Ivy Jane spent long summers at the home they had built on Irish Settlement Road in Underhill Center, Vermont, and moved there full time in 1977, when he retired for the second time. Starr's research entailed travel to archives all over North America but also to England, where he traced Colonel Grenfell's early career. When he failed to get needed materials from the Archives Nationales in Paris he sent his close friend, lawyer David DuVivier, to get them, regretting all the time that they didn't make the trip together.

He welcomed the many invitations to speak before Civil War Roundtable groups in the North and South. These were serious events, but also social events, for the custom was, and is, for speakers to offer thoughtful but engaging trifles suitable to the after-dinner format. Stephen Starr fulfilled this expectation but went far beyond it, producing for each presentation a publishable paper based on original archival research. Most of these papers were in fact published, but more often by local historical societies than by national scholarly journals.

Starr's desire to fill and overfill the expectations of his hosts, city by city, North and South, overrode larger ambitions he may have harbored to gain recognition on the national scholarly stage. This came in time, but as a result of his published books rather than separate papers or presentations.

Stephen Z. Starr, by Ivy Jane Starr, 1962. S.F. Starr

Starr carried on a large correspondence that was as much personal as scholarly. This was natural, since he considered his contact and interaction with fellow historians and historical enthusiasts to be as much the goal of the enterprise as achieving distinction as a scholar. His engaging correspondence with Col. Grenfell's heir Anthony Packe in Buckinghamshire, England, is preserved in the U.S. National Archives, and many equally valuable letters are preserved in the archive of the Cincinnati Historical Society.

Steve and Ivy Jane Starr transformed the inevitable visits to archives and Civil War battlefields into vacations. They both took particular delight in traveling to Baton Rouge, Louisiana, to visit the great historian of the South, T. Harry Williams. In Williams Starr found both an inspiring role model and a true friend. He dedicated the first volume of The Union Cavalry to Williams and Williams reciprocated by inscribing copes of his own books to his Cincinnati friend. Neither lived to see the third volume of The Union Cavalry in print, but it is clear from their correspondence on the subject that Williams saw the project as almost as much his own as the author's.

In his foreword to Colonel Grenfell's Wars Starr dropped a telling observation: "A project like this," he wrote, "bestows on the fortunate author the freedom of the City of Scholarship. All doors are open to him." In other words, the process of scholarship and especially of writing American history, gave Stephen Z. Starr entrée to America's intellectual society as a whole, a sense of belonging that had eluded him during his business career. He took unabashed and immense delight at being invited to join Cincinnati's venerable Literary Club, and faithfully produced paper after paper, to be read at the Club's 175-year-old home on East Fifth Street beneath the arch reading "Here Comes One With a Paper." This Hungarian immigrant, who had not known a word of English until he was thirteen and had not set foot in Cincinnati until his mid-thirties, took uncharacteristically immodest delight in the fact that at this very spot, where he stood so often, Charles Dickens, Oscar Wilde, and Samuel L. Clemens had all held forth.

In his dealings with all but a few close friends, Stephen Starr was formal and correct, as if following some increasingly out-of-date rule-book he had mastered back in Homer Messick's study in Cleveland. However, as he gained "the Freedom of the city of Scholarship" Starr relaxed, allowed himself to enjoy the company of other men, and even became something of a "Good Ole' Boy." For the Literary Club he produced papers on topics that he would earlier have considered frivolous, such as a talk on a nineteenth century female author from Michigan who, he proposed, was the worst poet of the century. His apogee in this genre was a paper entitled "Prosit!!! A Non-Cosmic Tour of the Cincinnati Saloon." For this engaging brew of urban social history, he commandeered from the Cincinnati Art Museum a large painting of a voluptuous nude by the Munich-trained Cincinnati artist Frank Duveneck (1848-1919) that had once hung behind the bar of a Vine Street saloon. Standing next to this classic, and beneath the famous arch, Starr, who had never hung out at *any* Cincinnati bar, concluded that:

> "…the neighborhood saloon, with its bar, its sitting room, its garden, and its glasses of mild beer for a nickel, brought people together and gave them a sense of belonging, of being part of a community. Much of that has been lost. Are we all together the better for it?"[237]

The demands of Starr's second career were heavy. Aside from writing some 2,500 printed pages—far more than most academic scholars produce in a lifetime—there was the research, the organization of materials, visits to relevant sites, and endless correspondence with archivists, librarians, historians and publishers. Obviously, this took a toll on family life. Starr was well aware of this, and tried his best to compensate. He exploited his professional travel to Europe, Japan, and China for private vacations with Ivy Jane, the two of them welcomed children and grandchildren to their home in Vermont, and together they spent happy days gardening, making hard cider, and enjoying quiet meals together in wintertime around their Franklin stove.

Nonetheless, the price Starr paid for his life as a historian was high and he knew it. No wonder, then, that he dedicated one of his books to his grandchildren, and his very first book to Ivy Jane:

"To I.J.E.S. In gratitude and love."

To this he added lines by Semonides of Amorgos,

"…in her hands life blossoms and bears fruit.
Beloved and loving, she grows old beside
Her husband, mother of children fair and honored;
Her name shines out among all womankind,
And on her ways a grace lies, like the gods'…"

Stephen Z. Starr did not live to see the final volume of <u>The Civil War Cavalry</u> in print. Several weeks after sending the third volume to his editor at Louisiana State University Press, he and Ivy Jane piled into their car to shop for groceries in Burlington and for him to get a haircut. Half-way to town Steve suffered a stroke. Four months later, having been frustrated by the arduous process of rehabilitation, he suffered a second stroke, which proved fatal. Stephen Z. Starr had provided for his family, toiled steadily and happily with his wife to raise and educate four children, and had become a respected and even beloved citizen of a deeply American city. Above and beyond all this, he successfully pursued his life-long dream of becoming an accomplished historian and scholar. He had achieved his life-long goals.

Ivy Jane Edmondson Starr, Artist

Ivy Jane Edmondson was supposed to become a pianist. This was the plan of her practical mother, who early foresaw that her son, George, would leave Cleveland to pursue a career elsewhere and knew from her own hardscrabble experience that husbands could die early or encounter financial difficulties that would leave their families with no source of support. As a house girl in music professor Charles Demuth's home in Oberlin she had watched her contemporary, Charlotte "Lottie" Demuth, being groomed for what would become a distinguished and remunerative career as a violinist. Minnie Edmondson decided early that her daughter Ivy Jane would follow the same kind of career as a pianist, and thus be able to provide for her mother in old age.

Ivy Jane hated practicing but found no alternative path until she met Miss Raymond, the art teacher at Hathaway Brown School. A competent etcher and watercolorist, Miss Raymond was quick to recognize her young student's abilities and soon had her doing linoleum-cut prints of domestic scenes and classical subjects. It was thanks to Miss Raymond's training in wood and linoleum block printing that Ivy Jane first gained recognition as an artist.

At age seventeen in 1926 she exhibited at the Cleveland Museum of Art's annual show and won a first prize. These early prints can be seen in the Museum's collection.

She drew themes for her linoleum block prints from the world of Greek mythology that she had studied at Hathaway Brown. One of them showed a naked, recumbent young woman partially obscured by the backside of a muscular man who was obviously enjoying the view. One wonders what her parents thought of it. And there were several of Iphigenia, a demure-looking young woman in a long-flowing robe. Iphigenia's father, Agamemnon, had offended the gods and needed to sacrifice his daughter to appease them. Agamemnon lured Iphigenia to the altar with the lie that she was going to be married to Achilles. But at the moment of sacrifice, the daughter was miraculously swapped for an animal and transported to an island, where she could live at a safe distance from her scheming father.

":Iphigenia," Ivy Jane Edmondson, age nineteen. Brad Edmondson

Another early print based on classical mythology depicts Persephone, the daughter of Zeus and Demeter, rising out of the ground. Persephone was so beautiful that Hades, the king of the underworld, stole her from her parents. The devastated Demeter, the goddess of the harvest, and caused the earth to become barren. Zeus ordered Hades to release Persephone and he did, but on the condition that she thereafter spend a third of each year in the underworld. This was the mythological origin of winter, and Persephone's annual rising signifies the onset of spring. Ivy Jane denied that she saw herself in Persephone, but her grand-nephew, writer Brad Edmondson, noted that in her later work she often returned to the theme of women for whom things were not quite as they should be.

Ivy Jane was fortunate to have close at hand a much more accomplished painter than Miss Raymond, and one who also took a keen interest in her progress, her Uncle Will (William J. Edmondson). By the 1920s Will had married and was living comfortably in Shaker Heights, thanks to money his wife had inherited. He had long since mastered the various types of portraiture favored by Cleveland's industrial magnates. His older brother George, Ivy Jane's father, had pushed him in this direction and for a quarter century he had honed his skill in scores of oil portraits of gravely solemn Cleveland males and their proper but elegantly turned out wives. Now, though, he took only commissions he wanted to do, and focused mainly on more colorful people from Cleveland's art world and his circle of friends. Portraits of artist Ora Coltman or of man-about-town Winsor French are among his best works. Most of the time Will Edmondson now indulged his passion for plein air landscape painting, traveling each summer to Virginia and New England to turn out serene landscapes that mirrored his gentle personality.

"Uncle Will" was delighted to coach his charming and eager young niece in both these artistic genres. Knowing that landscapes could never provide a steady income, Will Edmondson focused especially on portraiture, which accorded with Minnie Edmondson's career strategy for her daughter. Thanks to her Uncle Will, by her twenty-second-year Ivy Jane Edmondson was a skilled if rather traditional practitioner of this art.

Even though Ivy Jane already had two teachers, she was soon supplementing her studies with Saturday classes at the Cleveland School of Art (now Cleveland Institute of Art). At first she focused on drawing, but under the influence of the School's leading light, Henry Keller (1869-1949), a master watercolorist, she took up that medium. It was to become a main pillar of her life as a painter. Keller, born to a German family west of Cleveland, had trained in Dusseldorf and Munich. By the time Ivy Jane entered his studio he was the acknowledged dean of the Cleveland art world. Even though two of his paintings were included in the landmark Armory Show of 1913, where the new European avant-garde made its American debut, he was no modernist. Instead he focused, as did Uncle Will, on plein air watercolors. Later, when she was teaching art at Hathaway Brown, Ivy Jane Edmondson once more turned to Keller, who by then was teaching at the Huntington Polytechnic Institute.

Fifteen years before Ivy Jane arrived in Keller's studio, one of his students had been Charles Burchfield (1893-1967) from Salem, Ohio. By the time Ivy Jane was in her teens, Burchfield was riding high as a virtuoso watercolorist who specialized in Midwestern townscapes, rural scenes, and close-focus canvasses featuring wild plants and flowers. Will Edmondson liked Burchfield's work and befriended him. It was through her uncle that Ivy Jane made contact with Burchfield's paintings. Even though she met this artist only a couple of times (he left Cleveland in 1921 and only visited thereafter) and never studied with him, Burchfield's watercolors exerted a powerful influence on her art, and one that can be detected in her work over the next eighty years. Indeed, if we are to declare Ivy Jane Edmondson Starr a protégé of anyone, that person would be would surely be Charles Burchfieldand his landscape paintings.

Burchfield's neatly delineated and ghostly townscapes suggest the setting for Edgar Lee Master's <u>Spoon River Anthology</u> of 1915. His landscapes are realistic, but in a deeply lyrical way, thanks to his wild use of colors and his ability to simplify through the use of strong brush strokes. More than a few of his landscapes and paintings of flowers burst the bonds of realism to become ecstatic visions of nature. He used flashes of color to express the sounds of insects and frogs, and some of his flowers seem to take on grotesque human features. To such works he often appended an explanatory phrase or two. In later life Ivy Jane Starr treated Burchfield's memory with great respect and acknowledged her overall debt to him. But whether she actually derived these specific approaches and practices from him or she independently evolved along lines similar to those Burchfield had followed, remains unknown.

We have already seen how classes at the Cleveland Art School brought Ivy Jane Edmondson into contact with a talented and lively group of Hungarian immigrants, including the etcher and engraver Kalman Kubinyi. These relationships played an important role in freeing her from the conventional world of her family on East 96th Street, from Ivy Colson's proper soirees in Elyria, and the high-minded but straight-laced Hathaway Brown School. But they left no discernible mark on her art.

The next and final phase of Ivy Jane's training occurred when she spent 1931-1932 on a scholarship to the Art Students League in New York. She was assigned to the studios of Thomas Hart Benton and Hans Hoffmann. Several recent exhibitions and books identify Ivy Jane Starr as an artistic offspring of Benton, but she herself vigorously denied this honor. It is true that at least a few of her studio portraits reflect his realism, but she was more likely to apply it to the depiction of subjects like vegetables than to his preferred social and historical themes. It is also true that half century later she mined his 1930s populism and baroque planning ideas when she did her series "Women of the Old Testament." But all of this she could have picked up anywhere in the 1930s without help from Benton, whom she found to be an alcoholic boor who rarely appeared in his studio classes and even more rarely offered advice that was useful.

Hans Hoffmann had just emigrated to America from his native Bavaria, and the abstract works that were the source of his fame were still eight years in the future. But Ivy Jane found his drawing class useful, and also his view that some colors push out towards the viewer while others pull away. Such notions helped free her from her uncle Will Edmondson's rather conventional notions of color.

By the time of her marriage in 1933 Ivy Jane Edmondson had completed her training and was well launched on a career in art that would span eight decades. An inventory of her entire known oeuvre includes over six hundred entries. The total would have been higher yet had not scores of pieces, especially from the early period, been lost.

She was not in the habit of dating her work, and kept no inventory of them. When she got around to assigning dates to her work she did so by decade, but acknowledged that many of her dates were mere guesses.

Even with these caveats, her totals by decade are nonetheless interesting:

1920s   33
1930s   35
1940s   22
1950s   50
1960s   85
1970s   90
1980s   162
1990s   128
2000s   144

This long span divides naturally into five periods:

1) To the early 1930s, a period of training and preparation in Cleveland and New York.

2) From the early 1930s to the mid-1950s, when she was busy raising a family in New York and, after 1940, in Cincinnati. At the beginning of this period she did mainly portraits and a few rural scenes but by the end she had begun sculpting.

3) From the late 1950s to the mid-1970s, during which time she completed 122 works of sculpture. Down to the early 1980s she worked exclusively in hard stone, but by that decade 25 of 33 pieces were in clay and in the following decade 15 of 17 pieces.

4) From the completion of her children's high-schooling in the early 1960s to the death if her husband, Stephen Z. Starr, in 1987, full-time work as a painter and sculpture, mainly in Underhill Center, Vermont.

5) From 1987 to her death in 2012, Final sculpting in clay, intensive painting in oils, including several didactic pieces, works of fantastic realism, and several series, notably "Women of the Old Testament."

Of course, this periodization is much too facile, for it corresponds as much to the changing circumstances of Ivy Jane's life than to the evolution of her art. In some cases the two mesh, as for example, the rise and fall of her work as a sculptor, which corresponds, first, to a period of physical strength in her late forties, when she began sculpting in marble and even granite, and then to her gradual shift to clay as her physical strength waned and arthritis set in.

The biggest shortcoming of this chronology is that it obscures the continuities. For example, with the birth of her first son in 1934 she began a series of remarkably precise pencil sketches of newborn children, first her own, then her eight grandchildren, and finally a proliferation of great-grandchildren. A second major continuity were watercolors, mainly of landscapes and natural scenes but also of urban life. To be sure, these evolved over time. For instance, she made increasing use of ink or pencil in order to sharpen the images. But watercolor remained a constant feature of her production. Portraiture was another constant, as were self-portraits, of which she did twelve, which were concentrated at the beginning and end of her career. Any or all of these constants would merit an exhibition, for while they reveal the discontinuities caused by a demanding life and the process of aging, they also reveal continuities, both of form and content.

Two of Ivy Jane Starr's early portraits suggest that she was living simultaneously in two eras. Her fine and expressive portrait of Sister Marcelina, the Mother Superior of the hospital and nursing school where her mother had studied, could have come from her Uncle Will's brush, with its precise, sunlit, and sympathetic portrayal of the remarkable woman who was its subject. By contrast, her portrait of her friend Kate Lehman, is fully of its era, depicting a spoiled, self-indulgent, but savvy modern woman, lounging languidly on a couch. She was to do many other oil portraits during the next seventy years, ending with her large portrait of her grand-niece Emma Edmondson in 2008. Some of the best were charcoal sketches, including quickly captured images of her younger son and daughter, Fred and Diana. Several of the most sympathetic of her portraits show her husband, historian Stephen Starr, rendered in both oil and watercolor, at his typewriter, pursuing the career he had postponed for thirty years.

After the birth of her first son, George, in 1934, family life claimed more and more of Ivy Jane Starr's time and attention and would continue to do so over the next quarter century. This restricted the subjects of her paintings to daily life and even domestic themes. Immediately after she and Steve moved into an apartment on Morton Street in Greenwich Village she painted a large mural (long since painted over) depicting romantic scenes of urban life, replete with Hungarian restaurants and gypsy violinists. By contrast, her major painting of 1934 was a large oil showing her first son's baby carriage in front of the tall window on Morton Street. Using both watercolors and oils she painted scenes from her window both there and at 261 Seaman Avenue on the far northern tip of Manhattan Island, to which they moved in 1937.

The apartment on Seaman Avenue looked across the Harlem River to Spuyten Duyvil, the southern edge of the upper-class suburb of Riverdale. On the hillside stood a grand mansard-roofed residence from the 1880s that was under the wrecking ball. Ivy Jane painted the home before and during its demolition. In the 1960s she returned to this theme in a large canvas showing the half-demolished remains of a Mansarded Cincinnati mansion. She featured the steam shovels that were carrying out the operation, looking for all the world like the mechanical monsters they were This fascination with huge forces, both mechanical and organic, was to become a steady theme throughout Ivy Jane Starr's life, leading, among other works, to a series of watercolors of earthmoving machines, trucks, and graders working near her Pennswood retirement community around 2003.

During the 1940s and 1950s it was mainly during vacations that Ivy Jane found time to paint. The first of these was spent at her brother's farm near Medina, Ohio, in 1939. This return to the Midwest led her to paint a cycle of watercolors depicting the farmhouse, barns, outbuildings, and fields. They were done in a sun-lit realism that would have pleased Charles Burchfield, but without the element of expressionist fancy that crept into so many of Burchfield's later paintings and those of Starr herself.

(Left)Ivy Jane Starr in Medina, 1937 S.F. Starr
(Right) Barn at farm of G. Edmondson, Medina, Ohio, 1937. Brad Edmondson.

A second series was done during vacations at the Lake Erie home of life-long friends Charles and Catherine Sawyer. These move away from Burchfield's sunny realism but do not reach the looser watercolor style into which she settled later in Vermont. What clearly interested her most were subjects like the gnarled and fantastic driftwood that storms had driven onto the Erie shore. By the mid-1950s Ivy Jane was again painting during the year and finding many urban subjects in the old sections of Cincinnati.

The decision in 1952 to vacation in Underhill Center, Vermont, launched a fresh period of productivity and advances. During her first summers there, Ivy Jane Starr reveled in the beauty of the Green Mountains in sunlight and amidst storms, and did highly competent watercolor of broad vistas, as well as more focused renderings of such typical Vermont subjects as barns, houses, the winding Irish.

Pasture with Flowers, 1970s

Formerly owned by Lewis Lehrman and the Lehrman Foundation,

collection of anonymous owner, Colorado.

Settlement Road, and "sugarbushes," the wooden buildings in which maple sap is boiled to produce syrup. One of her most successful projects in this traditional vein was a series of watercolors of the home of Professor and Mrs. Peter Seybolt in Underhill Center. Compared with her earlier series on her brother's farm in Medina, Ohio, the Seybolt watercolors are freer and more spontaneous in conception and execution. But over time all these subjects began to pall and she was heard to quote Georgia O'Keefe's famous complaint that the New England landscape contained, "Too damn much green!"

Thaw in Vermont, ca. 1970. ArtNEO.

Having had her fill of what she felt had become ritualized landscapes and genre scenes, Ivy Jane Starr turned increasingly in new directions that arose not from established "schools" but from her own personality and vision. An early manifestation of this was a large watercolor of a collapsed house in Underhill Center, a scene of decay and dissolution presided over by a seated Jersey cow looking placidly at the viewer. Another stunning watercolor in the same vein was a close-up of a once solid maple tree, its trunk now ripped by lightning and standing as a silent monument to a past moment of drama.

Broken tree trunk, Vermont, 1970s. ArtNEO.

Increasingly, Ivy Jane Starr saw nature was a wild place exuding mysterious passions. Harkening back to a theme beloved by Charles Burchfield, she did a number of watercolors of sunflowers, some peacefully smiling at the sun and others blown by raging storms, their petals looking for all the world like wild white fingers in dramatic motion.

Thus transformed, Vermont nature appeared to her eyes not as something scenic or "pretty" but as a wild world. This was fully manifest in a large watercolor of a dark winter landscape covered with grey snow, which she represented with a large smear of oil paint an eighth of an inch thick. Other paintings present nature as teeming with semi-abstract representations of the animal or human world. Thus, an otherwise attractive watercolor scene of rolling hills as viewed in winter from her hillside home emerges as several giant, grey, and slumbering rhinoceroses. Yet another painting, this one in oil on Masonite, depicted the grey sky as a vast rolling curtain or swag, looming over the mountains. In a more positive vein, a brightly sunlit birch tree with fully leafed branches bent by the wind bears the title "Ballerina Birch," suggesting that the entire plant was in dizzying, joyful motion.

Vermont, 1970s, George A. Starr, Berkeley, Ca.

Ballerina Birch, 1960s, watercolor, ArtNEO.

This was not the first time that Ivy Jane Starr used words to explain what she considered the deeper essence of what she had painted. During her first summer in Vermont she painted a deep, narrow, steep-sided natural stone pool with one of her sons shown in silhouette climbing up its side. Ivy Jane saw this as a kind of allegory, and named it "Long Climb Up." Other such allegorical works were to follow later.

These and other new paths opened before Ivy Jane Starr in the 1950s as she finally found time to return to her art and after she had done her full share of Vermont landscapes and genre scenes. Pushed by her disenchantment with earlier subjects and techniques and pulled by the intriguing new directions that arose from her own imagination, she restlessly explored many new directions at once. One of these bears special emphasis, however: her infatuation with vegetables, roots, and buds as subjects for watercolors. Beginning with a still-life of broccoli and then turning to cucumbers, cockscombs, fiddle ferns, complex fennel roots, and gnarled buckeye buds she produced precise, close-up and portrait-like watercolors of unexpected subjects from nature. She was well-aware of the rich traditions of botanical art, and had leafed through the major collections dating back to the Renaissance. But she was less interested in documenting nature than in exploring the exotic and tangled three-dimensional forms that these vegetables, root plants, and buds assumed.

She painted each in turn, some of them several times, but in the end remained unsatisfied. Never a colorist, she was nonetheless a skilled delineator. Her dissatisfaction rested not in her representational skills but in the fact that the subjects called for a three-dimensional presentation, i.e. sculpture. However, with the exception of a pair of terra cotta bookends she had done in her teens, she had no prior experience working in three dimensions, whether in clay or stone. Yet beginning in the mid-1950s she came to feel that her true vocation was sculpting, and therefore set about retooling herself in that art.

To this end she turned to Cincinnati's reigning sculpture, Charles Cutler (1914-1971), and enrolled in his class at the Cincinnati Art Museum's Academy. Cutler's career was at its peak, and his sculptures of human forms emerging from raw rock were being shown in exhibitions in New York and Massachusetts. Cutler worked in bronze and wood but the preferred materials of this muscular and blunt-spoken artist were granite, basalt, and marble. Ivy Jane promptly equipped herself with cutting tools and both five and seven pound mallets.

Cutler in those years was producing pieces that seemed to emerge from the hard stone the way the fiddle ferns, fennel and other root vegetables emerged from the soil in Ivy Jane Starr's own paintings. It was a happy fit, and Cutler quickly passed on to her the carving and finishing techniques that enabled her to translate her vision into stone. From Cutler she also acquired a good knowledge of the best quarries in the eastern United States.

In spite of her small physique, Starr began turning out an avalanche of sculptures in granite, basalt, and marble. She reveled in the physicality of stone carving and spoke despairingly of those "so-called sculptors" like Henry Moore who molded their pieces in soft clay and handed them to others to cast in bronze. This, she devoutly believed, was not real sculpting. She sold oil portraits to fund the purchase of marble from Tennessee and Vermont, as well as granite. With her usual meager budget, she chased down massive un-quarried rocks from the Kentucky countryside, hauled them home in her station wagon, and attacked them with gusto.

At first she focused on birds in flight, penguins, dogs, cats, and other animals, including a cow's head, which she presented in simplified, abstracted and more elemental forms than they assumed in nature. One of these works, mounted on a metal rod, depicted several birds in flight while another, commissioned by the Cincinnati Zoo and now unfortunately lost, presented a row of penguins carved in profile from white marble with black wings by their sides rendered in epoxy.

True to her earlier practice, Starr found commissions for several portrait heads. But while these were successful, she concluded that they did not fully utilize the potential of stone. She overcame this in a sculpture of Elizabeth Ann Seton, the first American saint, commissioned by the Maryland shrine dedicated to her. But even this, she felt, was a mere extension of her earlier work as a portraitist and presented no new challenge. Instead of portraiture, Starr turned to the classical subjects of children and mother and child. Over the next decade she reverted again and again to these two themes, including a girl and dog, a black marble boy holding a piglet, and a crouching child figure. By the time she produced a small piece in marble of a girl in a flowing robe, she was clearly in full control of the medium and creating portraiture that was completely free of the painterly qualities she had been taught by her Uncle Will and had long been accustomed to revere.

Seated girl, 1970s, ArtNEO.

Undoubtedly Ivy Jane Starr's most popular work in this genre is a large marble of a young girl scrunched up in a sitting pose and reading a book. Librarians at the Cincinnati Public Library, which commissioned rhe work, report that children frequently sit to read on the floor next to her and are frequently photographed there.

Seated reader, Cincinnati Public Library, 1978, ArtNEO.

Starr was no fan of the abstract expressionism that reigned in high art circles during her middle and later years. She spoke disparagingly of the later work of her former teacher Hans Hoffmann and dismissed Jackson Pollack as a self-indulgent blow-hard. "He was supposed to come to the Art Students' League two days a week but usually came only once and sat in the hall and held forth. He was short, scrappy, and physically pugnacious." When he reviewed her work Pollock told Ivy Jane that it was "Really very good, but there is nothing I can do for you."[238] And that was that. But in spite of her visceral skepticism about abstractionism, the act of sculpting allowed, or forced Ivy Jane Starr to work at a much higher level of abstraction than her training in classical portraiture and twentieth century realism allowed her to achieve in oils or watercolors. The switch to sculpting freed her from polemics over avant-gardism and opened a path on which she was free to pursue her own true inclinations.

As she proceeded along this new direction Starr returned to the subjects of her many "vegetable" paintings. In sculpture she found an exciting new way to portray those fantastic fiddle ferns, fennel roots, broccoli and other plants. Her fascination with these organic forms as subjects for sculpture is evident from the fact that she did five different marble variants of fiddle ferns alone. Her numerous works in this vein are certainly realistic in in their origins but completely abstracted, lyrical variations or transpositions rather than mere representations.

The series of sculptures of roots and vegetables are surely among Ivy Jane Starr's most enduring works in any medium. Many, including a very different rendering of an African-American woman and child, and also a Japanese-themed garden sculpture, were executed in a Tennessee marble that was so hard that few sculptors had the sheer muscle to work it. The root and vegetables would have resonated with Charles Burchfield but not with her Uncle Will, with Charles Cutler but not Thomas Hart Benton or Hans Hoffmann. In the end, both the concept and implementation of works on this theme in both watercolor and in stone were hers alone.

(Left) Organic roots, granite, 1990. (Right) African woman and child, ArtNEO.

Monument to space exploration, granite, 2,OOO, Diana Starr Cooper.

Both in painting and sculpture Ivy Jane Starr during the 1960s and 1970s moved towards more abstract modes of presentations. Thus, after a trip with her husband to Japan she did a completely abstract oil of a tulip, evoking Japanese art, and in the same vein a Japanese screen featuring abstract fabric designs and young Japanese motorcyclists. An important marble sculpture from these same years came to her mind when she and her husband attended a baseball game at Crosley Field in Cincinnati. Indifferent to the game itself, Ivy Jane was nonetheless fascinated by the sight of kneeling players as they waited to come to bat. With her trip to Japan fresh in her mind, she saw this canonic moment as a kind of oriental ritual, and presented the two figures as such in a work of sculpture.

Though barely two feet tall, Ivy Jane Starr's "Baseball Players" is her most monumental work of sculpture. Consisting of seven separate pieces of rough-hewn granite mounted on a wooden base, it is abstracted but not fully abstract, suggestive of its heroic subject without a touch of realism. If this fine piece were to be rendered in three-meter-high stone or bronze it could provide a stunning and commanding monument at the entrance of a major baseball park.

Waiting to Come to Bat, granite, 1985. S.F. Starr

From 1969 to 1987 Ivy Jane and Steve Starr lived and worked in a house they had built for themselves on the Irish Settlement Road in Underhill Center, Vermont. The view was breathtaking in all seasons, but the climate severe.

They maintained a large garden in the summer and huddled around a wood stove in the dark winter, when they relied on each other and a small coterie of neighbors and friends for company. Both focused single-mindedly on their work, he on his multi-volume history of the Union cavalry and she on sculpting and painting. While there is little doubt that it was Steve who found this austere yet beautiful environment most appealing, Ivy Jane also threw herself into it. She discovered sources of excellent cut marble in Proctor, Vermont, and used her station wagon to pick up large hunks of quarried but unused black marble from quarries on Isle La Motte, the northernmost island in Lake Champlain. Quarrying had long since ceased on this picturesque island so the unused marble slabs and chunks were free for the taking. Famed for its use at Radio City in New York, this marble takes a high polish but is hard and unyielding to hand tools. Undaunted, Ivy Jane did a number of large pieces from this flinty material, including a black Madonna.

If there was any doubt that the Starrs had planted themselves on their Vermont hillside with the intention of spending their lives there it was removed when Ivy Jane sculpted from a five-foot marble plinth a Lar, the Roman god of the hearth. A Lar was supposed to protect all within the locale they surveyed. Like their related household deities, the Penates, they watched over the domus, which Romans conceived as a universe in miniature. The Starr's gave this monument pride of place in their Vermont dooryard. It was an act of faith, certainly in the present, but also in the future. By the time they had erected the Lar they had lived seven decades, almost half a century of that time together. Both had emerged healthy from bouts of cancer and now they had work to do. A hopeful radiance suffused this autumnal phase of their life together. Yet within a decade he was dead and she was involuntarily launched on a totally new phase of her life.

Lar, god of the hearth, marble, 1989. S.F. Starr

Stephen Z. Starr died in the cold autumn of 1987. Ivy Jane, unwilling to face the harsh Vermont winter alone, sold the house and by the next spring was living in Princeton, New Jersey, near her daughter and son-in-law, Ivy and Dennis Minely. In the early Princeton months she did a small portrait sculpture of her late husband in clay, a number of sketches of her father's studio on East 96th Street in Cleveland, and evocative recollections of Cincinnati, as well as two self-portraits.

It was at this time that she had cataracts in both eyes surgically removed. For some years she had been using the new and intense acrylic colors. Once her cataracts were gone she discovered that they had distorted her color sense. She therefore destroyed scores of her recent Vermont watercolors and steered away from doing traditional landscapes thereafter. For several years she was adrift, shifting her attention to drawing in pencil and charcoal and to sculpting.

Another constraint at this time was the development of arthritis in both her shoulders and hands. Whether this was a consequence of years of wielding a five-pound sledge hammer, as she thought, or of a congenital condition, as seems likely, it effectively ended her career working hard stone. It was at this fortuitous moment that her younger daughter Diana asked her to illustrate a book she had written on the interaction of animals and trainers in The Big Apple Circus. Night After Night (1994) featured twenty-five sketches done in pen, charcoal, and wash and a cover in color. Starr announced that it "got Vermont landscapes out of my mind" and renewed her interest in sketching.

Increased travel in her eighth decade gave rise to a flood of watercolors and pencil sketches. A visit to her old neighbors the Burgesses in Vermont produced a series on their house, a trip to the Bellstrom family in Spain inspired ten watercolors, while a vacation at the Arizona home of her friend Catherine "Kit" Sawyer gave rise to twenty watercolors of the desert. A visit to her son and daughter-in-law in Oberlin, Ohio, inspired her to do small paintings on the architecture of that historic mid-western town, a series that eventually numbered sixteen paintings. To produce these she devised a small, hand-held easel that enabled her to stand in front of the building and paint, without drawing attention as a normal easel would have done.

In her restless search for subjects during the 1990s, Ivy Jane Starr mined her old sketch books. This led to the production of a number of intriguing paintings of the Budapest home of her son and daughter-in-law George Starr and Julia Bader, and also three excellent paintings on New Orleans, two of them showing the construction of the traditional Christmas-eve bon fires on the levees up-river from the city and a third, a large composite work in oil entitled "Laissez les bon temps rouler," showing a highly stylized young horn player. The latter piece, bold and celebratory, now hangs in the Hogan Jazz Archive at Tulane University. Paired with this is a large canvas of a jazz-playing "Gabriel."

"Gabriel," ArtNEO.

The early 1990s were a period of intense and many-sided activity. Ivy Jane produced a burst of new portraits, including of her son George and his daughter Klari, and oil portraits or portrait sketches of daughter Diana seated informally at a table, and a new crop of baby sketches of grandchildren. As if searching for sitters, she did an oil painting of granddaughter Anna based on a snapshot, and a formal portrait of Oberlin alumnus and pioneer Black office-holder John Mercer Langston, based on a century-old photograph. The Mercer portrait hangs today in the Cox Building at Oberlin College. And she even did two careful portraits of dogs, her daughter Diana's Labradors Sophie and Henry.

These were years in which Ivy Jane Starr completed her last sculptural works in stone. A white marble Fallen Angel, Kneeling Woman (in black Brazilian marble), and further Fennel Bulbs continued earlier explorations, albeit in smaller formats, while a larger columnar "Boy with a Ball" also built on earlier themes.

The discovery of new waxes and clays opened stunning fresh vistas to Starr's sculpture. Thus, she did a grotesque "Boulevardier" with his smiling head on one side. a pair of dancers (inspired by a ball she attended in Oberlin many years earlier), and a further Fallen Angel, all sculpted first in clay. When her daughter-in-law Julia Bader arranged for these and several other pieces to be cast in bronze in Hungary, their monumental character was immediately evident. And several other pieces executed in wax, including a pianist seated at a grand piano, a cellist, and a boy driving a go-cart, showed a whimsical spontaneity and dynamism that would have been impossible to achieve in stone.

"Fallen Angel," bronze, originally clay. S.F. Starr

"Boulevadier," cast bronze. S. F. Starr

(Left) "Dancers", 1984. S.F.Starr. (Right) "Smiling Children," terra cotta, 1975. S.F. Starr

A Concert in Princeton, 1989 S.F. Starr

This last and most plastic phase of Ivy Jane's sculpture enabled her to achieve the highest degree of expressiveness. A plaque depicting three smiling figures, deeply sculpted and slightly tinted in the spirit of Luca della Robbia (1399-1482), epitomized her work of this period.

A small piece in baked clay entitled "Steve [Starr] Putting on His Shirt" merits special note. A mere nine inches tall, it shows a refinement and balance between strain and repose, stretched cloth and the human form beneath, that is impressive by any measure. Like many other works from this period, this is pure sculpture and in no sense mere three-dimensional painting.

"Steve Putting On His Shirt," terra cotta, 1979. S.F. Starr

During the 1990s Starr also ventured into several new directions in watercolor and oil paintings. Thus, an oil painting of thawing snow done just before she left Vermont features a heavy band of white paint mixed with grey clay, as if offering the viewer tactile contact with the earliest onset of spring.

Genre paintings with ghostly figures that are both present and absent also make their appearance. This trend began back in the 1960s, when she commemorated the sixtieth anniversary of Cincinnati's women's literary circle, the Noonday Club, meeting at her home. Ivy Jane Starr described the group as "having been founded by several prominent Jewish ladies who had finished college and come back to Cincinnati. They didn't want to go to seed, so they met and wrote papers, serious papers." A founding member of the group, Gertie Friedlander, now wheel-chair bound and accompanied by a nurse, attended this session. Ivy Jane painted the gathered women as outlines, and inside the outlines she put clouds and hills. When her great-nephew Brad Edmondson asked her why she had done this she replied, "Because they weren't really there." She explained that, "They were so busy paying court to Gertie that they were somehow absent," so she reduced them all to mere silhouettes, blank shadows with no reality. About the same time, a carefully painted scene in oil looking forward in a bus running from Princeton to New York used the same method, as did a large canvas of a crowded bus at Christmastime entitled "Pax Express." All are allegories, for all carry explicit comments or messages that the artist wished to convey.

The shift to clay gave rise to a whole series of painted stick-like figures conveying various messages. One, a commission for the Department of Women's Studies at Princeton, showed a realistic but tumbled and utterly confused assemblage of letters representing the writings produced by scholars of the department. Did those who commissioned the work grasp its criticism? Another shows a headless and armless human bowing before a half dozen strange and distorted columns representing The Law. This same satirical attitude towards the law emerged in a large and abstract human head in marble, featuring a half dozen dinner knives fastened to its brow like an Indian head dress and entitled "Legal Beagle."

The Law. S.F. Starr

During her last three decades Ivy Jane Starr embraced a kind of magic realism. The roots of this style can be traced back to her paintings of broken trees and fennel, and to the sculptures of fiddle ferns and other roots. But it was only in her eighth and ninth decades that it reached full flower, and then most fully in one work: "The Mysterious Forest." This single work consists of two separate components: a work of baked and painted clay representing three dark trees in silhouette, the outline of their deep green foliage describing an oval with serrated edges, highly stylized; and a background painting in oil representing the deeper forest of which the sculpted trees are a part. Together, they present what seems like a dream or some deep recollection from the past.

Study for "The Mysterious Forest," S.F. Starr

Ivy Starr's earliest representations of the natural world were entirely benign, the kind of expressions of nature that derive from a happy summer vacation. After living year-round in Vermont for more than a decade, Nature's more ominous face pressed in upon her. If "The Mysterious Forest" has a vaguely sinister aura about it, her representations of earthworms as Nature's agents of decay and regeneration are far more disquieting. As she put it, "Ashes to ashes, dust to dust!"

This was the message also of a watercolor dating from her last days in Vermont, where a thawing snow reveals the decaying statues of leaders that did not survive the winter's cold. Here was a frozen version of poet **Percy Bysshe Shelley's** 1818 poem of decay, "Ozymandias," which the artist came across at this time:

> I met a traveler from an antique land
> Who said: "Two vast and trunkless legs of stone
> Stand in the desert. Near them, on the sand,
> Half sunk, a shattered visage lies, whose frown,
> And wrinkled lip, and sneer of cold command,
> Tell that its sculptor well those passions read
> Which yet survive, stamped on these lifeless things,

The hand that mocked them and the heart that fed:

And on the pedestal these words appear:

My name is Ozymandias, king of kings:

Look on my works, ye Mighty, and despair!'

Nothing beside remains.

Closely related to these sculptures and painting is a series of nearly a dozen human heads sculpted out of the same material, baked, and unpainted. Many were flattened or distorted in the same way that a rotting watermelon sags and decays. All have eyes but are otherwise featureless, and certainly devoid of human qualities. One has its tongue hanging out. They are three-dimensional shadows, and were intended to be placed on the ground, amidst her sculpted worms or in small groupings of their own and bearing the same message: "Ecce homo!" or "Behold the man!" the words spoken by Pontius Pilate as he presented a scourged Jesus Christ to the mob.

Grotesque Heads of Baked Clay, late 1970s.

The dark ruminations that informed these works also led to an expansion of the didactic trend that we detected earlier. Back in 1972 the so-called Club of Rome had issued dire warnings about "The Limits of Growth" and traced those limits to the uncontrolled expansion of human populations worldwide. In the late 1980s numerous reports on the growth of world population made the point that humans had proliferated more in the past three generations than in the preceding half millennium. Reading such claims, Ivy Jane Starr concluded that a crisis was at hand. In 1990, she undertook a large canvas depicting overpopulation, not of human beings but of every conceivable type of organism and life form. Showing a benign Vermont landscape teeming and overrun with fanciful organisms and insects, the work features a nineteenth-century style banner title on which is written, "Too Many of Us." Nearly two centuries earlier the Quaker painter Edward Hicks had painted the several dozen versions of his "Peaceable Kingdom" while living only three miles from Ivy Jane Starr's home in Newtown, Pennsylvania. Her "Too Many of Us," completed in 1993, is a kind of Peaceable Kingdom in reverse.

A similar feeling of impending disaster infused a second didactic painting of these years. The inspiration for this work came from a 1994 New York Times article, one of several that had appeared since the late 1980s, detailing the collapse of amphibian populations worldwide. Ivy Jane Starr concluded that the unexplained extinction of Golden Toads and Harlequin Frogs were a signal to mankind, like the proverbial canaries in a coal mine. Several scientists expressed reservations about this theory, but she nonetheless painted a large canvas teeming with frogs and toads and bearing the title, again emblazoned on a nineteenth century banner spreading across the canvas, "What the Frogs Are Teaching Us."

"Just Too Many of Us," oil on canvas, late 1990s. ArtNEO.

"What the Frogs are Teaching Us," 1995, ArtNEO.

When asked about the ominous message of several of her later works Ivy Jane Starr would point to several others which, in her view, presented a slightly more sanguine views of the future. Among these were a pair of heads of baked clay. One with one hand over its sad face, is peering into the past. The other, with a non-committal look of expectation, looks to the future. It is not clear whether these preceded or followed the darker works discussed above.

"Looking to the Past" and "Looking to the Future," baked clay, date uncertain, Art NEO.

During her ninth decade Ivy Jane Starr's art was increasingly informed by her reading, which now included reexamination of both classical and religious texts she had read in school and which she now reread. This resulted in a painting of Icarus, showing his wings melting in the sun, an oil of Moses handing down the Ten Commandments, and a triptych entitled "Three Religions," featuring the ancient Greek gods, Christianity, and contemporary man.

"Moses handing down the Law," oil on canvas, 1980s, ArtNEO.

By comparison, an oil based on a trip the artist made to Assisi and showing a young St. Francis on the streets of his home town, but in modern dress. This opened to her a promising new avenue. Over the next four years this approach led to the creation of a twenty-eight-canvas cycle of oil paintings devoted to "Women of the Old

Testament," in modern dress. She named the cycle "Daughters of Eve." Here is the artist's own introduction to these works, from the published catalogue:

Ivy Jane Starr at 100.

"What led a painter who had spent a lifetime on secular subjects to do these paintings of the Old Testament women? What was the incentive behind these paintings? Up to the age of eighty-five my knowledge of the Bible was limited to childish Sunday-school versions of the major stories. But now I decided to read the Bible straight through. It was now or never.

Beyond the grand creation myth in Genesis I anticipated mild boredom. But I began my reading at just the time our press was full of reports of infertile women who had hired surrogate mothers, and all the noisy discord that followed. Wasn't that what I had just been reading about in the Bible? The story of Sarah, Abraham, and Hagar also intrigued me because it was so like the news of today. Amazing! No less fascinating was the discovery that Abraham was not so admirable in his early life, yet he developed into a fine person.

All this I found engrossing. I read on, pondering why the characters, and especially the women, behaved as they did. In their tribal, patriarchal society, they managed as best they could. These women present pictures of good behavior and bad. At times they are heroic, at other times sneaky and conniving, and at still others they emerge as helpless victims.

I wanted to paint these women without passing judgment on them. After all, what was acceptable conduct back in early Biblical times for both sexes is quite different from the standards we live by now. Yet for all the differences between the circumstances and moralities of their time and our own, their emotional problems are similar to ours.

I don't call these pictures illustrations, for they do not pictorialize the high points of the stories. …I chose, rather, to present those situations that showed best how these women might appear in today's world. I realize full well that the concentration on subject matter and a more literary approach puts the project outside the field of most contemporary art. So be it…"

Daughters of Eve" Cycle, ca. 1985, ArtNEO

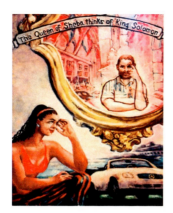 

"Daughters of Eve" includes many arresting paintings, which are rendered more compelling by their close adherence to the Biblical texts and by Ivy Jane Starr's wry published commentaries. The style throughout hearkens back to the 1930s and to Thomas Hart Benton, not just in its narrative and heroic character but in the deliberate use of the dramatic Baroque angles of perspective so beloved by Benton. Exhibited only once, the series is preserved at the ArtNEO Gallery in Cleveland and amply warrants future exhibitions.

In her ninth decade Ivy Jane Starr continued at her customary whirlwind pace. Statements and texts appeared on several canvases, including "Literary Pursuits" on a watercolor of children reading, or "I Bet He Did It" on a painting of the interior of her son George's home in Budapest after what appeared to have been a miner domestic theft. A cartoon-like watercolor of people reading newspapers during the 2004 US election campaign flaunts the banner "How Much Can We Believe?" She also returned to a number of old fascinations. Among these were depictions of earth-moving machines, which she had depicted in sinister tones sixty years before. Observing such machines from her home at Pennswood, she now presented then in a more positive light, calling the series "Builders' Ballets." Some of these late paintings were charming evocations of daily life, such as her canvas depicting people on a bus to New York.

"A Bus Ride to New York," 1999. ArtNEO.

Throughout her nineties Ivy Starr continued to sketch and paint, including her last self-portraits and some thirty-one watercolors of views near her Quaker retirement home in Pennsylvania and a remarkable series of five pen and watercolor vistas from the roof of her son Fred's home in Washington. In 2008 she did an ink sketch of Lafayette Square in Washington, with a ninety-two-year-old Robert McNamara, the former U.S. Secretary of Defense, striding purposely across it. When her son Fred introduced the two nonagenarians they carried on a spirited conversation on the politics of the day, in spite of the twenty-degree temperature.

The composer Brahms is said to have done counterpoint exercises each morning down to the end of his life. Ivy Jane Starr did the same, except by painting flowers. Friends and family brought her flowers daily, and whenever possible she would have them wheel her into the Pennswood flower gardens. She would paint the same flower again and again, especially her beloved amaryllises. Her last painting, done at age 102, was a watercolor of xenias done for her daughter-in-law Christina Starr as a birthday card.

Ending

In music, harmony or disharmony can arise from two notes that are close to one another on the scale or octaves apart. Stephen and Ivy Jane Starr had married for love, but then recognized how profoundly their aspirations differed from each other. Over the decades they forged a harmony that embraced rather than papered over the deep differences between their personalities and temperaments. This harmony deepened in the course of the five decades they spent together.

Humor, or at least irony, played a very real, if carefully bounded role in both their lives and in their life together. Writing about his great aunt, Ivy Jane, Brad Edmondson ascribed to her:

> "a nuanced sense of humor that had equal appreciation for the low forms (slapstick and puns), old chestnuts (which she delivered like important messages from the early 20th century), and more modern, absurdist jokes. Many of her wisecracks took aim at the stupidity, snobbery, and other character weaknesses she had seen in people. I eventually understood that she often used humor to sweeten bitter memories. But she was not a bitter person."

For Steve, by contrast, humor was something like wine, which softened and sweetened the vicissitudes of life. His sense of humor may not have been inborn but it greatly expanded and ripened with age. A trip to Baton Rouge and New Orleans that the two of them made in 1981 saw it in full flowering, as he detected endless subjects for merriment and shared them with Ivy Jane and anyone else who was inclined to laugh with him. During those same later years, humor also became for him a gateway to joviality and comradery with male friends.

Above all, it was the glue of a large family that held the couple together through rocky times. For all their differences, they were dedicated parents who worked as a team, loving without suffocating, providing without building dependence. All this is amply documented in the thousands of letters they wrote to each of the children once they left for college. In the end, a serene and harmonious contentment seems to have prevailed between them. "Fortunately, we grew more together," wrote Ivy Jane. The marriage endured more than half a century and ended only with the death of Stephen Starr in his seventy-sixth year. By then both had achieved their goals: as a couple, as a family, and as artist and historian.

Afterword

By this point, a reader might well ask what possible justification could there be for offering detailed histories of two such different families as the Csillags/Starrs and Edmondsons, and for following the lives of their members over three centuries. One possible answer might be that these family stories reveal certain inborn traits of personality and character that endured and revealed themselves through the generations. Those who are paying to have laboratories analyse the DNA in their spit may have sought such continuities in this book. But they must be disappointed. Those readers who seek to make the case for either side of the Nature-Nurture split will come away from these pages with little to show for their efforts.

This is scarcely surprising, given the immense diversity that exists within this one American family. During the period of recorded history, members of the Edmondson and Csillag/Starr families conducted their lives in at least seven languages, including English, Hungarian, Latin, Hebrew, French, Yiddish, and both High and Alsatian German. Over the same centuries these very different families also professed a wide range of religions, including Catholicism, Anglicanism, Judaism, Quakerism, Methodism, and Unitarianism, not to mention free thinking and skepticism. Amidst such a hodgepodge of change, is it any wonder that it is all but impossible to discern continuities, whether genetic or passed down by custom?

At the same time, there are some striking parallels and similarities. The two early families were separated by language, religion, culture, and by more than 1,000 miles across Europe as the crow flies. Yet down to the seventeenth century in the case of the Edmondsons and to the eighteenth century in the case of the Csillags they both led similarly traditional lives. This meant that they were all farmers or petty tradesmen who remained close to the land. During the late medieval and early modern eras, people across Europe shared traditional forms of work and worship that changed only when kings and their advisors wanted them to change.

Since the lives of both families went completely unrecorded during those pre-modern centuries, we are free to speculate that they lived idyllic lives or, alternatively, that they suffered under the heel of landowners and governments. The fact is that we don't know. The earliest known Edmondson appears in the written records of Cumbria only in the late sixteenth century, while the earliest known Csillag, who didn't yet go by that name, was the younger son of a Moravian family who was forced to leave Moravia in the eighteenth century and settled in eastern Hungary. Prior to those dates, the records are silent. "History" as we conceive it began only when changes were imposed on both families from above.

The powerful forces that eventually upturned the lives of these two families were the English Revolution of the seventeenth century and the great reforms instituted by Charles VI and Joseph II of Austria in the eighteenth century. These forces brought wrenching change and prodded many to action. Brothers and uncles of the early Edmondsons left an indelible and important mark on the new world that was emerging in their lifetimes; the proto-Csillags left no such footprints in history. Yet following the initial shock of change, several generations of both Edmondsons and Csillags settled peacefully into the new modes of life. This curious condition endured down to the birth in 1797 of George Edmondson, the Russianist and educator, and to the birth of Csillag Sandor, the future lawyer, eighty-one years later. These two men fundamentally changed the trajectories of their families.

From these dates to the present both families have remained in a state of constant whirl. They became highly mobile, moving restlessly from location to location. Their communities were swept up in dramatic changes that caused various internal fractures. As this happened, the more ambitious men of both families headed for the big cities. In neither case was this move forced upon them. Rather, they embraced urban life as a means of fulfilling their personal aspirations.

The upheavals found expression in their religious life. The Edmondsons had abandoned Catholicism and embraced Quakerism in the seventeenth century, while the Csillags abandoned Judaism for Catholicism only at the dawn of the twentieth century. Quaker Edmondsons of the early nineteenth century had no inkling that within a generation the family would turn its back on the Quakers and become Methodists and then Unitarians. Nor did Sandor Csillag in 1920 suspect that within a few decades his children would abandon his newfound Catholicism for Methodism, Unitarianism, or agnosticism. Until it happened, neither family could have suspected how their descendants would be swept into the secularism that increasingly prevailed in the Western world.

Both families eventually fled from the Old World to the New World, but their decisions to cross the ocean traced less to hope than misfortune: being disowned by his father in the case of George William Edmondson and political strife in Germany and Hungary in the cases of Peter Niesen and Csillag Sandor. None of these men were rebellious by nature, nor were any other members of their immediate families, once they had abandoned their traditional faiths in favor of Quakerism in the case of the Edmondsons and Catholicism in the case of the Csillags.

Once in America the immigrants found themselves disoriented and professionally at sea. Whatever hopes they may have had for a new life were soon dashed. George William Edmondson, the one who arrived in Norwalk, Ohio, via northern Montreal and Quebec City, worked hard but eventually failed. As the years passed his marriage broke up, he took to drink, and he came to depend on his son George M. Edmondson for support. His contemporary Peter Niesen from the Rhineland village of Wallersheim came to a worse end. After marrying and launching a family of five children he returned to Germany, never to be heard from again. His wife, Regina, having become a de facto widow, wailed, "Why did we ever come to this awful country?" As to Csillag Sandor, he fled to America after the collapse of his Hungarian world but never adjusted to his new country. The fascist Horthy government and his own fear of a second world war made a return to Hungary impossible, but he looked down on much of his new environment with condescension and hauteur.

Only with the emergence of the next generation did these families produce men and women who embraced American life and thrived in it. George Mountain Edmondson and his three siblings, Peter Niesen Jr. and his sister Minnie Niesen Edmondson, and Stephen Z. Starr and his two siblings all achieved success in their careers and lives and came to epitomize American values. But this happy outcome occurred only after the passage of several difficult decades.

By the nineteenth century members of both families were seeking new professions. Csillag Sandor chose the law and two of his three children followed him into that profession. Meanwhile, following the death of the educator George Edmondson, members of three further generations of Edmondsons devoted their lives to painting, photography, and sculpture, a tradition that continues down to the present.

By the twentieth century these professional developments were accompanied by new spiritual quests. Stephen Starr eventually found his true vocation as a historian, in which role he gained national distinction. But while history reigned in his mind, music ruled in his heart. He adored Mozart and the Viennese classics and considered opera to be a realm of magic to which he had direct access via the radio. Never did his eyes twinkle more brightly than in humming along with classical music. Similarly, Ivy Jane Starr found her vocation in painting and sculpture, but these were far more than roadmaps for making her way in the practical world. For at the heart of her being was beauty as such, whether in nature or in the works of great artists. The fact that in her 102nd year she was still painting evocative miniatures of her beloved amaryllis attests to this truth. For both Stephen and Ivy Jane Starr the appreciation of beauty in nature and in humankind's greatest achievements was a kind of religion, grounding and brightening their lives.

Down to the nineteenth century the known history of both families deals mainly with the men. But the women were there, and often played significant roles. Their task, aside from giving birth to children, raising them, and clothing and feeding the family, was to do whatever was necessary to enable the family to survive in the face of actions their menfolk took in the external world. Women in both families lived by Marcus Aurelius' maxim "to endure whatever wind blows." Their lives went largely unrecorded, and are known to us only to the extent that descendants passed down stories of their actions and words. However, during the late nineteenth and twentieth century all this changed. As a result, the lives of more recent womenfolk were not only more eventful in ways extending beyond the family, but are, thankfully, far better documented. In many ways the relentlessly self-educating "Minnie" Edmondson, and the tireless journalist Irene Friedenberg Starr epitomized the upward striving that changed the expectations of American women in the twentieth century.

While stressing the whirlwind of change over the past two-hundred years, should we not also be seeking out the continuities? Of course they exist, but some of the most important ones-- those having to do with appearance, voice, personality, and temperament—can only be detected from a distance. Some doubtless emerge from these pages. But family members, including the present author, are too close to the story to identify or appreciate them.

With the exception of the early Edmondsons' support for Cromwell and the Quakers, both families were loyal citizens. But whereas Csillag Sandor aspired to enter the higher ranks of Austro-Hungarian public life and society, most of the Edmondsons after George Edmondson the educator focused single-mindedly on their painting and photography. Neither family looked to government to clear a path for them, and neither had more than a passing or forced relationship to politics.

Two noteworthy characteristics that emerge from this review of the arch of family history are aspiration and independence. Both sides of the family in which I was raised were hard-working, of course, but less as an end in itself than to make something of themselves. Csillag Sandor reached his goals as a lawyer and judge, but within the Austro-Hungarian system that was slowly and gracefully crumbling. His decision after World War I to uproot himself and his family and settle in America proved fatal for his career and brought hardship and misery to himself and his wife, Irene. But he deserves all honor and respect, for that same decision saved his family from almost certain extinction in the Holocaust.

Grandfather George Edmondson showed similar guts when, after enduring the deaths of his wife and their two daughters, he managed to work his way back to life, to form a new family and build to what became a successful career in photography. Unlike Grandfather Starr/Csillag, he lived to enjoy the benefits of his success.

Aspiration drove both sides of the family but neither pursued it at all cost. Both in the end limited their aspirations to what could be achieved while not becoming dependent on others. Csillag's aspirations came to naught in America but his second wife made up for this by successfully combining aspiration and hard work. George Edmondson thrived in his solo career in photography. The children of both couples, Stephen and Ivy Jane, inherited this drive for independence, made it the cornerstone of their family life, and successfully passed it down to all four of their children.

This, then, is a story of hard work and of solid if middling achievement extending over several generations. Theirs is a tale neither of "rags to riches" nor of "riches to rags." Taking the late nineteenth and twentieth centuries as a whole, the economic curve for both families bent upward, but in the moderate and careful way that typified them both. In 1932 the two families became linked through the marriage of Stephen Z. Starr and Ivy Jane Edmondson. The new family they created achieved a longer period of stability and relative freedom from economic want than either family had ever known.

The story we have told demands humility from all their many descendants. Both George M. Edmondson the photographer and Csillag Sandor the lawyer had experienced crushing personal losses early in their lives, tragedies far beyond anything members of the next generation have known. Both overcame them through sheer hard work for the sake of their families. This was so viscerally a part of George M. Edmondson's mentality that he felt no need to express it or embody it in a conscious plan. Csillag, whose personal loss was compounded by the collapse of the entire world he had known, was the one member of either family to make an important decision on the basis of a long-term plan: he emigrated because he didn't want either of his sons to fight in the next war, which he was certain would break out soon. His decisive action saved both himself and his family.

In light of their complex and often difficult histories, it is not surprising that both the Edmondsons and Csillags were serious people. Anyone searching for a trace of humor in either family down to the late nineteenth century will be disappointed. However, George William Edmondson, who moved to America, came to appreciate the droll and humorous sides of life once he overcame the split with his father. His son, photographer George Mountain Edmondson, barely survived the deaths of his first wife and children but after remarrying developed a wholesome, knee-slapping joviality that he passed on to his son, also named George. As to Stephen Z. Starr, after he had refashioned himself as an American and after he and his wife, Ivy Jane, successfully raised and educated their four children, also allowed himself to revel in life's lighter sides. Only then would he easily tell a joke or smilingly raise a toast with a glass of his beloved Wehlener Sonnenuhr Riesling. So let us now, in that spirit, conclude this history.

Gallery:

A Selection of Self-Portraits by Ivy Jane Edmondson Starr

c. 1928.

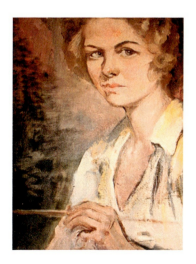

Oil on canvas, ca. 1930, Diana and Peter Cooper., Bethany, Ct.

1930, ArtNEO.

Self-Portrait, early 1940s, oil on canvas, ArtNEO.

Self-portrait, 1990s, oil on canvas, ArtNEO.

Footnotes:

Chapter I

[1] For authoritative information on the Hungarian legal profession I am indebted to Victor Karady's fine paper, "Jews in the Hungarian Legal Profession and Among Law Students from the Emancipation till the Shoah," <u>Iskolakultura Online</u>, 2007, pp-37-47.

[2] http://data.jewishgen.org/wconnect/wc.dll?jg~jgsys~community~-863067

[3] "A Brief Outline of the History of the Jews of Hungary," A speech delivered on 13 December 1992 at the 4 Temple Emanu-El Beth Solom, Westmount, Quebec, Canada.

[4] Karady, "Jews in the Hungarian Legal Profession," p. 36.

[5] Personal communication from Victor Karady to SFS, December 21, 2015.

[6] Irene reported to several U.S. census takers that she had been born in 1891, whereas she in fact was born on 3 February, 1887.

[7] George A. Starr, Csillig Sandor's grandson and a part-time resident of Budapest, describes Szondi ut as "a street of merely so-so apartments in a respectable district (the 6th)." GAS to SFS, 2012.

[8] As reported by Ivy Jane Starr, based on what Stephen Z Starr had told her. Letter to SFS, 1991.

[9] Karady, "Jews in the Hungarian Legal Profession," p. 36.

[10] Ibid., pp.41-42.

[11] Alon Rachamimov, <u>POWs and the Great War: Captivity on the Eastern Front</u>, Oxford, 2002, Intro., Ch.5.

[12] https://muse.jhu.edu/login?auth=0&type=summary&url=/journals/kritika/v006/6.3gatrell.html

[13] Alon Rachamimov, POWs and the Great War: Captivity on the Eastern Front, NY, 2002.

[14] Karady, "Jews in the Hungarian legal Profession…," pp. 43-44.

[15] Certificate of Naturalization, No, 2452981. Csillag was 49 years of age, 5 feet 9 ½ inches tall, and blonde.

[16] Probate Court, Doc. 214, No. 177745.

[17] Letter from SZS TO SFS, October 10, 1963.

[18] Encyclopedia of Jewish Life, 2001, New York, vol. II, p. 916.

[19] Moshe Eliahu Gonda, Mea shana le-yehudei Decrecen, Tel Aviv, 1970, p. 323.

[20] Text provided by Dr. Joan Ellen Friedenberg, Professor Emeritus of Education at Florida International University, a collateral descendent of Irene Starr's father.

Chapter II

[21] On this family see MC 19/2/1702 Horton in Ribblesdale Parish Registers, North Yorkshire Record Office, North Allerton.

[22] Copy of Register of Marriages, 1680-1702.

[23] International Genealogical Index for Westmoreland and Yorkshire, MC 19/2/1702 at Horton in Ribblesdale.

[24] Dent Copy Register Baptisms, 1714-1738, preserved at Kendal Records Office.

[25] Dent Parish Registers, Ref:WPR/70/4. Kendal Records Office.

[26] Quarterly Meeting of Westmoreland Births, Sedbergh.

[27] Baptized at Dent, Dent Parish Register, Ref. WPR/70/2+4) at Kendal Records Office. Agnes Edmonson was widowed and died at Gibbs Hall in 1810, Quarterly Meeting, Westmoreland Burieals, Digested copy of the registers of burials of the Quarterly Meeting of Westmoreland, 1635-1837, book 1227, p. 53.

[28] Kendal Records Office, Copy Register of Baptisms, Marriages and Burials, 1556-1800, Horton in Ribblesdale.

[29] George Fox, Journal of George Fox, Philadelphia, 1978, p. 38.

[30] Hugh Barbour, J. William Frost, The Quakers, New York, 1988, p. 28.

³¹ The registration of marriages and deaths in the two Musgraves began in 1539, and of baptisms in 1572.

³² On William Edmondson see William Edmundson (sic.), <u>A Journal of the Life, Travels, Suffering, and Labour of Love in the Work of the Ministry, of that Worthy and Faithful Servant of Jesus Christ, William Edmundson</u>, London, 1829, and "Edmundson, William." <u>Dictionary of National Biography</u>. London: Smith, Elder & Co. 1885-1900, vol. p. , and Frank Edmundson, MD, "William Edmundson, 1627-1712. Some New and Little Known Memorabilia," <u>A History of the Edmundson Family</u>, Henry Horne Edmondson, ed., Mountain City, Tennessee, 1981.

³³ Edmundson, <u>A Journal of the Life, Travels,</u> Sufferings, p. 54, ff.

³⁴ <u>Ibid.</u>, p. 39.

³⁵ <u>Ibid.</u>, p. 62.

³⁶ Fox, <u>Journal of George Fox</u>, p. 627.

³⁷ Edmundson, <u>A Journal of the Life, Travels, Sufferings</u>, pp. 63-65.

³⁸ On Shelter Island see Mac Griswold, <u>The Manor, Three Centuries at a Slave Plantation on Long Island, Shelter Island, New York</u>, New York, 2013.

³⁹ John Garrett, <u>Roger Williams, Witness Beyond Christendom, 1603-1683</u>, London, 19_, pp. 218-9.

⁴⁰ <u>Ibid.</u>, p. 67.

⁴¹ Quoted in Hugh Thomas, <u>The Slave Trade</u>, p. [ ] fn. 26.

⁴² Edmundson, <u>A Journal of the Life, Travels, Sufferings</u>, p. 128.

⁴³ <u>Ibid.</u>, p. 627.

⁴⁴ Quoted in Garrett, <u>Roger Williams</u>, p. 215.

⁴⁵ <u>Ibid.</u> p.

⁴⁶ <u>Ibid.</u>, p.

⁴⁷ John Wesley,

⁴⁸ Sedbergh monthly meeting, Leayet/Dent Mens's Preparation Meeting Minute Book, 1708-1724.

⁴⁹ Hugh Thomas, <u>The Slave Trade</u>, New York, 1958, p. 120.

⁵⁰ <u>Ibid.</u>, p.

[51] The one more authoritative source on this structure is Kenneth L. Carroll, Three Hundred Years and More of Third Haven Quakerism, Easton, 1984.

[52] Frank B. Edmundson, Emerson B. Roberts, "John Edmondson – Large Merchant of Tred Haven Creek," Maryland Historical Magazine, vol. 50., no. 3, pp. 220, ff.

[53] Ibid., p. 227.

[54] Ibid., pp. 222-226.

[55] The best sources on Edmondson's personal life are the essay by Edmundson and Roberts, noted above, and M. Patricia Humphreys, "John Edmondson of Talbot County, Maryland," in Henry Horne Edmondson, A History of the Early Edmondson Family, Data on Edmondson's will, drawn from the Maryland Hall of Records, Wills, Liber 6, folio 97, 96, 95, folio 95, are to be found in Humphreys' article.

[56] See above, f.n. 32, also Carroll, Three Hundred Years and More of Third Haven Quakerism, p. 23.

[57] Edmundson and Roberts, "John Edmondson – Large Merchant of Tred Haven Creek," p. 221.

[58] Ibid. p. 228.

[59] Henry Horne Edmondson, A History of the Early Edmondson Family, p. 15. This same descendent claims that Thomas Edmondson of Little Musgrave, born in 1645, also emigrated to America, dying at Essex, Virginia, in 1689.

Chapter III

[60] JB (Jane Edmondson Benson), From the Lune to the Neva Sixty Years Ago; With Ackworth and "Quaker" Life by the Way, London, 1879, p. 13. All details of GM's life not otherwise documented are from this volume.

[61] No author, A History of Ackworth School, n.p., 1853, pp. 7-9.

[62] Ibid.

[63] Pliny Earle, Memoirs of Pliny Earle, M.D., with extracts from his diary and letters (1830-1892) and selections from his professional writings (1839-1891), Boston, 1898, p.68 (courtesy of Brad Edmondson).

[64] These dialects are documented by Alan C. Crosby, The Lancashire Dictionary of Dialect, Tradition and Folklore, Otley, West Yorkshire, 2000.

⁶⁵ *Mentor and Amander, or a Visit to Acworth's School by a Late Teacher*, London, 1814.

⁶⁶ JB, *From the Lune to the Neva*, p. 40.

⁶⁷ JB, *From the Lune to the Neva*, pp. 37-38.

⁶⁸ On Quakers in Russia see Richenda, G. Scott, *Quakers in Russia*, London, 1964, and Arnold B. McMillan, "Quakers in Early Nineteenth Century Russia," *Slavonic and East European Review*, 1973, October.

⁶⁹ Grellet, Stephen, *Memoirs of the Life and Gospel Labours of Stephen Grellet*, London 2 vols., 1851, citations from vol. I, ch. XXIX, XXX. Also extract of letter from Mary Fisher, 22 June 1814, *Quaker Pioneers in Russia*, p.

⁷⁰ *Ibid.*.

⁷¹ Wheeler, Daniel, *Memoirs of the Life and Gospel Labours of the Late Daniel Wheeler*, London, 1852, on Wheeler's early life see Ch I.

⁷² Wheeler, p. 60. Wheeler's letters contain detailed accounts of his several meetings with Alexander I, cf. pp. 92-3, etc., including one involving Edmondson, p. 99.

⁷³ JB, *From the Lune to the Neva*, p. 86.

⁷⁴ Edmondson to his parents John and Anne Edmondson, 27 June 1818, Quaker Historical Society, London.

⁷⁵ *Ibid.*.

⁷⁶ Edmondson to Singleton, n.d., Quaker Historical Society,

⁷⁷ Edmondson to his parents, Sept. 18, 1818, Quaker Historical Society, London.

⁷⁸ Edmondson to his parents, 16 July 1818, Quaker Historical Society, London.

⁷⁹ *Ibid.*.

⁸⁰ Arnold B. McMillan, "Quakers in Early Nineteenth Century Russia," Slavonic and *East European Review*, 1973, October, p. 575.

⁸¹ Grellet, *Memoirs of the Life and Gospel Labours of Stephen Grellet*, vol. I, p. 365.

⁸² Wheeler, *Memoirs of the Life and Gospel Labours*, p. 53.

⁸³ Alexander Pushkin, *Eugene Onegin*, Walter Arndt, transl., New York, 2002, p. 198.

84 Edmondson to William Singleton, 9 September, 1819, Quaker Historical Society, London.

85 McMillan, "Quakers in Early Nineteenth Century Russia," p. 22.

86 Edmondson letter to Singleton, 4 July 1818. Quaker Historical Society, London.

87 Edmondson to his parents, 18 July 1818, Quaker Historical Society, London.

88 Edmondson to his parents, 9 February 1819, Quaker Historical Society, London.

89 Ibid..

90 Wheeler, Memoirs of the Life and Gospel Labours, p. 62.

91 Edmondson to his parents, 9 February 1819, Quaker Historical Society, London. Also in Arnold B. McMillin, "Quakers in Nineteenth Century Russia," Slavonic and East European Review, 1973, October, p. 571.

92 Susan P. McCaffray, "Confronting Serfdom in the Age of Revolution: Projects for Serf Reform in the Time of Alexander I," The Russian Review, 64.1, 2005, January, pp. 8-12.

93 Wheeler, Memoirs of the Life and Gospel Labours, p. 52.

94 Ibid., p. 110-111.

95 On all aspects of Wheeler's plan see Memoirs of the Life and Gospel Labours, p. 62, ff.

96 Benson, From the Lune to the Neva, p.113.

97 Edmondson to Anne Singleton, Friends Library, Portfolio 41/154, 4 September 1819.

98 Ibid..

99 Anne Edmondson to her sister, either letter or Lune to Neva

100 Benson, From the Lune to the Neva, p. 34.

101 Ibid., p, 112.

102 Wheeler, Memoirs of the Life and Gospel Labours, p. 76-83.

103 Ibid., p. 99.

104 Edmondson to Agnes Singleton, 5 November 1824, Quaker Historical Society; quoted McMillan, "Quakers in Early Nineteenth Century Russia," p. 578.

[105] Ibid.

[106] Wheeler, Memoirs of the Life and Gospel Labours, pp. 111-112.

[107] Blackburn Mail, 5 May 1826, quoted by D. Thompson, "George Edmondson, 1798-1863," Friends Quarterly, 1956, January, p. 26.

[108] "The Story of Queenwood College in Hampshire," p. 9. Also Thompson, "George Edmondson, 1798-1863," p. 27.

[109] n.a., "The Story of Queenwood College, Hampshire," unpubd. ms, ca. 1915, courtesy of Michael and Callie Edmondson, p. 9.

[110] Joseph Clayton, Robert Owen: Pioneer of Social Reforms, London, 1908, p. 43.

[111] F. Podmore, Robert Owen, London, 1906, p.569; also Thompson, "George Edmondson, 1798-1863," p. 27.

[112] F. Podmore, Robert Owen, London, 1906, p.569; also D. Thompson, "George Edmondson, 1798-1863," p. 27.

[113] H. E. Armstrong, The Teaching of Scientific Method, London, 1910, p. 81, quoted in Thompson, "George Edmondson 1797-1863," p. 29.

[114] "The Story of Queenwood College, Hampshire, n.p., mentioned also in Thompson, "George Edmondson, 1798-1863," p. 28.

[115] "Terms &c. of Queenwood College near Stockbridge, Hants., Conducted by George Edmondson," reproduced in "The Story of Queenwood College in Hampshire."

[116] D. Thompson, "Queenwood College in Hampshire," Annals of Science, 1955, p. 248.

[117] J. Tyndall, Fragments of Science, 2 vols., London, 1879, II, p. 353.

[118] Ibid., II, p. 338.

[119] Thompson, "Queenwood College, Hampshire," p. 251.

[120] Tyndall, Fragments of Science, II, p. 353, ff.

[121] Thompson, "Queenwood College, Hampshire," p. 249.

[122] N.A., "The Story of Queenwood College in Hampshire," unpubd. MS, property of Brad and Michael Edmondson, p. 2.

123 Mrs. Tyndall, Preliminary Drafts for a Life of John Tyndall, 1820-1854, London, 1856, p. 169; quoted by Thompson, "Queenwood College, Hampshire," Annals of Science, 1955, pp.248-249.

124 Ibid.

125 Queenwood Reporter, 15 October 1848, cited by Thompson, "George Edmondson, 1797-1863," p. 28. And "The Story of Queenwood College, Hampshire," p.7.

126 Tyndall, Preliminary Drafts for a Life of John Tyndall, pp. 163 ff.

127 Reprinted from scrapbook G.W. Edmondson gave to his son, G.M. Edmondson, about 1907, property of Brad Edmondson,

128 Dictionary of National Biography, London, 1885, Vol. 16, pp. 394-395

Chapter IV

129 Annotated scrapbook given by George William Edmondson to his son George Mountain Edmondson in 1907. Property of S.F. Starr.

130 Recalled by Ivy Jane Edmondson Starr to the author, 1987, and by John Edmondson, as recalled by his father George William Edmondson (II).

131 Property of Brad Edmondson.

132 The Life and Letters of Frederic Shields, Ernestine Bell Mills, ed., London, New York, 1912, p. 64.

133 Letter from Mr. Huw Thomas, Royal Geographical Society to S.F.S, 7 December 1999.

134 George Charles Wallich, The North Atlantic Sea-Bed: Comprising a Diary of the Voyage on Board HMS Bulldog, London, 1862. "Surveys of H.M.S. Bulldog." Proceedings of the Royal Geographical Society, V., 1860–1861, pp. 62–70.

135 New York Times, 23 August, 1860.

136 Confirmed by Norwalk Daily Reflector, 8 October 1897, "Death of Mrs. John Mountain." Mrs. Mountain was born in 1813. The Mountains had six children, John, William, Thomas, Anna, Sophia, and Mary Jane (Mrs. G.W. Edmondson."

137 Anthony Pack, an English descendent of the visitor, George St. Leger Grenfell, to Stephen Z. Starr, who was writing a life of Grenfell, Colonel Grenfell's Wars, Baton Rouge, 1995.

¹³⁸ Quoted by Ivy Jane Edmondson Starr, 1989, to SFS.

¹³⁹ Norwalk Reflector, 30 September, 14 October, 1862.

¹⁴⁰ Information on the Mountains in Norwalk can be gleaned from U.S. Census, 1880, p. 3141, at which time six members of the family were there, Immigration data is in Probate Court of Huron County, Declaration and Record of First Papers, 1864-1875m Huron County Probate Court. 205, 319. etc. and also Naturalization Records. See also Norwalk Daily Reflector, 8 Oct 1877, 20 January 1880.

¹⁴¹ Declaration and Record of First Papers, 1864-1875, Huron County Probate Court, Naturalization Records. Edmondson applied for citizenship on 4 March 1869 and received it in 1873. Naturalization Records 1864-1884, Huron County Probate Court, nos. 273 277.

¹⁴² "Did You Know?" a weekly column on Norwalk history by J. H. Williams, apparently ca. 1930, clipping file, Firelands Historical Society. Williams erroneously claims Edmondson arrived from Plymouth.

¹⁴³ J.H. Williams, "Did You Know?" (same clipping file) lists a Mrs. Allen in 1863; Miss Brumbaker and D. L. Heath in 1864; J. H. Potter, Mrs. Mary Allen and C. H. Ballou in 1865; and Barnes and Cornell in 1866. Port Clinton boasted J. E. Duigman, Sandusky had H. J. Eppler, and P. M. Pool worked in Fremont.

¹⁴⁴ Abraham J Baughman, History of Huron County, Cleveland, 1879, p. 194.

¹⁴⁵ Joseph Forward and W.A. Smith and a man named Weatherby.

¹⁴⁶ Reverse side of an 1872 photograph of G.M. Edmondson, age 6. S. F. Starr collection. Identified by Ivy Jane Edmondson Starr.

¹⁴⁷ Ivy Jane Edmondson Starr, "Role Models?? (written while reading Alice Walker's "In Search of Our Mothers' Gardens." 1999, archive of SFS.

¹⁴⁸ Huron County Chronicle, 1 October 1875.

¹⁴⁹ Ibid.

¹⁵⁰ Includes (from left to right) Anne Mountain, Mary Jane Mountain (seated), Ivy Edmondson (foreground), Cousin Louisa Smith (standing), Sophia Mountain, and two others, unidentified. Undated note from Ivy Jane Edmondson Starr, SFS archive.

151 Norwalk Reflector, 20 November 1878; Norwalk Experiment, 25 November 1878

152 The American Cyclopedia, 1879, p. 50; 1890, p.195.

153 Reminiscence of Ivy Jane Edmondson Starr, to SFS, 1987.

154 "J. and J. Mountain, Merchant Tailoring," Norwalk Experiment, 18 July 1867.

155 Memo on "Role Models???" by Ivy Jane Edmondson Starr, 1999. Archive of SFS.

156 Ivy Jane Edmondson Starr to SFS, Brad Edmondson, and others.

157 Mary Sayre Haverstock, Artists in Ohio Before 1900, Kent, 2000, pp.209-210.

158 J. H. Wiilliams, "Did You know?" Norwalk Reflector, 15 November 1948.

159 A History of Cleveland, Ohio, 3 vols., Chicago-Cleveland, 1910, III, p. 1004.

160 n.a., A History of Cleveland, Ohio, III Biographical, Chicago, Cleveland, 1910. p. 1004.

161 Edmondson had several signed and dedicated books from Hubbard's Roycroft press in his library. Property of SFS.

162 J.H. Williams, "Did You Know?" Norwalk Reflector, undated clipping (1930s?), Ivy Jane Edmondson Starr to SFS.

163 Letter from William J. Edmondson to Ivy Jane Edmondson Starr, 6 January 1956. Archive of SFS.

164 Ulrich W. Hiesinger, Childe Hassam, American Impressionist, New York, 1994, p. 32.

165 Robert S. Pozner, "Asheville's Growth Began With 19th Century TB Treatment," Asheville Citizen-Times, 20 July 2015.

166 Cleveland Museum of Art, http://clevelandart.org/art/1917.400Mu,[hs: https://www.1stdibs.com/art/paintings/william-john-edmondson-untitled-neoclassical-dance-scene/id-a_66318/

167 James M. Wood, Out and About with Winsor French, Kent, 1916.

168 Ivy Jane Edmondson Starr to SFS, 1999, n.d.

169 American Magazine of Art, 11 December 1920, pp. 490-502.

170 Edan Hughes, Artists in California, 1786-1940.

171 Karl Grossman, A History of Music in Cleveland, Cleveland, 1972, pp..141-142.

172 "Colson Equipment Company," Interchange (newsletter of the Marmon Group), January, 1904, pp.2, ff.

173 G Frederick Wright, A Standard History of Loraine County, Ohio, Cleveland, 1916, p. 782.

[174] Ivy Jane Edmondson Starr to SFS, 2003.

[175] Property of the author.

[176] Ivy Jane Edmondson Starr to SFS, 1987. The main sources on GME are Frederick Starr, Art in the Veins: The Legacy of the Edmondson Family in Cleveland, Cleveland, 2009; David D. van Tassel and John J. Grabowski, Encyclopedia of Cleveland History, Cleveland, 1987.
1910 A History of Cleveland, Ohio, Cleveland, 1910, Biographical, p. 1004.
A History of Cleveland and its Environs, Chicago, 1918, III, pp. 468-469; n.a., Ohio Photographers: 1839-1900, Nevada City, California, 1998, p. 14.

[177] Norwalk Experiment, 19 October 1988.

[178] Norwalk Daily Reflector, 9 July 1900,

[179] See Jan Cigliano's important, Showplace of America: Cleveland's Euclid Avenue, 1850-1910, New York, 1991, based on photographs by G.M. Edmondson and dedicated to his memory.

[180] Ivy Jane Edmondson Starr to SFS, 2006.

[181] Photo-Era Magazine, Vol. XXXVI, 1916, p. 196; Ohio Photographers: 1839-1900, Nevada City, California, 1998, p. 14.

[182] "Edmondson is specializing these days in photographing estates." Undated clipping from the Cleveland Plain Dealer, estimated by Ivy Jane Edmondson Starr as 1930.

[183] Norwalk Daily Reflector, 9 July 1900.

[184] Ibid.

[185] M. Brown, Margaret Bourke-White: The Cleveland Years, 1927-1930, New Gallery of Contemporary Art, Cleveland, 1976.

[186] Ivy Jane Edmondson Starr to SFS, 2006.

[187] Probate Judge Henry L Kennan. Huron County Probate Court, Marriage records, vol. 5, p. 155, 17 October 1888.

[188] Norwalk Daily Reflector, 18 Feb 1899.

[189] Norwalk Daily Reflector, 18 February 1899.

[190] Norwalk Daily Reflector, 9 March 1904.

191 Ibid.

192 Germans to America: Passenger Data File, 1850-1897, Ira A. Glazier and P. William Filby, eds., Wilmington, 1988, vol. 19. pp. 293.

193 Lorain County Court House, Elyria, Probate Court, 3 November 1867.

194 Roger Huss, 24 White Birch Terrace, Kinnelon, NJ, 07405, to SFS, nd, 1003. Huss's daughter Susan Huss-Lederman, also visited Wallersheim: hussleds@uwwvax.uww.edu, Huss's contacts in Wallersheim included Albert Niesen, am Bruhl, 254597 Wallersheim, Germany, who had a son, Alois, who live across the street from the original Niesen house. Albert Niesen's daughter, Maria Niederprum, lives in Hersdorf. Other sources are Herman Bungartz's writings on the Eifel region; Thomas A. Pick's homepage: Births and Marriages in the Eifel, and a further Huss correspondent, andreas.sesterhenn@mainz.sema.slb.com.

195 Latter Day Saints records, film no. 1258482.

196 Correspondence from Roger Huss of New Jersey (rogerhuss@optonline.net), with SFS Huss is a descendent of Johann and Elizabeth Niesen Huss.

197 Ruth Rockwood Dougherty heard this from her mother Mathilda ("Tillie") Niesen, and passed it to Ivy Jane Edmondson Starr.

198 See below, p. 84.

199 Estate of Peter Niesen, Lorain County Probate Court, April 16, 1881. In 1911 John Niesen inherited the substantial sum of $3,200 after the death of a relative in Wallersheim. It is not ruled out that this person was Peter Niesen and that he had lived on and prospered. Katie Robinson to Roger L. Huss, 3 March 1999, letter in papers of SFS.

200 Ivy Jane Edmondson Starr to SFS, 10 January 1981.

201 Ibid.

202 1880 U.S. Census.

203 G Frederick Wright, A Standard History of Lorain County, Ohio, 2 vols., Chicago and NY, 1916, II p. 882.

204 Reported by her sister Mathilda (Tilly) to Ivy Jane Starr, note to SFS, 20 August 2008.

205 This woman is variously identified as "Grandma Plato" and "Grandma Westbecker." The fact that the Plato (Plothe) family was so closely linked with Regina Kracht argues for the former. But Minnie's

daughter Ivy Jane clearly recalled the name as Westbecker, a family from Baden related to the Niesens only by marriage.

[206] Ivy Jane Edmondson Starr to SFS, 20 August 2008. The sister was Matilda "Tillie" Niesen Delfing.

[207] Ibid.

[208] Minnie Niesen to "Cousin Johann" Niesen, in Wallersheim, Germany, 15 January 1899, translated by Albert Niesen. Courtesy of Roger Huss.

[209] "Wages of Farm Labor, 1866-1909, U. S. Department of Agriculture, Bulletin No.99, 1912. p. 28.

[210] Applications for Appointment of a Guardian for Idiot, Imbecile, Lunatic, or Drunkard," Loraine County, pp. 1173-1174, 6 January 1896, No. 117. (Lorain County Probate Court, film 16, no. 1981).

[211] Lorain County Reporter, 13 February 1897.

[212] Letter of 11 February 1897, translation by the late Albert Niesen of Wallersheim, who discovered it in a family residence there. Niesen's address was Am Bruhl 2, 54597 Wallersheim, Germany. Courtesy of Roger Huss (see above). Regina Niesen's grave is in St. Joseph Cemetery on North Ridge Road, Amherst.

[213] Minnie Niesen to "Cousin Johann" Niesen, in Wallersheim, Germany, 15 January 1899, translated by Albert Niesen. Courtesy of Roger Huss.

[214] "Note to Additional Note," undated copy of note to Brad Edmondson.

[215] Oberlin News, reprinted in the Norwalk Reflector, 13 April 1901.

[216] "Note to Additional Note," undated copy of note to Brad Edmondson.

[217] Ivy Jane Edmondson Starr, "'Role Models??' (Written while reading Alice Walker's In Search of Our Mothers Gardens)" 1999, SFS papers.

[218] IJES to SFS, 1999, and her essay "Role Models (Written While Reading Alice Walker's "In Search of Our Mothers' Gardens"): Wilhelmina Niesen."

[219] IJES to SFS, 3 September 2006.

[220] Scribner Fauver, the son of one of these eligible Elyrians, later served as Oberlin's attorney during my time as president of the College and we were colleagues and good friends. SFS.

[221] Interview with Brad Edmondson,

[222] Ibid.

[223] Stephen Z. Starr, "Louis Kossuth and the War of 1859," unpubd. MS, library of the author, p. 1.

[224] "William Charles Macready vs. Edwin Forrest," Bulletin of the Historical and Philosophical Society of Ohio, 7.3, July 1959, pp. 167-180.

[225] "Camp Dennison, 1861-1865," Bulletin of the Historical and Philosophical Society of Ohio, 19.3, July 1961, pp. 167-190.

[226] "Grant and Thomas: December, 1864," Cincinnati Civil War Roundtable, April 27, 1961. Printed MS, property of SFS.

[227] Ibid., p. 2.

[228] "The Saber and the Union Cavalry," Civil War History, 11.2, June, 1965, pp. 142-59.

[229] Ibid., p. 47.

[230] "Colonel George St. Leger Grenfell: His Pre-Civil War Career," Journal of Southern History, 30.3, August, 64, pp. 277-97; Colonel Grenfell's Wars: The Life of a Soldier of Fortune, Baton Rouge, 1971.

[231] Unpublished Ms, copy in possession of SFS.

[232] Jennison's Jayhawkers: A Civil War Cavalry Regiment and Its Commander, Baton Rouge, 1973, p. xii.

[233] "The Other Pickett: Col. John T. Pickett," Civil Wear Roundtable of Kentucky, 1966, November.

[234] "The First Massachusetts Volunteer Cavalry, 1861-1865, a Fresh Look," Proceedings of the Massachusetts Historical Society, LXXXVII, 1975, pp. 88-104; "The Inner Life of the First Vermont Volunteer Cavalry, 1861-1865," Vermont History, 46.3, Summer 1978; "The Third Volunteer Cavalry: A View From the Inside," Ohio Historical Journal, vol;.85, no.4, 1976, pp. 306-318; "The Grand Old regiment," Wisconsin Magazine of History, XLVIII, 1964, autumn; "The Second Michigan Volunteer Cavalry: Another View," Michigan History, vol. 69, summer, 1976.

[235] "The First Massachusetts Volunteer Cavalry…," p. 104.

[236] "The Last Days of Rebellion," Bulletin, Cincinnati Historical Society, 35.1, 1977, pp. 5-30.

[237] "Prosit!!! A Non-Cosmic Tour of the Cincinnati Saloon," Bulletin of the Cincinnati Historical Society, 36.3, Fall, 1978, pp. 174-191.

[238] Conversation of Ivy Jane Edmondson Starr with the author, 18 April 2005.